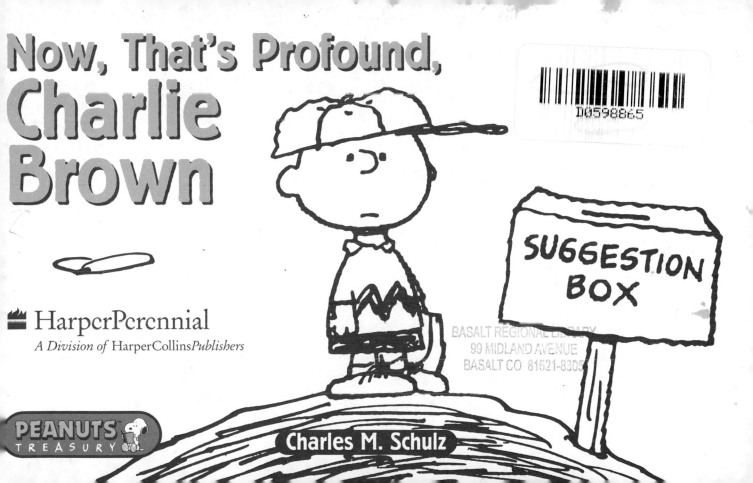

Now, That's Profound, Charlie Brown

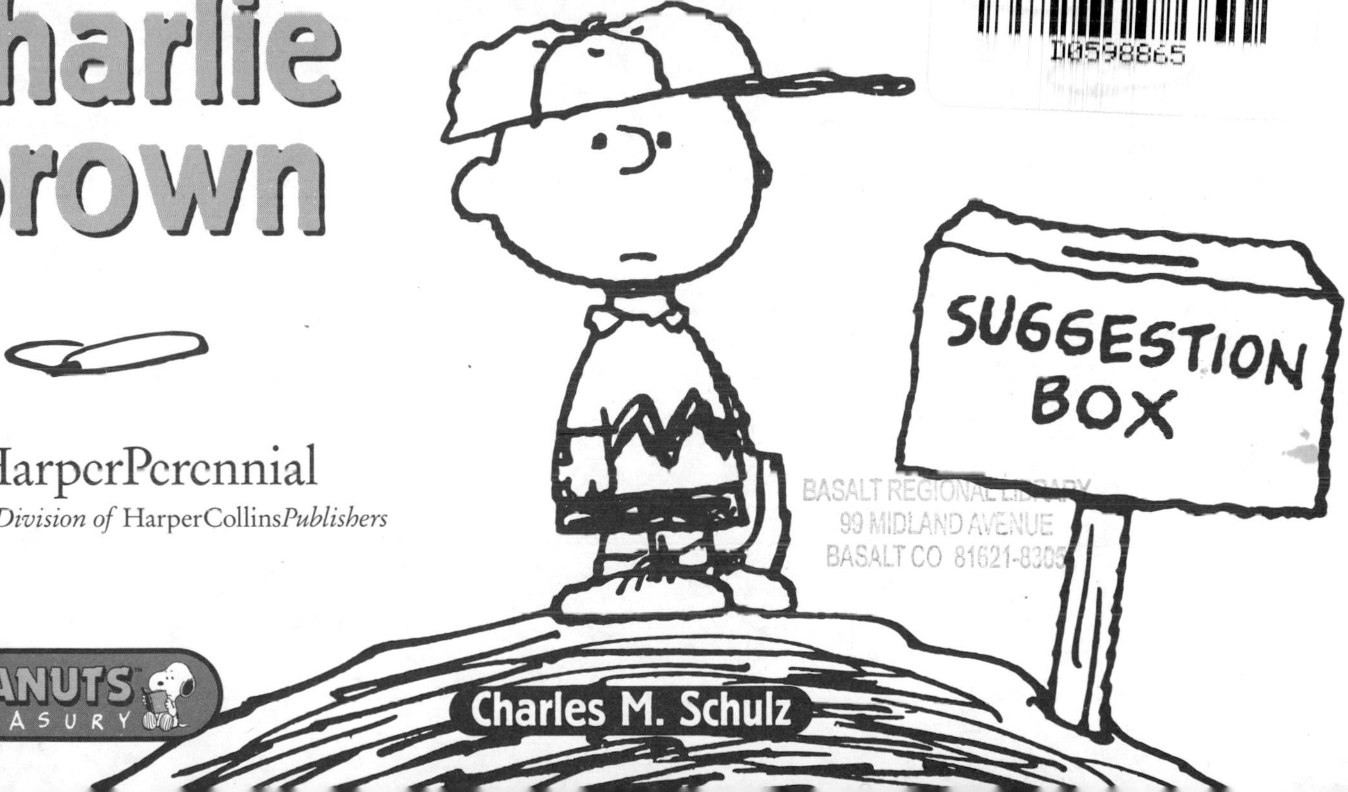
SUGGESTION BOX

HarperPerennial
A Division of HarperCollins*Publishers*

PEANUTS TREASURY

Charles M. Schulz

HarperCollins books may be purchased for
educational, business, or sales promotional use.
For information please write to:
Special Markets Department, HarperCollins Publishers, Inc.,
10 East 53rd Street, New York, NY 10022

http://www.harpercollins.com

Designed by Christina Bliss, Staten Island

ISBN 0-06-107561-2

Printed in U.S.A.

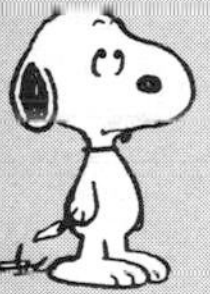

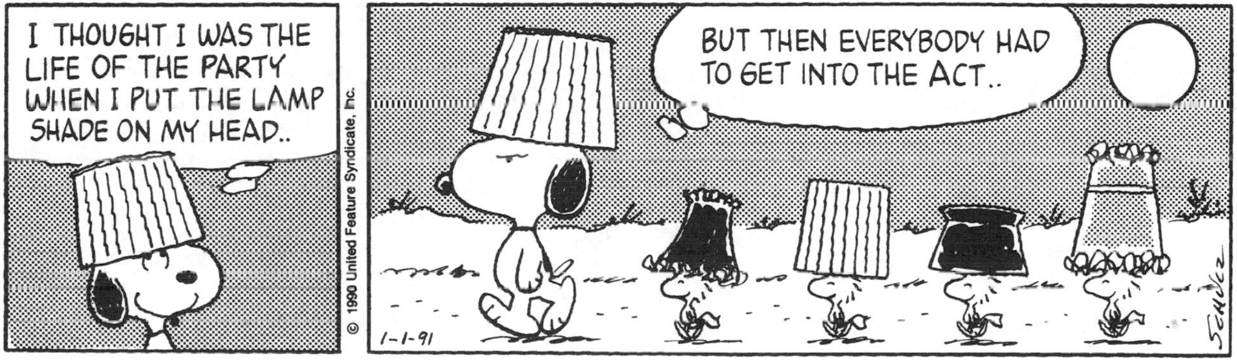
I THOUGHT I WAS THE LIFE OF THE PARTY WHEN I PUT THE LAMP SHADE ON MY HEAD..
© 1990 United Feature Syndicate, Inc.
BUT THEN EVERYBODY HAD TO GET INTO THE ACT..
1-1-91

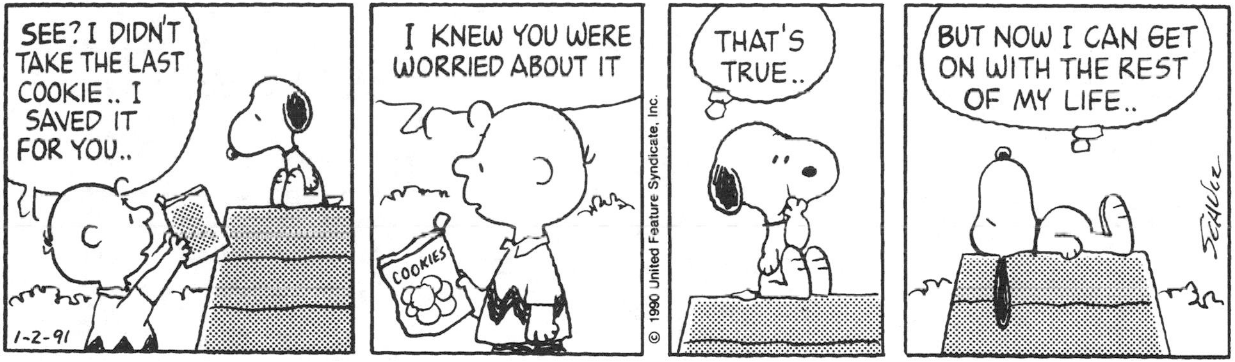
SEE? I DIDN'T TAKE THE LAST COOKIE.. I SAVED IT FOR YOU..
1-2-91
I KNEW YOU WERE WORRIED ABOUT IT
COOKIES
© 1990 United Feature Syndicate, Inc.
THAT'S TRUE..
BUT NOW I CAN GET ON WITH THE REST OF MY LIFE..

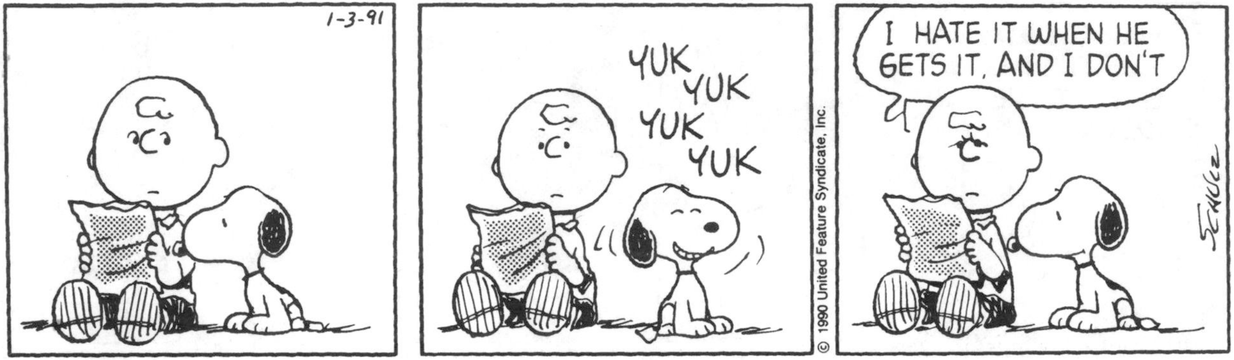
1-3-91
YUK YUK YUK YUK
© 1990 United Feature Syndicate, Inc.
I HATE IT WHEN HE GETS IT, AND I DON'T
SCHULZ

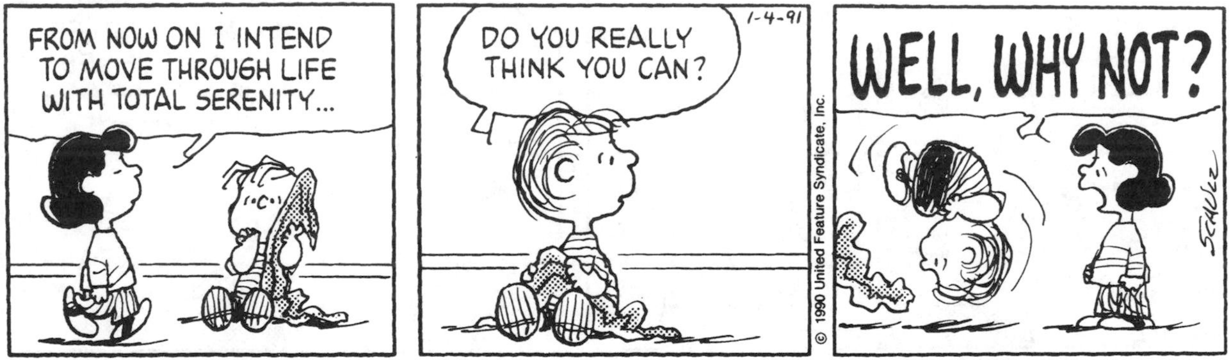
FROM NOW ON I INTEND TO MOVE THROUGH LIFE WITH TOTAL SERENITY...
1-4-91
DO YOU REALLY THINK YOU CAN?
© 1990 United Feature Syndicate, Inc.
WELL, WHY NOT?
SCHULZ

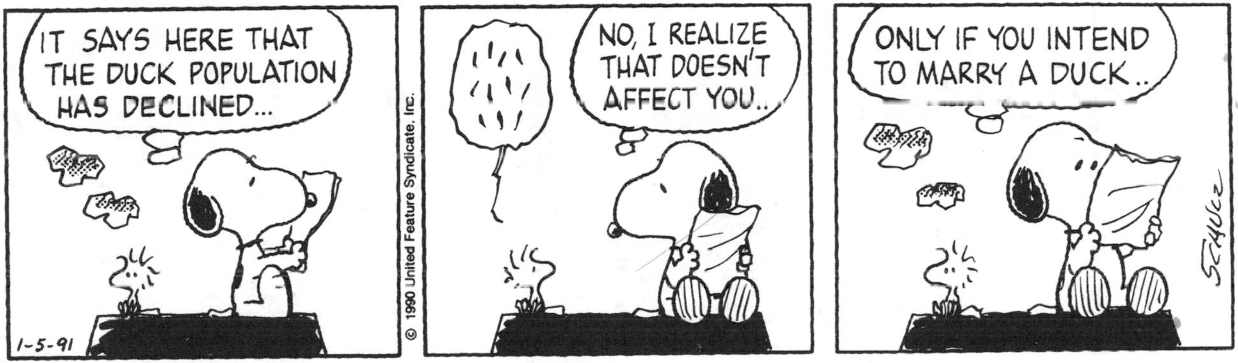
IT SAYS HERE THAT THE DUCK POPULATION HAS DECLINED...
NO, I REALIZE THAT DOESN'T AFFECT YOU..
ONLY IF YOU INTEND TO MARRY A DUCK..
1-5-91
© 1990 United Feature Syndicate, Inc.
SCHULZ

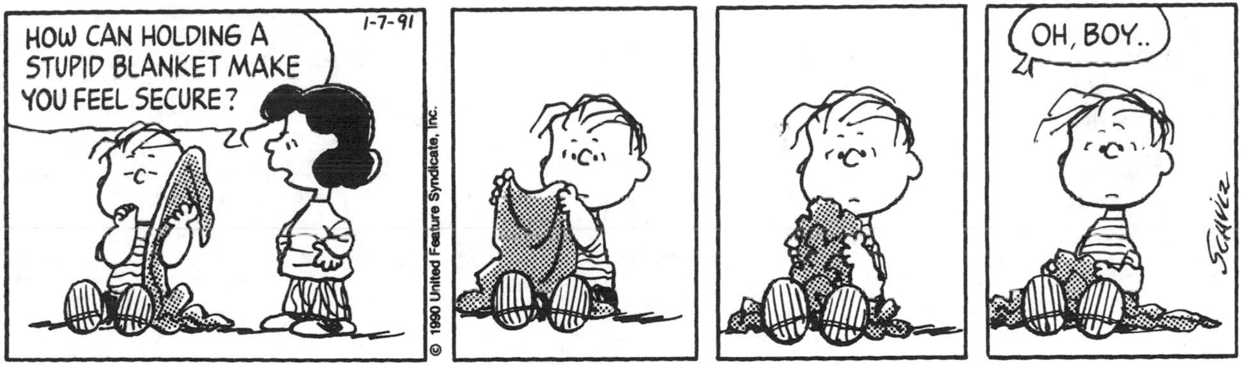
HOW CAN HOLDING A STUPID BLANKET MAKE YOU FEEL SECURE?
OH, BOY..
1-7-91
© 1990 United Feature Syndicate, Inc.
SCHULZ

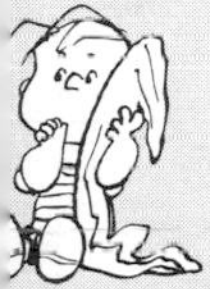

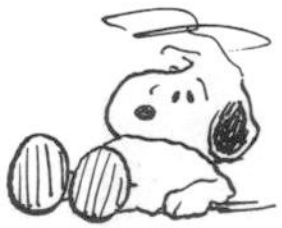

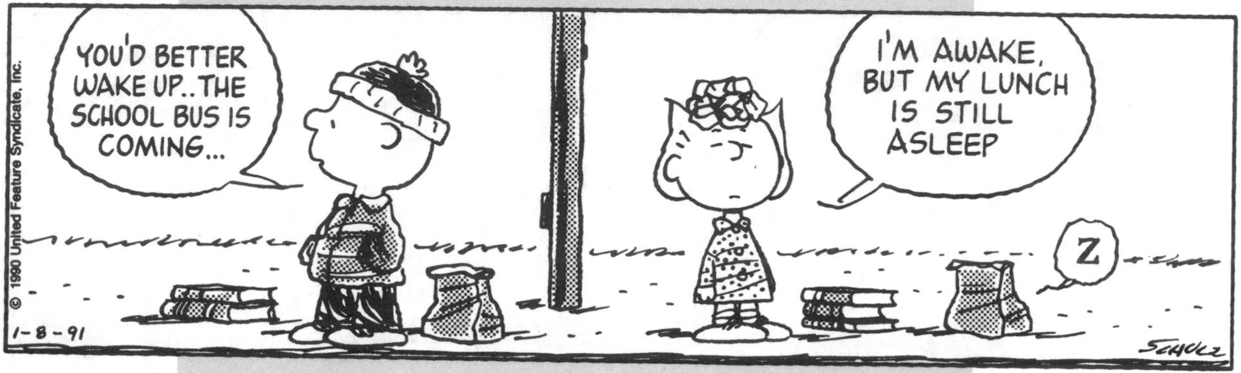

YOU'D BETTER WAKE UP.. THE SCHOOL BUS IS COMING...
© 1990 United Feature Syndicate, Inc.
1-8-91
I'M AWAKE, BUT MY LUNCH IS STILL ASLEEP
Z
SCHULZ

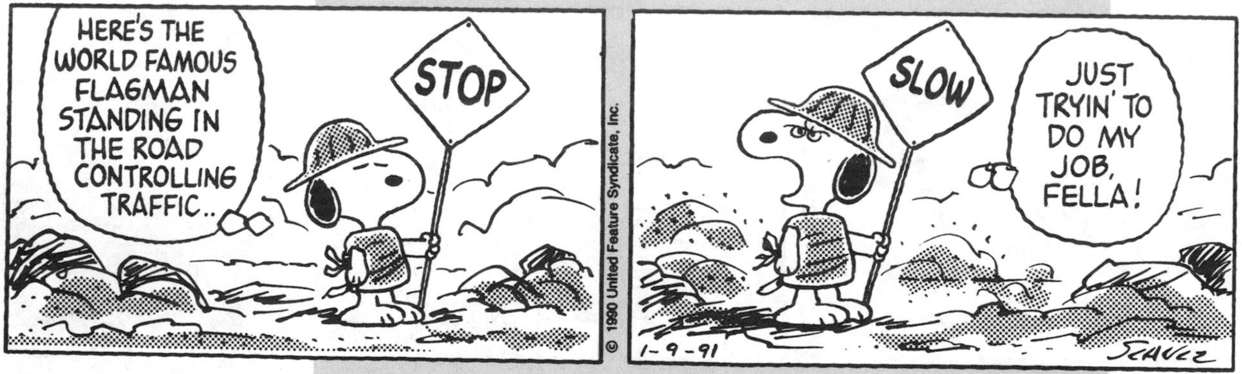

HERE'S THE WORLD FAMOUS FLAGMAN STANDING IN THE ROAD CONTROLLING TRAFFIC..
STOP
© 1990 United Feature Syndicate, Inc.
SLOW
JUST TRYIN' TO DO MY JOB, FELLA!
1-9-91
SCHULZ

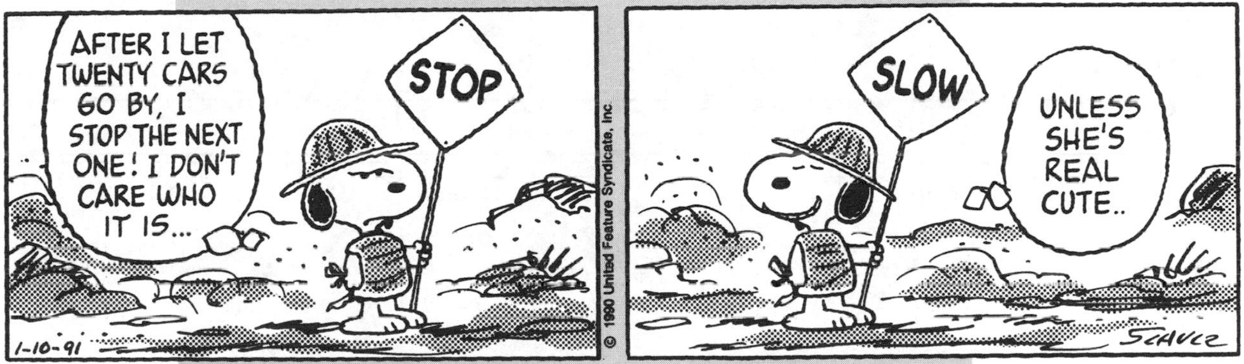
AFTER I LET TWENTY CARS GO BY, I STOP THE NEXT ONE! I DON'T CARE WHO IT IS...
STOP
1-10-91
© 1990 United Feature Syndicate, Inc.
SLOW
UNLESS SHE'S REAL CUTE..
SCHULZ

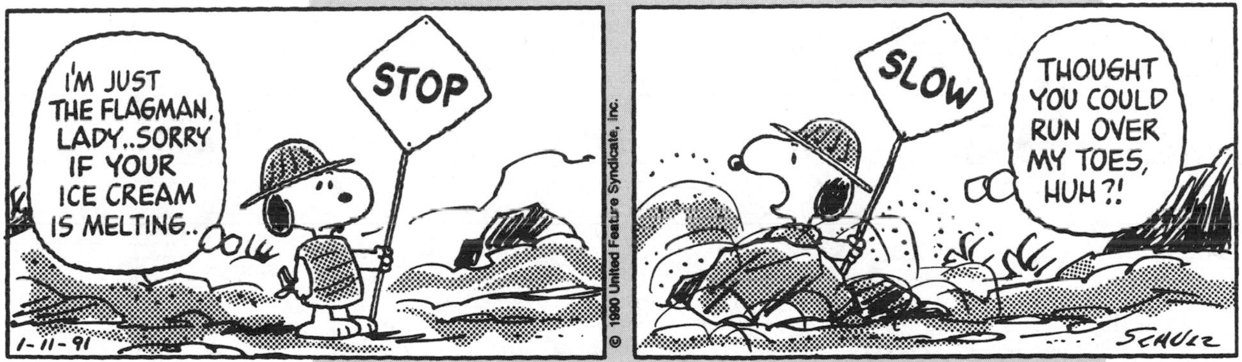
I'M JUST THE FLAGMAN, LADY..SORRY IF YOUR ICE CREAM IS MELTING..
STOP
1-11-91
© 1990 United Feature Syndicate, Inc.
SLOW
THOUGHT YOU COULD RUN OVER MY TOES, HUH?!
SCHULZ

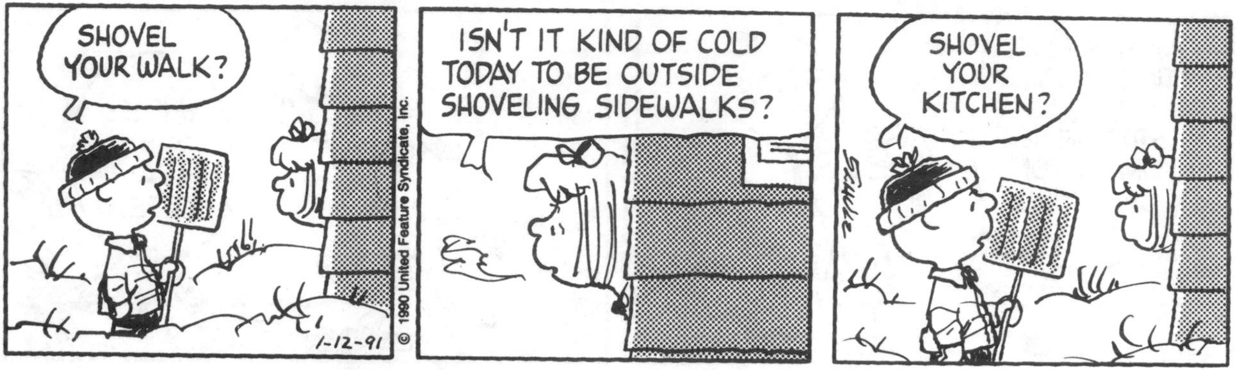
SHOVEL YOUR WALK?
1-12-91
© 1990 United Feature Syndicate, Inc.
ISN'T IT KIND OF COLD TODAY TO BE OUTSIDE SHOVELING SIDEWALKS?
SHOVEL YOUR KITCHEN?
SCHULZ

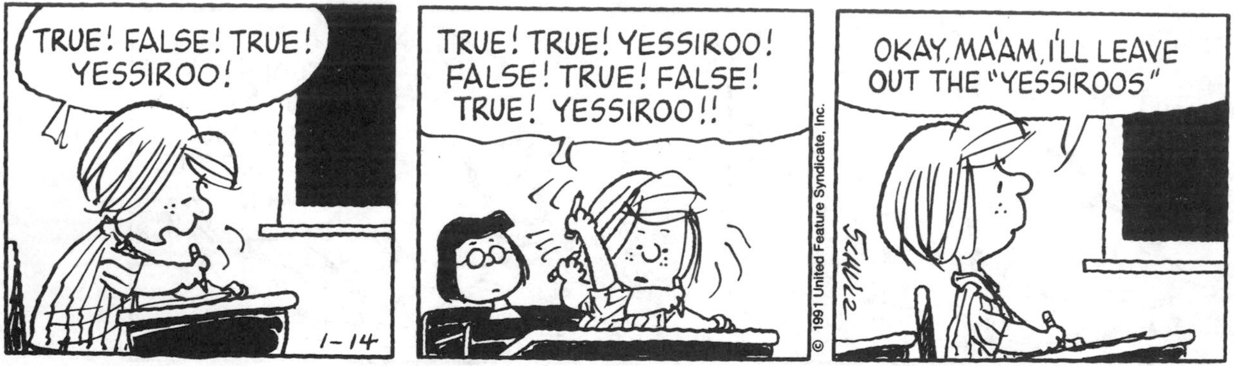
TRUE! FALSE! TRUE! YESSIROO!
1-14
TRUE! TRUE! YESSIROO! FALSE! TRUE! FALSE! TRUE! YESSIROO!!
© 1991 United Feature Syndicate, Inc.
SCHULZ
OKAY, MA'AM, I'LL LEAVE OUT THE "YESSIROOS"

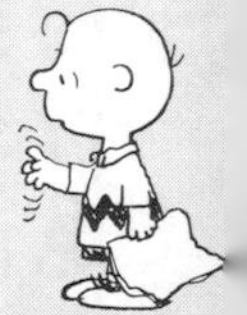

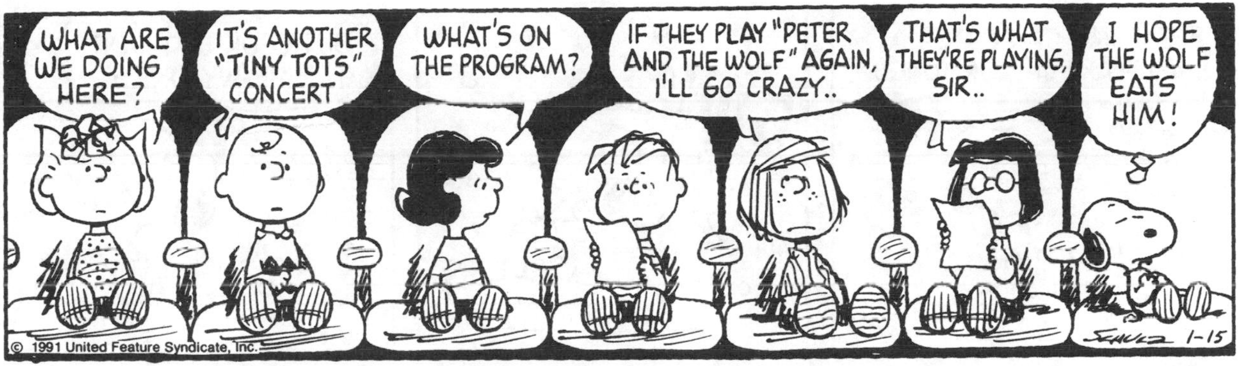
WHAT ARE WE DOING HERE?
IT'S ANOTHER "TINY TOTS" CONCERT
WHAT'S ON THE PROGRAM?
IF THEY PLAY "PETER AND THE WOLF" AGAIN, I'LL GO CRAZY..
THAT'S WHAT THEY'RE PLAYING, SIR..
I HOPE THE WOLF EATS HIM!
© 1991 United Feature Syndicate, Inc.
SCHULZ 1-15

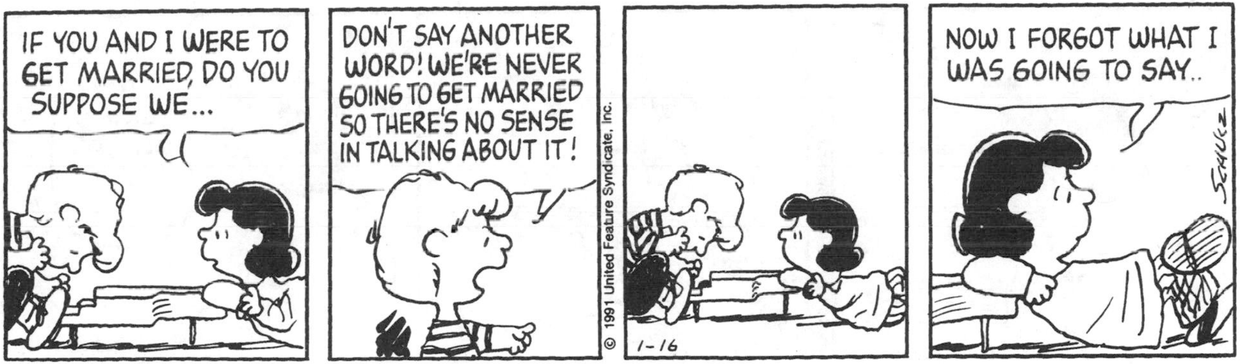
IF YOU AND I WERE TO GET MARRIED, DO YOU SUPPOSE WE...
DON'T SAY ANOTHER WORD! WE'RE NEVER GOING TO GET MARRIED SO THERE'S NO SENSE IN TALKING ABOUT IT!
© 1991 United Feature Syndicate, Inc.
1-16
NOW I FORGOT WHAT I WAS GOING TO SAY..
SCHULZ

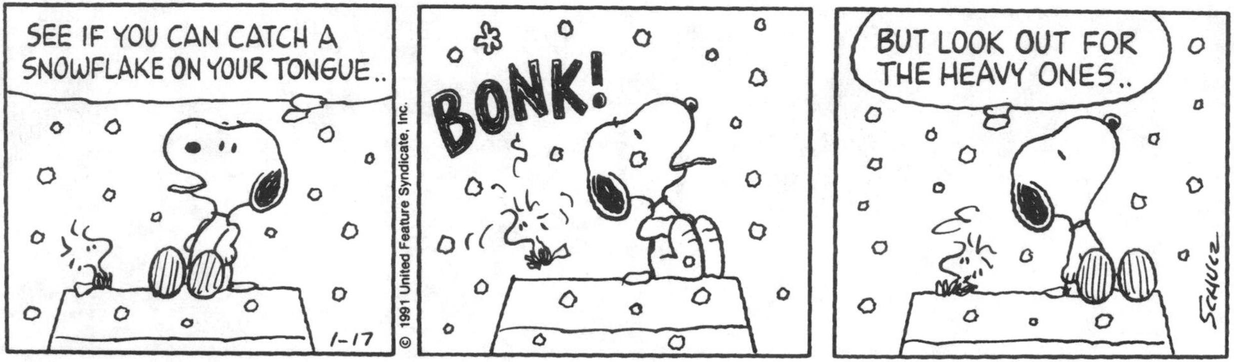
SEE IF YOU CAN CATCH A SNOWFLAKE ON YOUR TONGUE..
1-17
© 1991 United Feature Syndicate, Inc.
BONK!
BUT LOOK OUT FOR THE HEAVY ONES..
SCHULZ

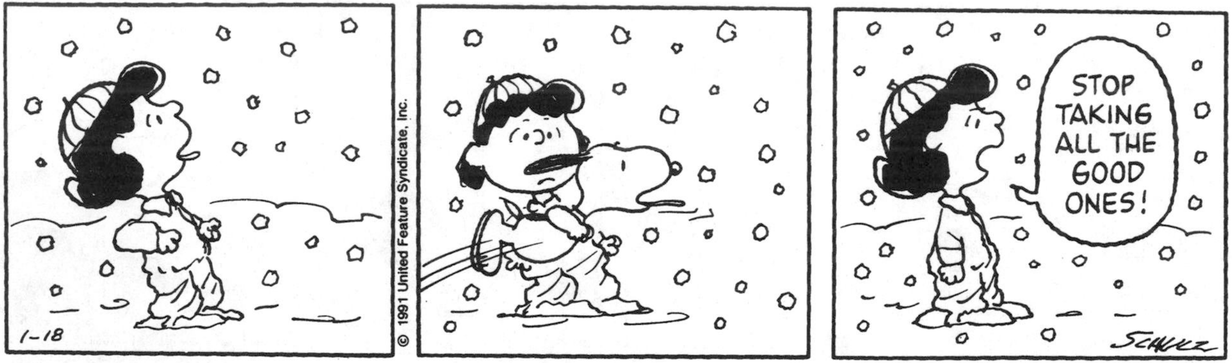
1-18
© 1991 United Feature Syndicate, Inc.
STOP TAKING ALL THE GOOD ONES!
SCHULZ

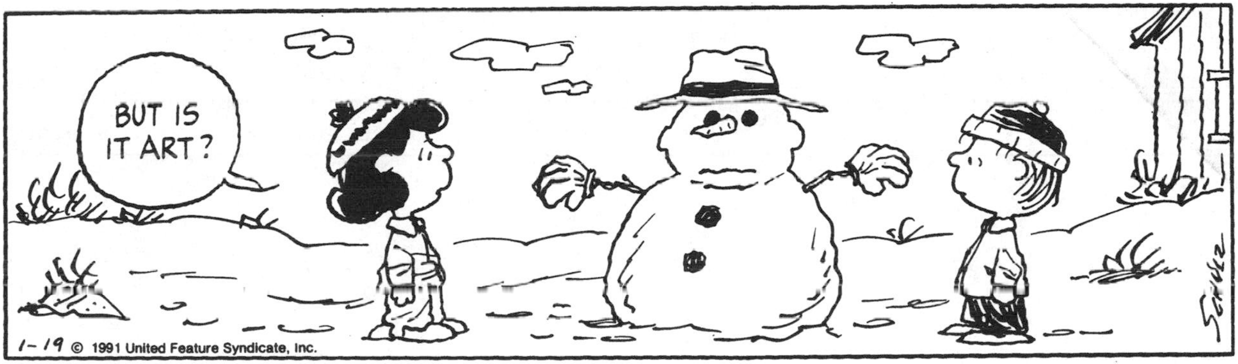
BUT IS IT ART?
1-19 © 1991 United Feature Syndicate, Inc.
SCHULZ

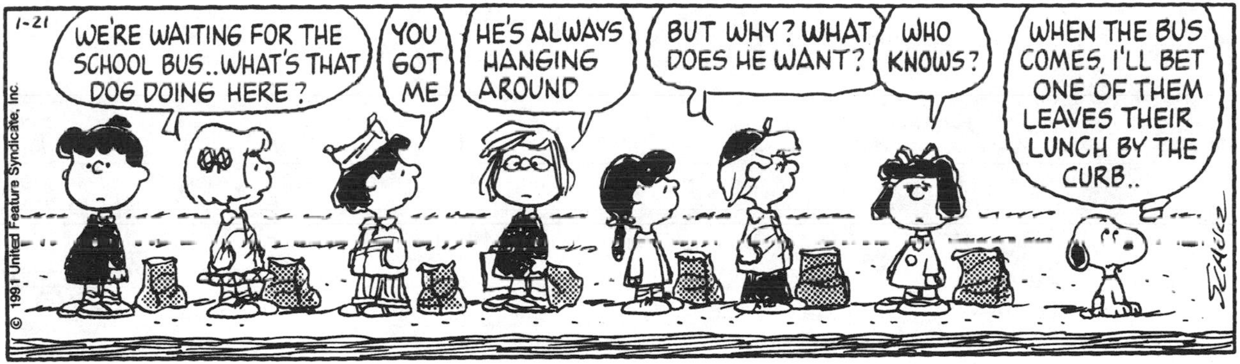
1-21
WE'RE WAITING FOR THE SCHOOL BUS..WHAT'S THAT DOG DOING HERE?
YOU GOT ME
HE'S ALWAYS HANGING AROUND
BUT WHY? WHAT DOES HE WANT?
WHO KNOWS?
WHEN THE BUS COMES, I'LL BET ONE OF THEM LEAVES THEIR LUNCH BY THE CURB..
© 1991 United Feature Syndicate, Inc.
SCHULZ

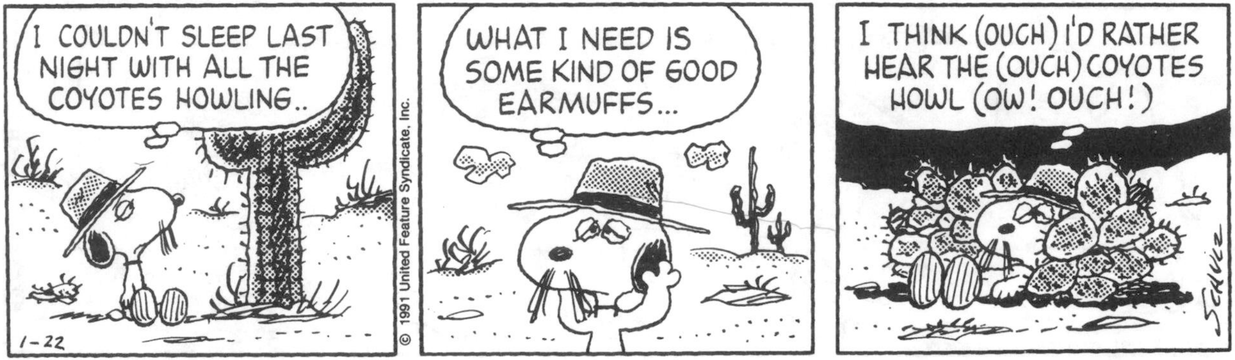
I COULDN'T SLEEP LAST NIGHT WITH ALL THE COYOTES HOWLING..
1-22
© 1991 United Feature Syndicate, Inc.
WHAT I NEED IS SOME KIND OF GOOD EARMUFFS...
I THINK (OUCH) I'D RATHER HEAR THE (OUCH) COYOTES HOWL (OW! OUCH!)
SCHULZ

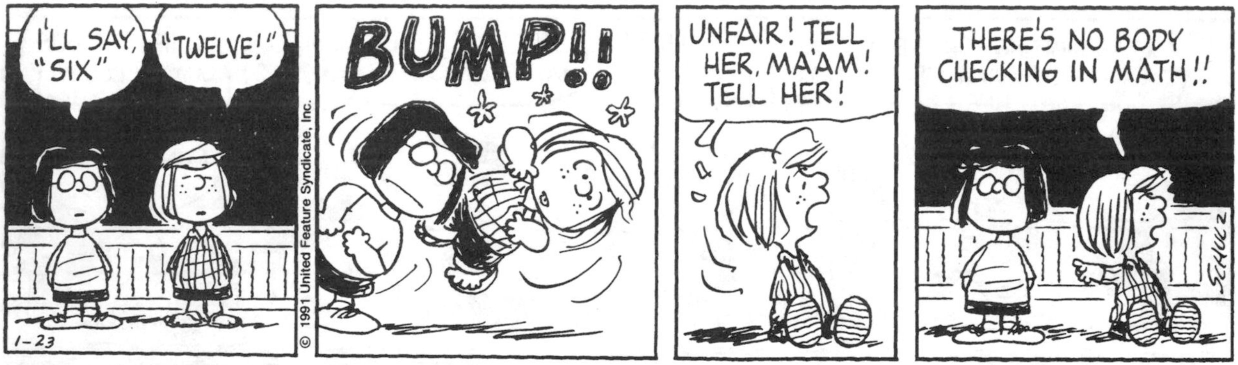
I'LL SAY, "SIX"
"TWELVE!"
1-23
© 1991 United Feature Syndicate, Inc.
BUMP!!
UNFAIR! TELL HER, MA'AM! TELL HER!
THERE'S NO BODY CHECKING IN MATH!!
SCHULZ

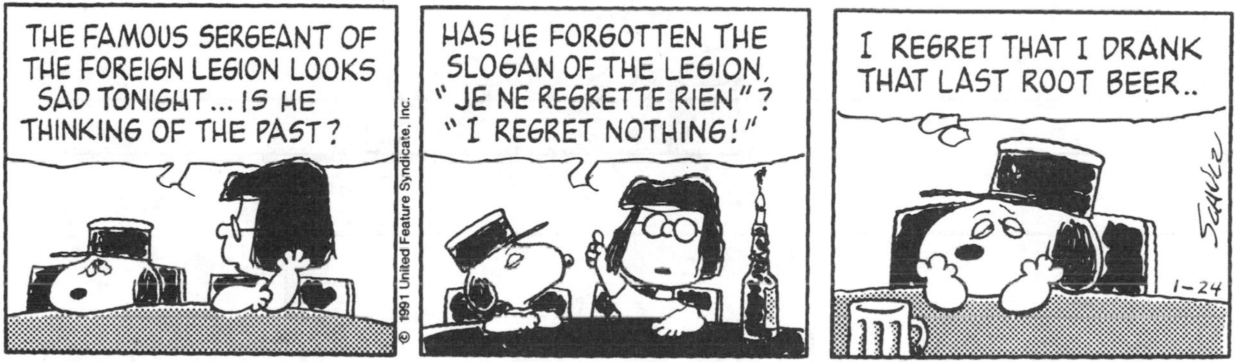
THE FAMOUS SERGEANT OF THE FOREIGN LEGION LOOKS SAD TONIGHT... IS HE THINKING OF THE PAST?
HAS HE FORGOTTEN THE SLOGAN OF THE LEGION, "JE NE REGRETTE RIEN"? "I REGRET NOTHING!"
I REGRET THAT I DRANK THAT LAST ROOT BEER..
SCHULZ
1-24

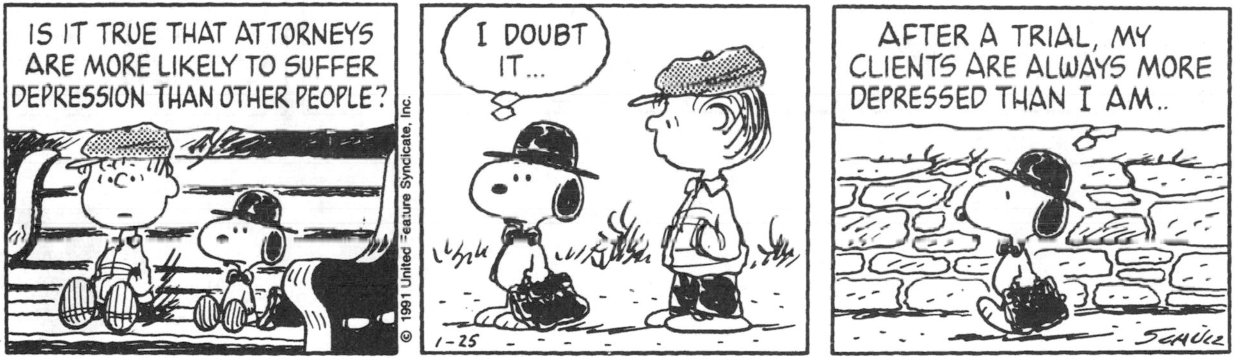
IS IT TRUE THAT ATTORNEYS ARE MORE LIKELY TO SUFFER DEPRESSION THAN OTHER PEOPLE?
I DOUBT IT...
1-25
AFTER A TRIAL, MY CLIENTS ARE ALWAYS MORE DEPRESSED THAN I AM..
SCHULZ

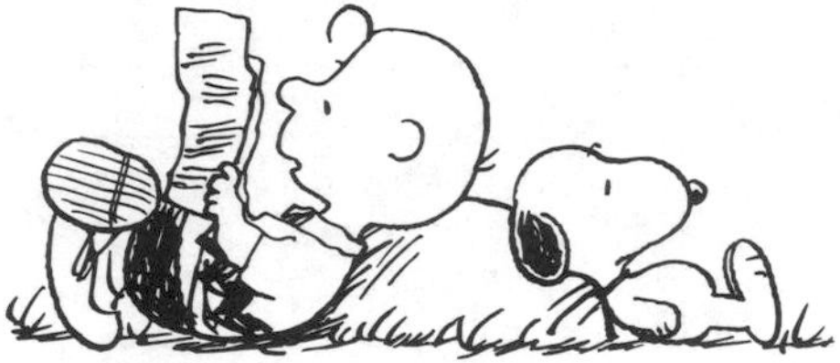

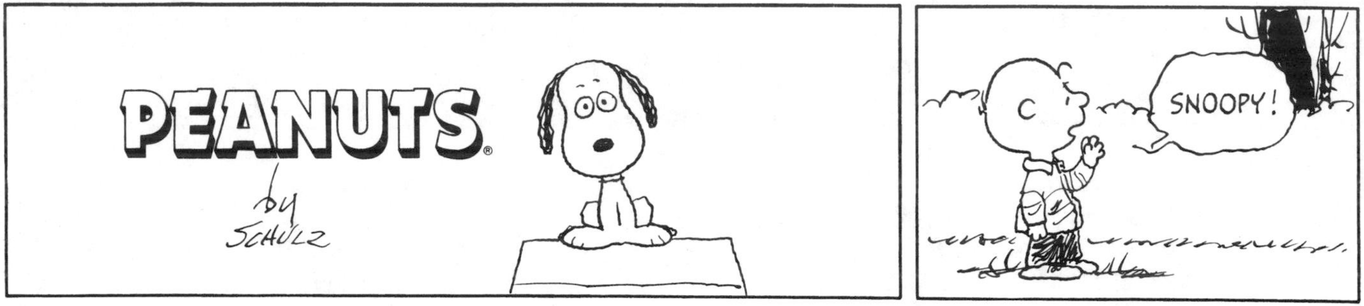
PEANUTS®
by SCHULZ
SNOOPY!

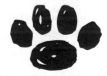

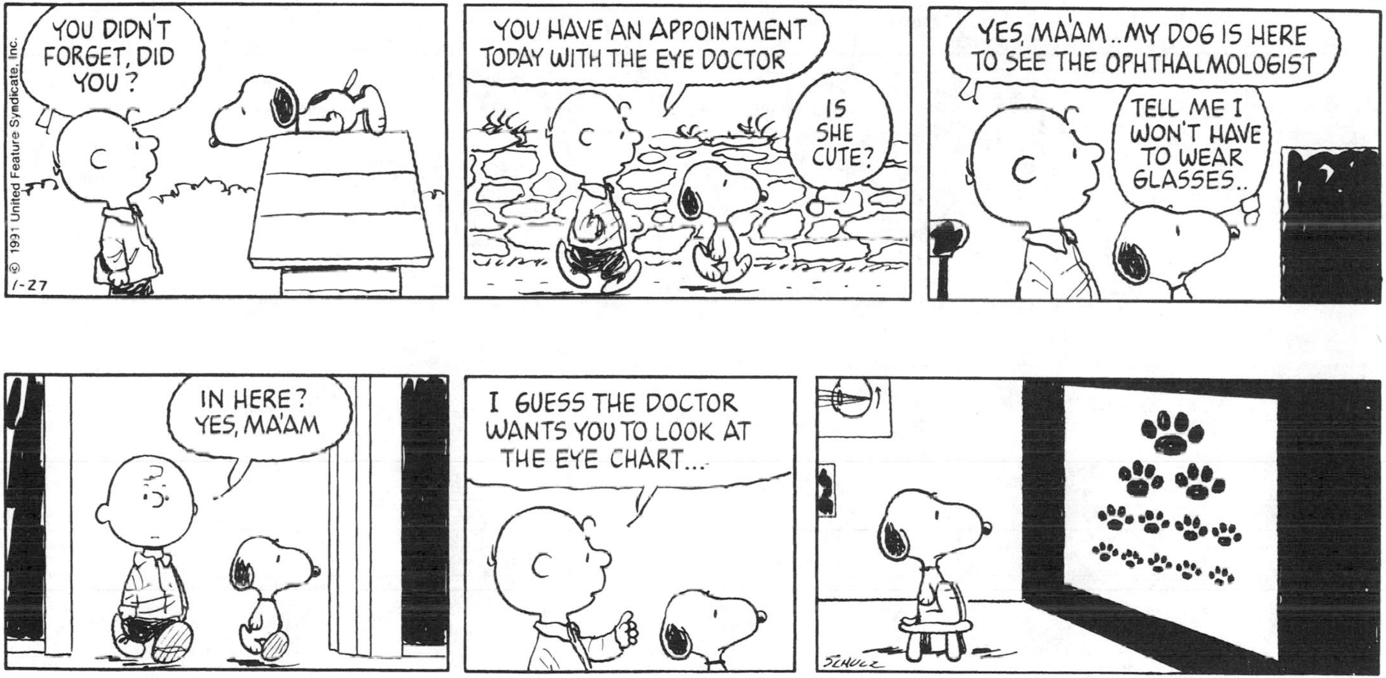
© 1991 United Feature Syndicate, Inc.
1-27
YOU DIDN'T FORGET, DID YOU?
YOU HAVE AN APPOINTMENT TODAY WITH THE EYE DOCTOR
IS SHE CUTE?
YES, MA'AM.. MY DOG IS HERE TO SEE THE OPHTHALMOLOGIST
TELL ME I WON'T HAVE TO WEAR GLASSES..
IN HERE? YES, MA'AM
I GUESS THE DOCTOR WANTS YOU TO LOOK AT THE EYE CHART...
SCHULZ

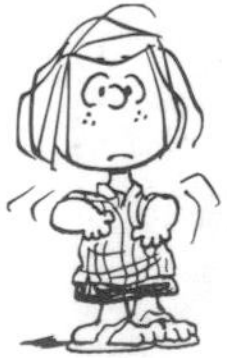

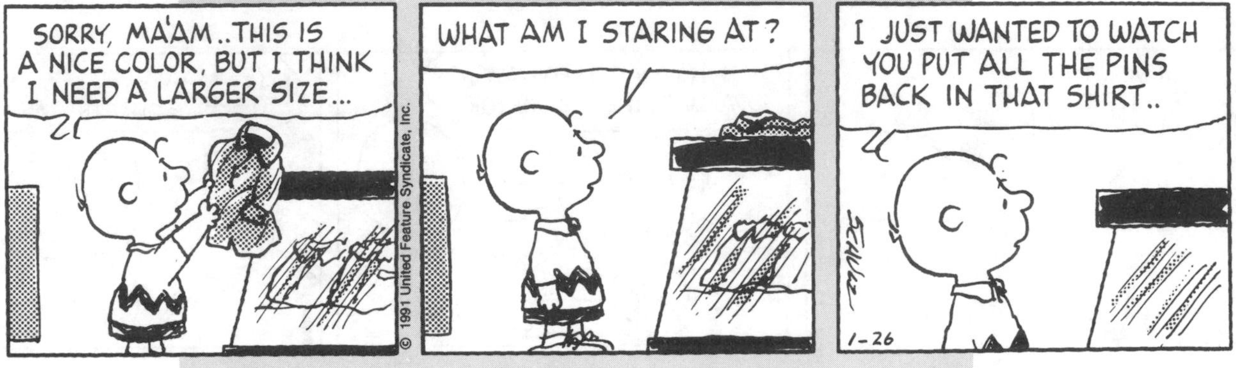
SORRY, MA'AM..THIS IS A NICE COLOR, BUT I THINK I NEED A LARGER SIZE...
WHAT AM I STARING AT?
I JUST WANTED TO WATCH YOU PUT ALL THE PINS BACK IN THAT SHIRT..
1-26

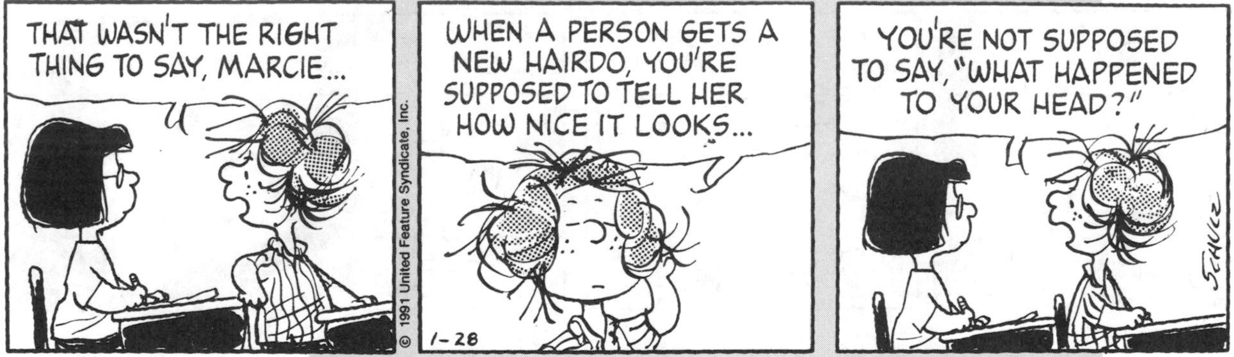
THAT WASN'T THE RIGHT THING TO SAY, MARCIE...
WHEN A PERSON GETS A NEW HAIRDO, YOU'RE SUPPOSED TO TELL HER HOW NICE IT LOOKS...
YOU'RE NOT SUPPOSED TO SAY, "WHAT HAPPENED TO YOUR HEAD?"
1-28

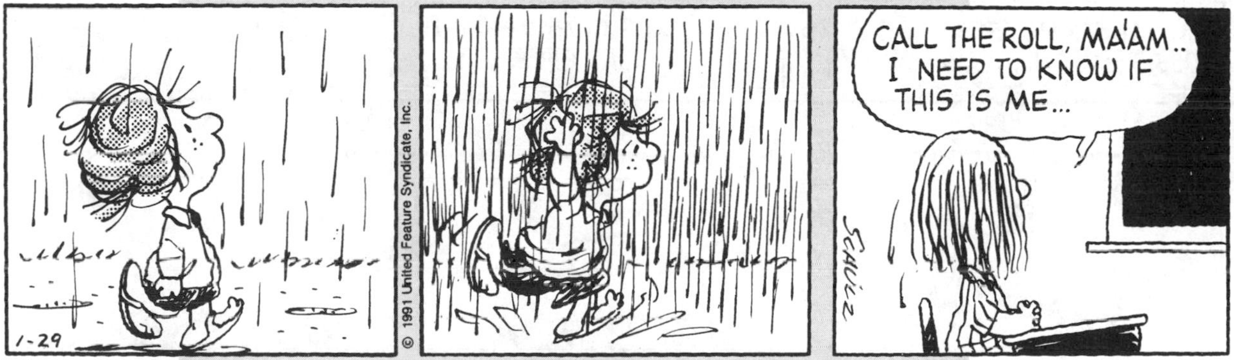
1-29
© 1991 United Feature Syndicate, Inc.
CALL THE ROLL, MA'AM.. I NEED TO KNOW IF THIS IS ME...
SCHULZ

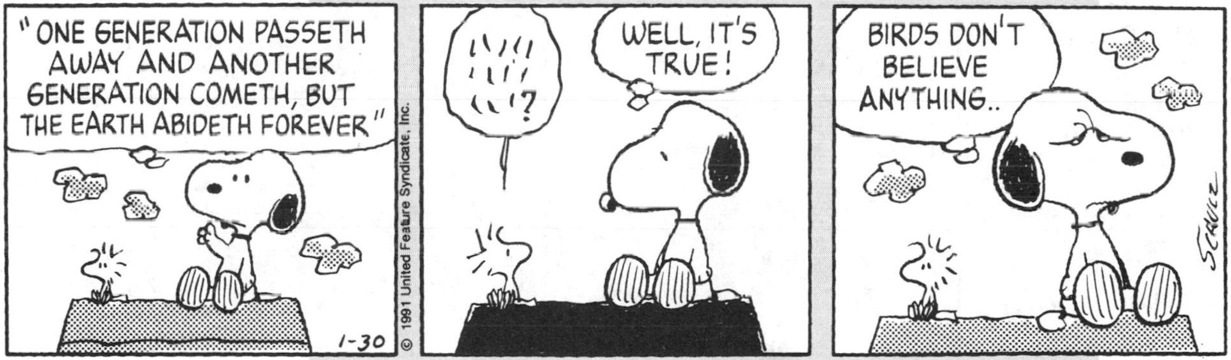
"ONE GENERATION PASSETH AWAY AND ANOTHER GENERATION COMETH, BUT THE EARTH ABIDETH FOREVER"
1-30
© 1991 United Feature Syndicate, Inc.
?
WELL, IT'S TRUE!
BIRDS DON'T BELIEVE ANYTHING..
SCHULZ

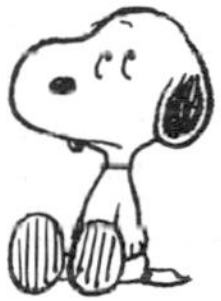

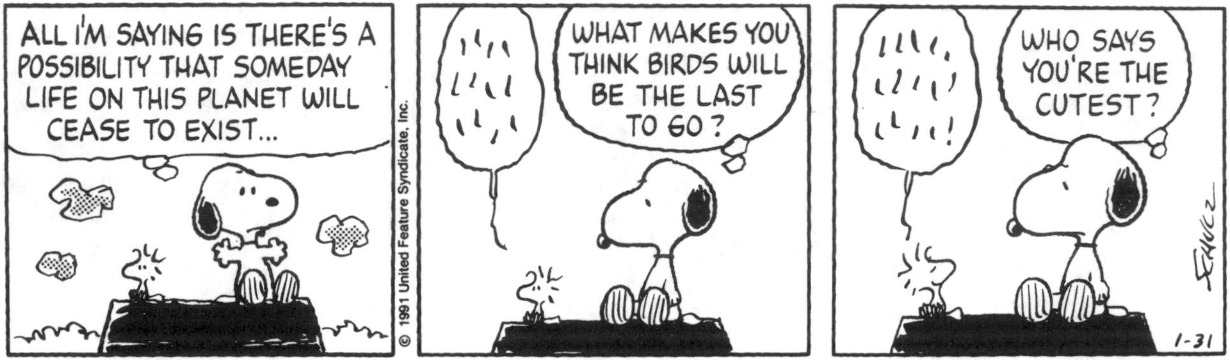
ALL I'M SAYING IS THERE'S A POSSIBILITY THAT SOMEDAY LIFE ON THIS PLANET WILL CEASE TO EXIST...
© 1991 United Feature Syndicate, Inc.
WHAT MAKES YOU THINK BIRDS WILL BE THE LAST TO GO?
WHO SAYS YOU'RE THE CUTEST?
SCHULZ
1-31

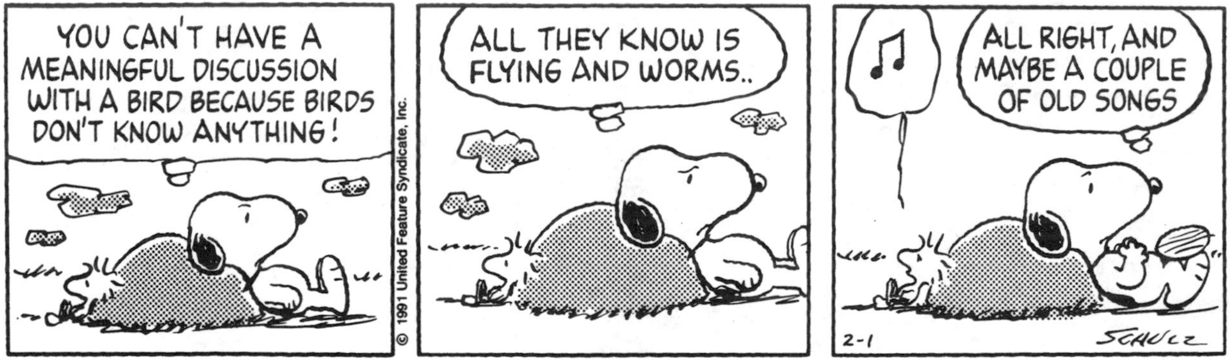
YOU CAN'T HAVE A MEANINGFUL DISCUSSION WITH A BIRD BECAUSE BIRDS DON'T KNOW ANYTHING!
© 1991 United Feature Syndicate, Inc.
ALL THEY KNOW IS FLYING AND WORMS..
ALL RIGHT, AND MAYBE A COUPLE OF OLD SONGS
2-1
SCHULZ

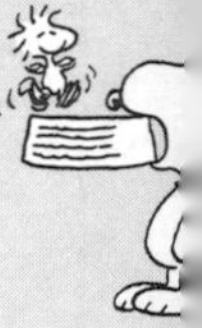

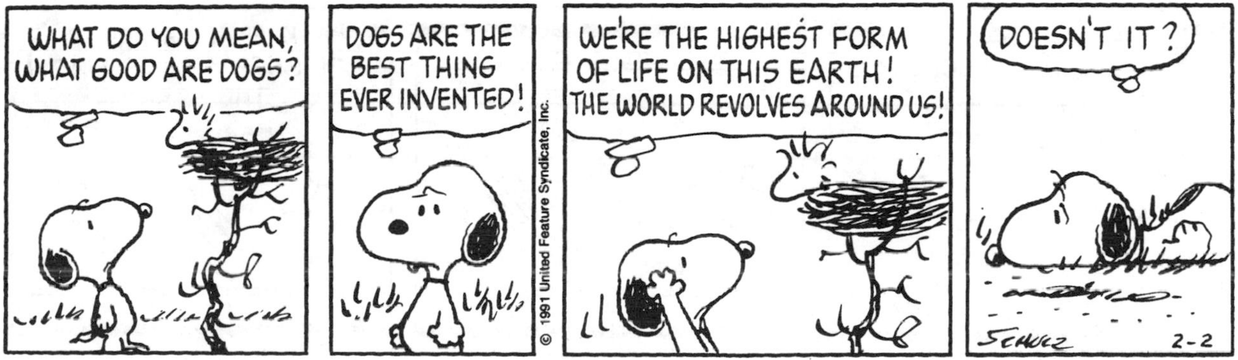
WHAT DO YOU MEAN, WHAT GOOD ARE DOGS?
DOGS ARE THE BEST THING EVER INVENTED!
© 1991 United Feature Syndicate, Inc.
WE'RE THE HIGHEST FORM OF LIFE ON THIS EARTH! THE WORLD REVOLVES AROUND US!
DOESN'T IT?
SCHULZ 2-2

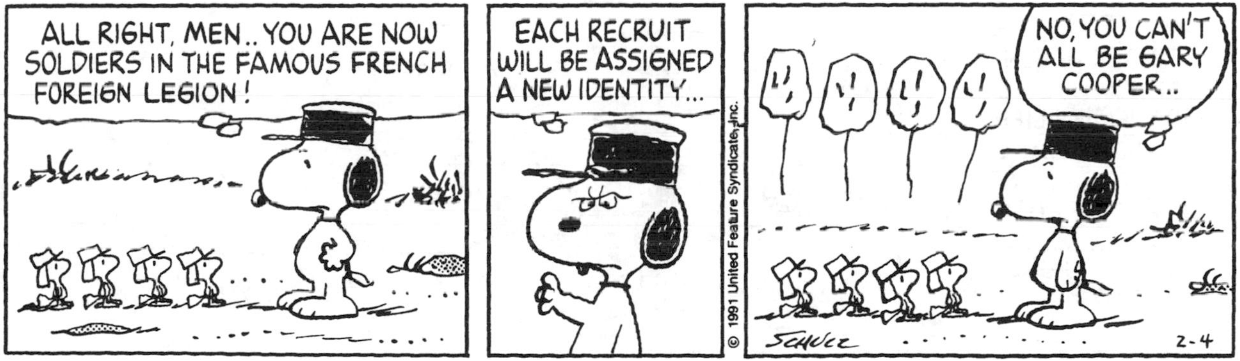
ALL RIGHT, MEN.. YOU ARE NOW SOLDIERS IN THE FAMOUS FRENCH FOREIGN LEGION!
EACH RECRUIT WILL BE ASSIGNED A NEW IDENTITY...
© 1991 United Feature Syndicate, Inc.
NO, YOU CAN'T ALL BE GARY COOPER..
SCHULZ 2-4

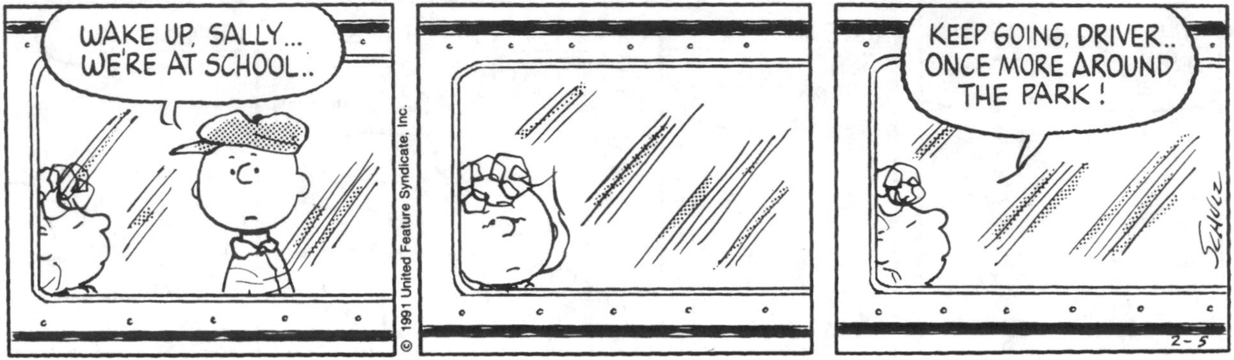
WAKE UP, SALLY... WE'RE AT SCHOOL..
© 1991 United Feature Syndicate, Inc.
KEEP GOING, DRIVER.. ONCE MORE AROUND THE PARK!
SCHULZ
2-5

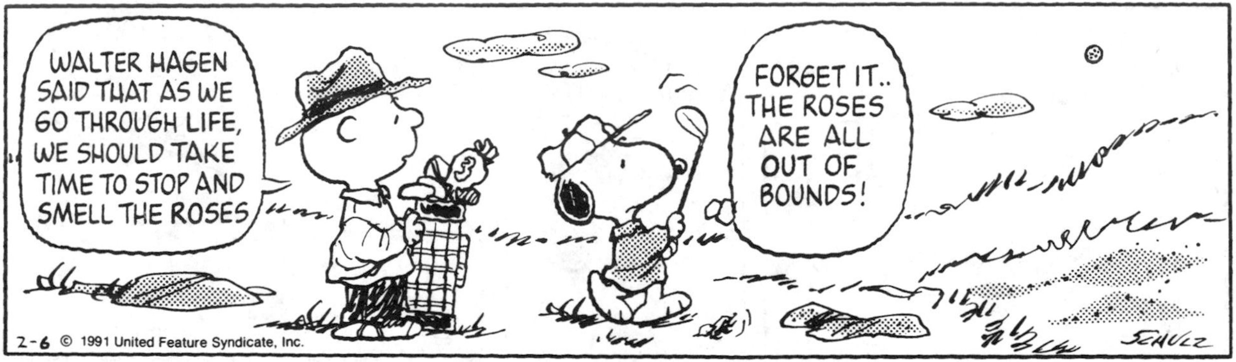
WALTER HAGEN SAID THAT AS WE GO THROUGH LIFE, WE SHOULD TAKE TIME TO STOP AND SMELL THE ROSES
FORGET IT.. THE ROSES ARE ALL OUT OF BOUNDS!
2-6 © 1991 United Feature Syndicate, Inc.
SCHULZ

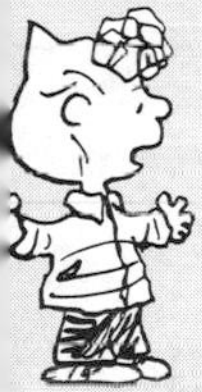

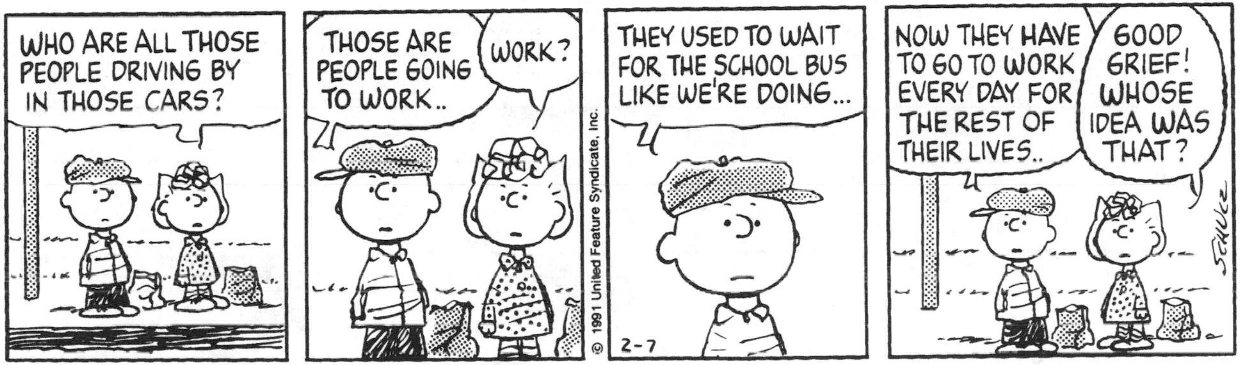

WHO ARE ALL THOSE PEOPLE DRIVING BY IN THOSE CARS?
THOSE ARE PEOPLE GOING TO WORK..
WORK?
THEY USED TO WAIT FOR THE SCHOOL BUS LIKE WE'RE DOING...
NOW THEY HAVE TO GO TO WORK EVERY DAY FOR THE REST OF THEIR LIVES..
GOOD GRIEF! WHOSE IDEA WAS THAT?
© 1991 United Feature Syndicate, Inc.
2-7
SCHULZ

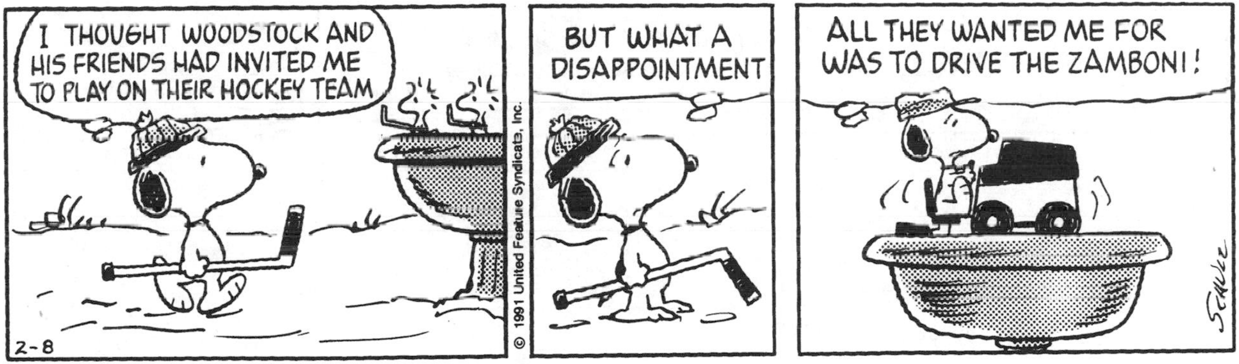

I THOUGHT WOODSTOCK AND HIS FRIENDS HAD INVITED ME TO PLAY ON THEIR HOCKEY TEAM
BUT WHAT A DISAPPOINTMENT
ALL THEY WANTED ME FOR WAS TO DRIVE THE ZAMBONI!
© 1991 United Feature Syndicate, Inc.
2-8
SCHULZ

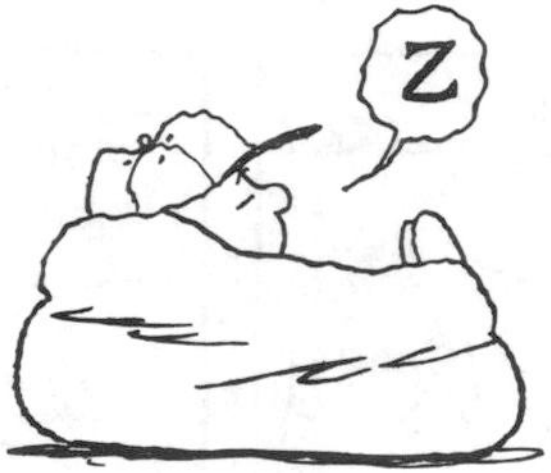
Z

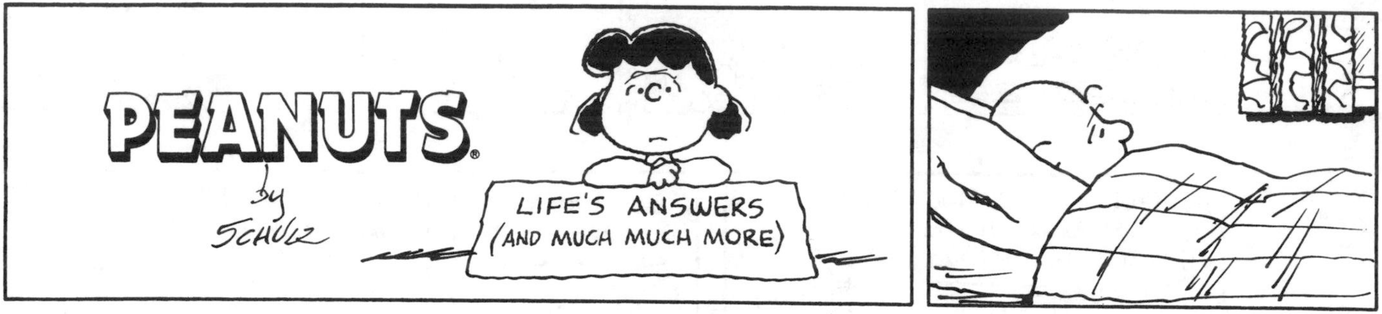
PEANUTS
by SCHULZ
LIFE'S ANSWERS
(AND MUCH MUCH MORE)

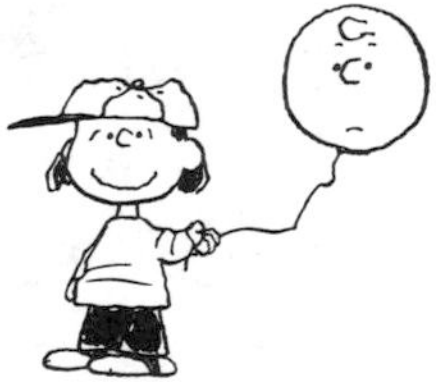

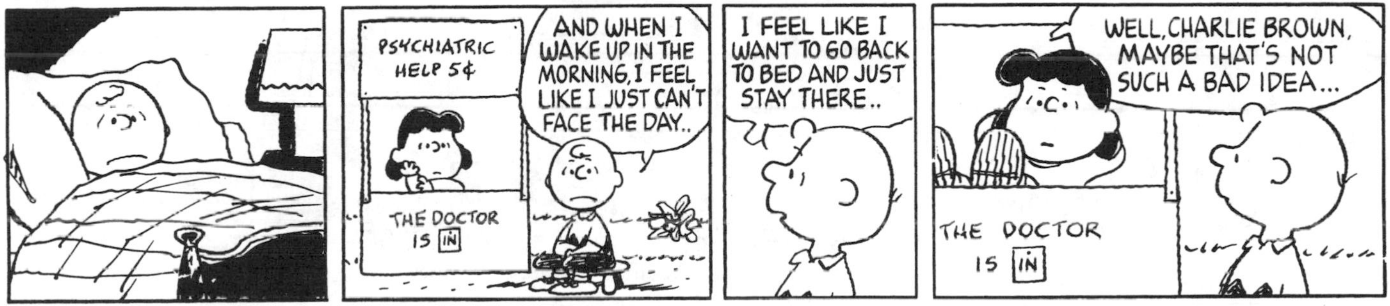
PSYCHIATRIC HELP 5¢
THE DOCTOR IS IN
AND WHEN I WAKE UP IN THE MORNING, I FEEL LIKE I JUST CAN'T FACE THE DAY..
I FEEL LIKE I WANT TO GO BACK TO BED AND JUST STAY THERE..
WELL, CHARLIE BROWN, MAYBE THAT'S NOT SUCH A BAD IDEA...
THE DOCTOR IS IN

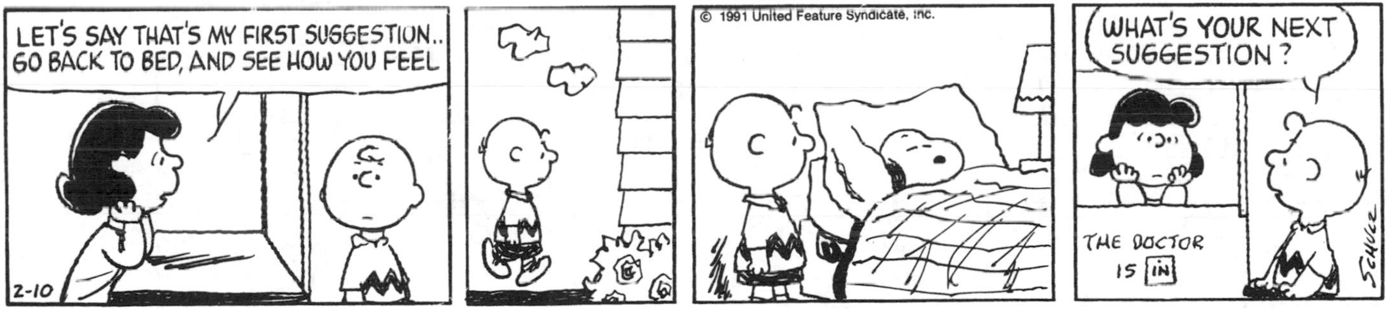
LET'S SAY THAT'S MY FIRST SUGGESTION.. GO BACK TO BED, AND SEE HOW YOU FEEL
2-10
© 1991 United Feature Syndicate, Inc.
WHAT'S YOUR NEXT SUGGESTION ?
THE DOCTOR IS IN
SCHULZ

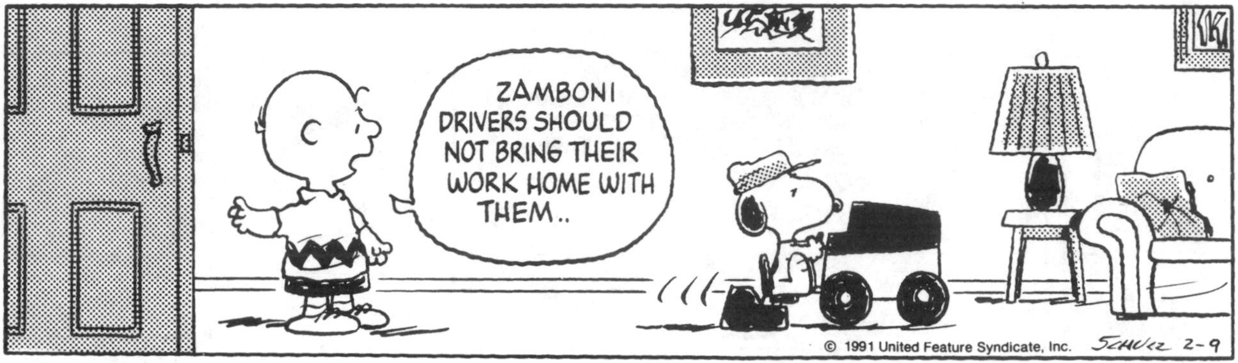
ZAMBONI DRIVERS SHOULD NOT BRING THEIR WORK HOME WITH THEM..
© 1991 United Feature Syndicate, Inc.
2-9

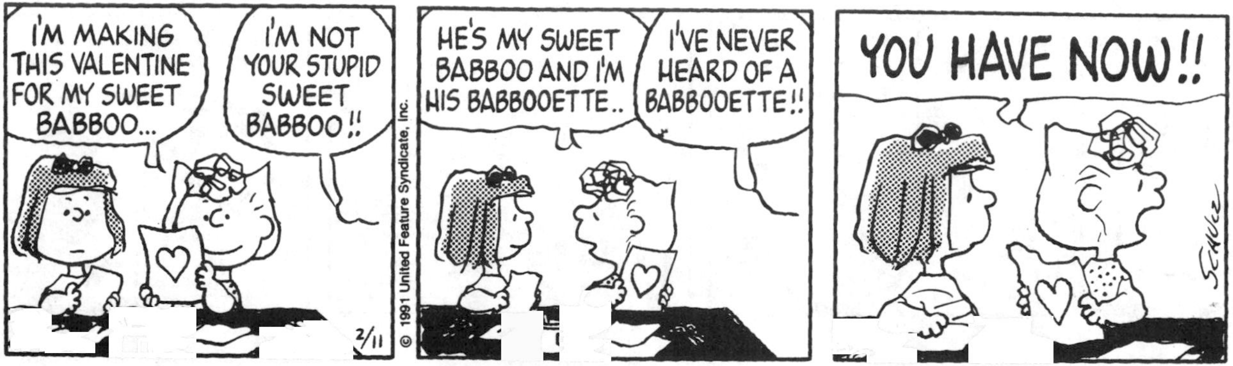
I'M MAKING THIS VALENTINE FOR MY SWEET BABBOO...
I'M NOT YOUR STUPID SWEET BABBOO!!
© 1991 United Feature Syndicate, Inc.
2/11
HE'S MY SWEET BABBOO AND I'M HIS BABBOOETTE..
I'VE NEVER HEARD OF A BABBOOETTE!!
YOU HAVE NOW!!

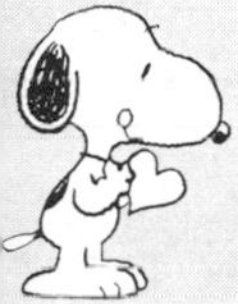

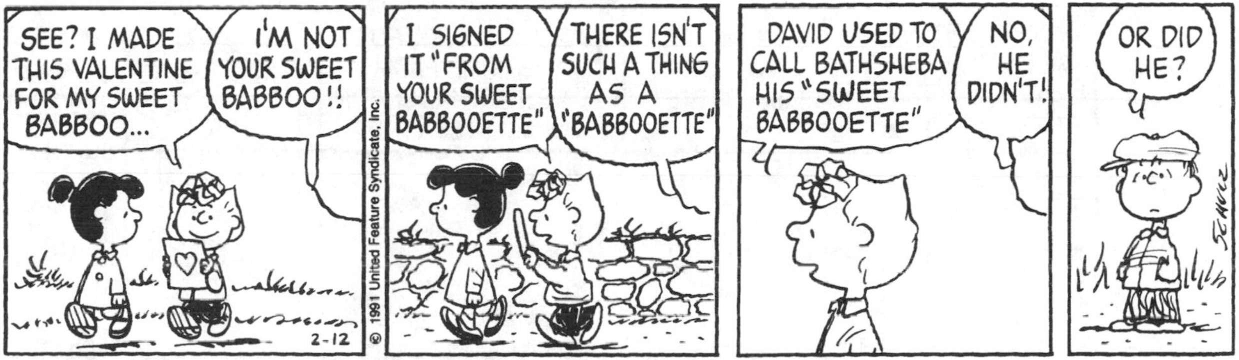

SEE? I MADE THIS VALENTINE FOR MY SWEET BABBOO...
I'M NOT YOUR SWEET BABBOO!!
2-12
© 1991 United Feature Syndicate, Inc.
I SIGNED IT "FROM YOUR SWEET BABBOOETTE"
THERE ISN'T SUCH A THING AS A "BABBOOETTE"
DAVID USED TO CALL BATHSHEBA HIS "SWEET BABBOOETTE"
NO, HE DIDN'T!
OR DID HE?
SCHULZ

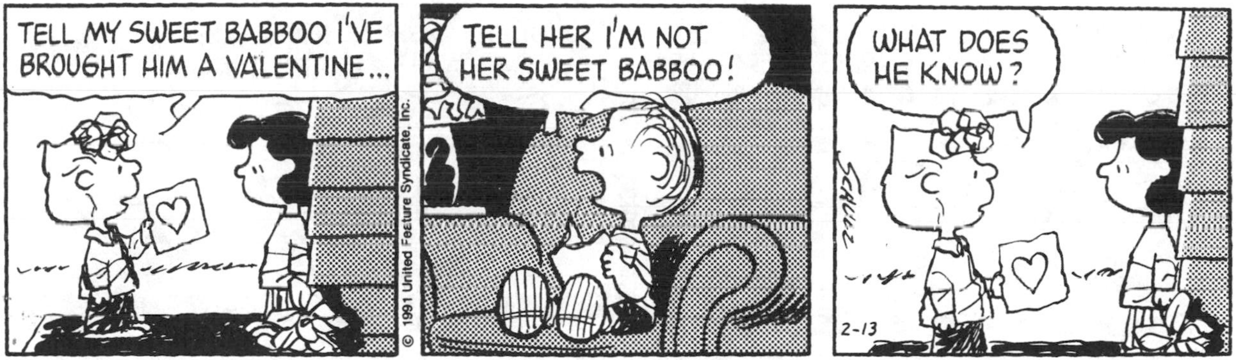

TELL MY SWEET BABBOO I'VE BROUGHT HIM A VALENTINE...
© 1991 United Feature Syndicate, Inc.
TELL HER I'M NOT HER SWEET BABBOO!
WHAT DOES HE KNOW?
SCHULZ
2-13

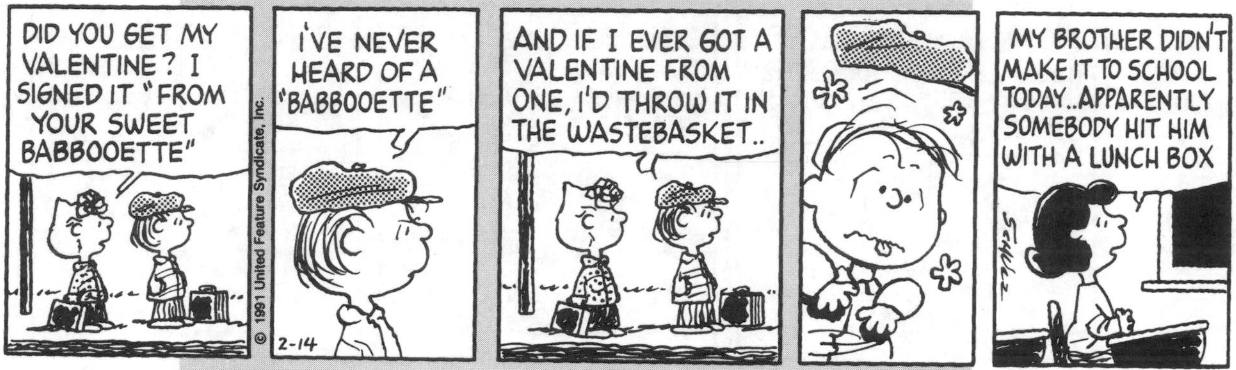
DID YOU GET MY VALENTINE? I SIGNED IT "FROM YOUR SWEET BABBOOETTE"
I'VE NEVER HEARD OF A "BABBOOETTE"
© 1991 United Feature Syndicate, Inc.
2-14
AND IF I EVER GOT A VALENTINE FROM ONE, I'D THROW IT IN THE WASTEBASKET..
MY BROTHER DIDN'T MAKE IT TO SCHOOL TODAY..APPARENTLY SOMEBODY HIT HIM WITH A LUNCH BOX
SCHULZ

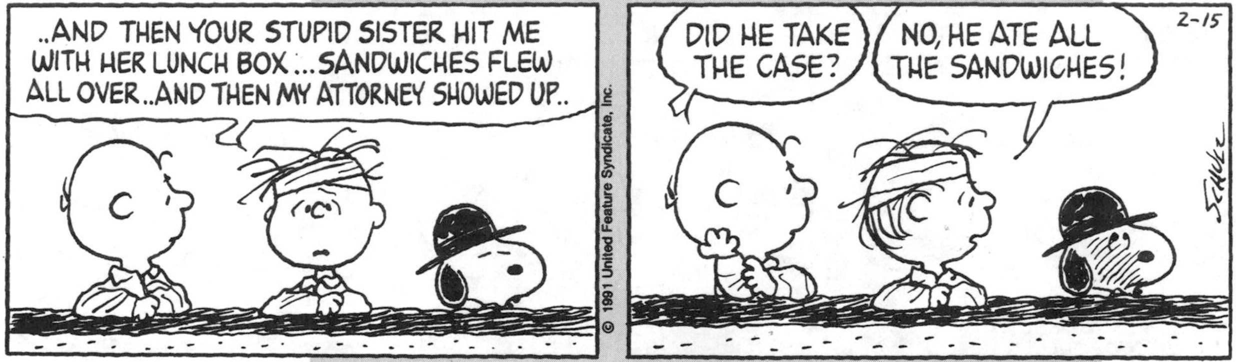
..AND THEN YOUR STUPID SISTER HIT ME WITH HER LUNCH BOX...SANDWICHES FLEW ALL OVER..AND THEN MY ATTORNEY SHOWED UP..
© 1991 United Feature Syndicate, Inc.
2-15
DID HE TAKE THE CASE?
NO, HE ATE ALL THE SANDWICHES!
SCHULZ

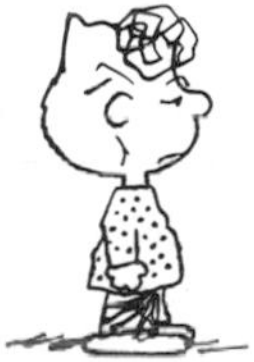

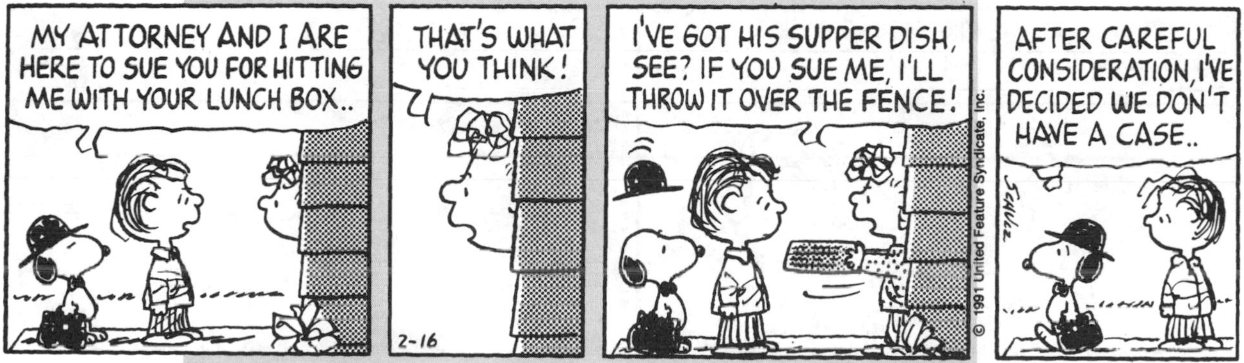

MY ATTORNEY AND I ARE HERE TO SUE YOU FOR HITTING ME WITH YOUR LUNCH BOX..
THAT'S WHAT YOU THINK!
2-16
I'VE GOT HIS SUPPER DISH, SEE? IF YOU SUE ME, I'LL THROW IT OVER THE FENCE!
© 1991 United Feature Syndicate, Inc.
AFTER CAREFUL CONSIDERATION, I'VE DECIDED WE DON'T HAVE A CASE..
SCHULZ

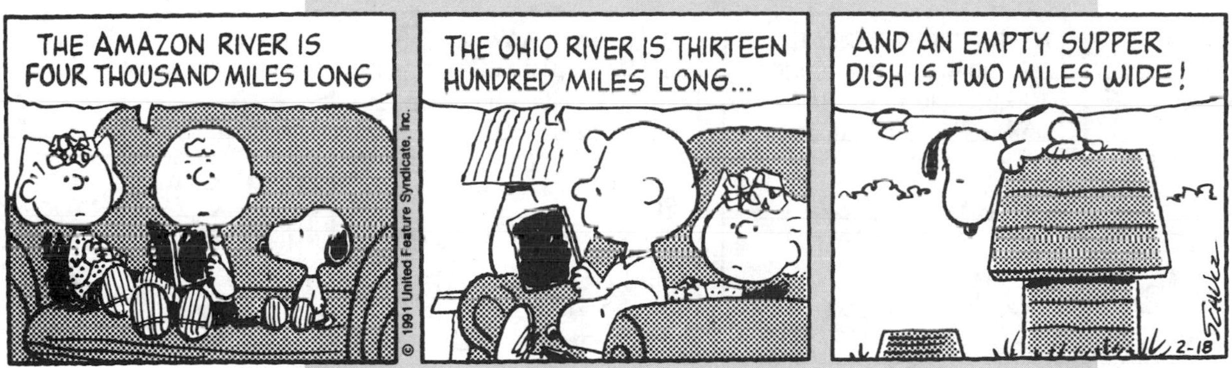

THE AMAZON RIVER IS FOUR THOUSAND MILES LONG
© 1991 United Feature Syndicate, Inc.
THE OHIO RIVER IS THIRTEEN HUNDRED MILES LONG...
AND AN EMPTY SUPPER DISH IS TWO MILES WIDE!
SCHULZ
2-18

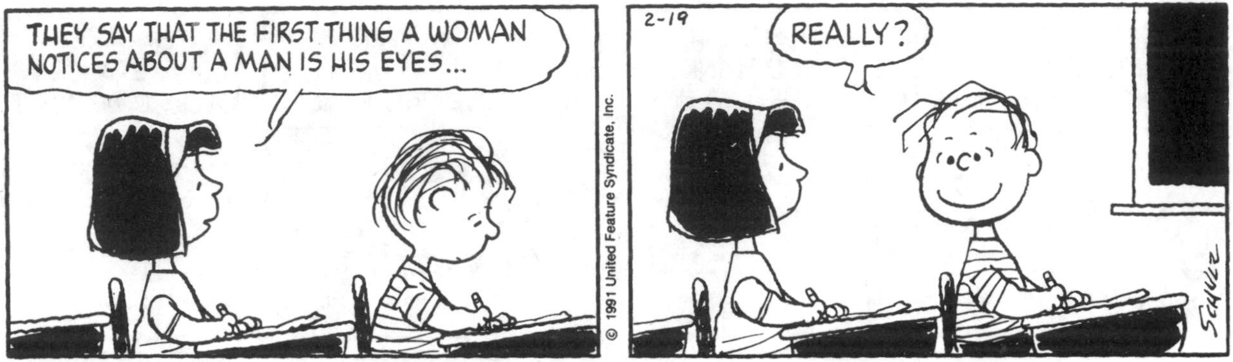
THEY SAY THAT THE FIRST THING A WOMAN NOTICES ABOUT A MAN IS HIS EYES...
© 1991 United Feature Syndicate, Inc.
2-19
REALLY?
SCHULZ

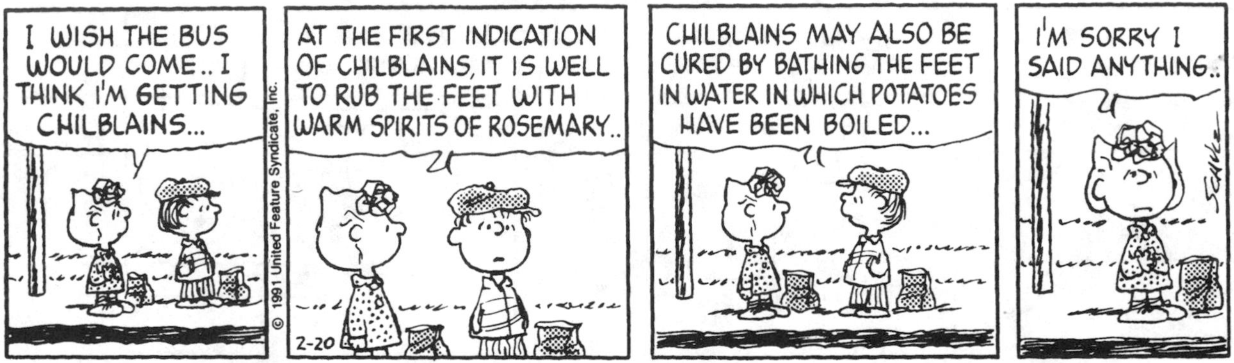
I WISH THE BUS WOULD COME.. I THINK I'M GETTING CHILBLAINS...
© 1991 United Feature Syndicate, Inc.
AT THE FIRST INDICATION OF CHILBLAINS, IT IS WELL TO RUB THE FEET WITH WARM SPIRITS OF ROSEMARY..
2-20
CHILBLAINS MAY ALSO BE CURED BY BATHING THE FEET IN WATER IN WHICH POTATOES HAVE BEEN BOILED...
I'M SORRY I SAID ANYTHING..
SCHULZ

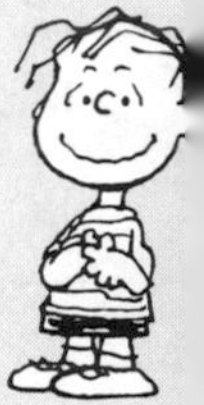

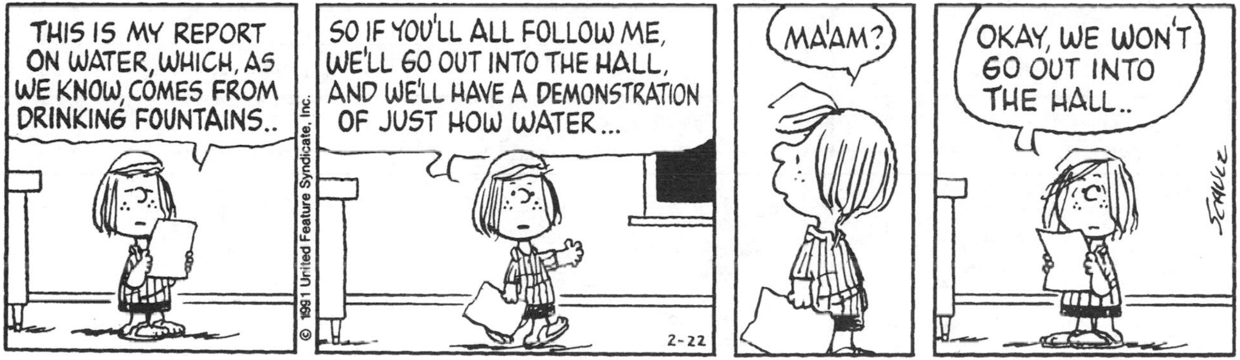
THIS IS MY REPORT ON WATER, WHICH, AS WE KNOW, COMES FROM DRINKING FOUNTAINS..
© 1991 United Feature Syndicate, Inc.
SO IF YOU'LL ALL FOLLOW ME, WE'LL GO OUT INTO THE HALL, AND WE'LL HAVE A DEMONSTRATION OF JUST HOW WATER...
2-22
MA'AM?
OKAY, WE WON'T GO OUT INTO THE HALL..
SCHULZ

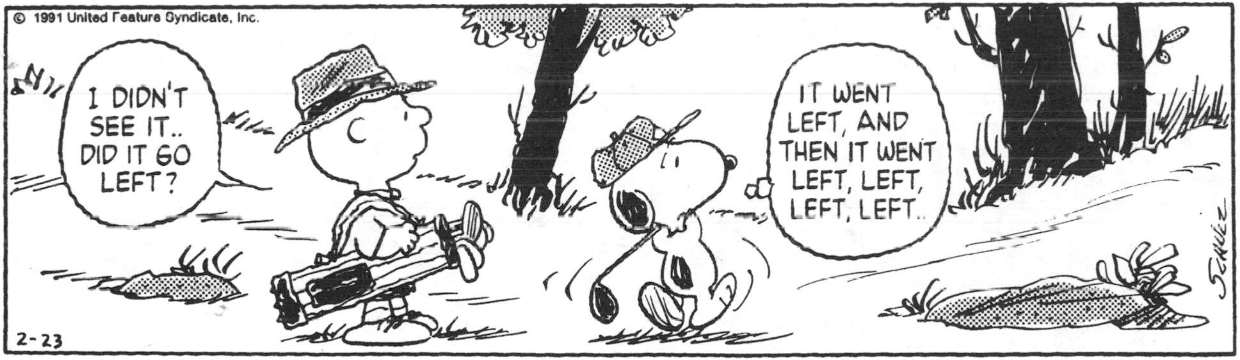
© 1991 United Feature Syndicate, Inc.
I DIDN'T SEE IT.. DID IT GO LEFT?
IT WENT LEFT, AND THEN IT WENT LEFT, LEFT, LEFT, LEFT, LEFT..
SCHULZ
2-23

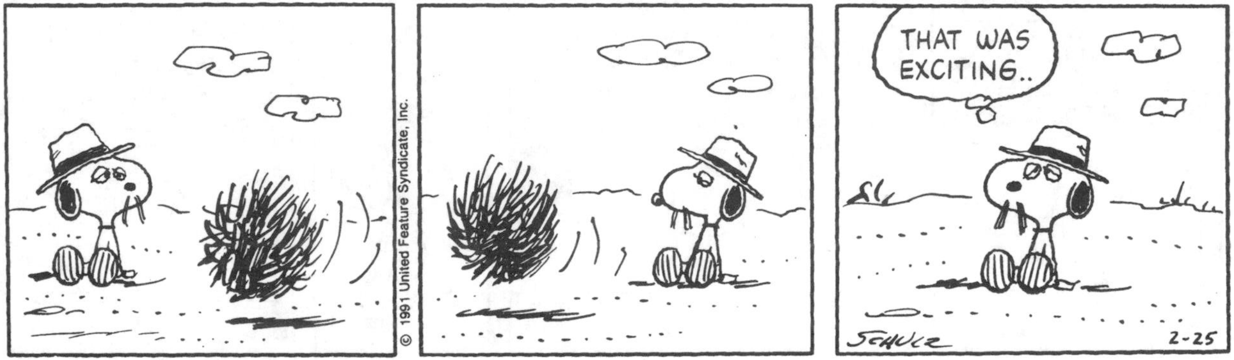
© 1991 United Feature Syndicate, Inc.
THAT WAS EXCITING..
SCHULZ
2-25

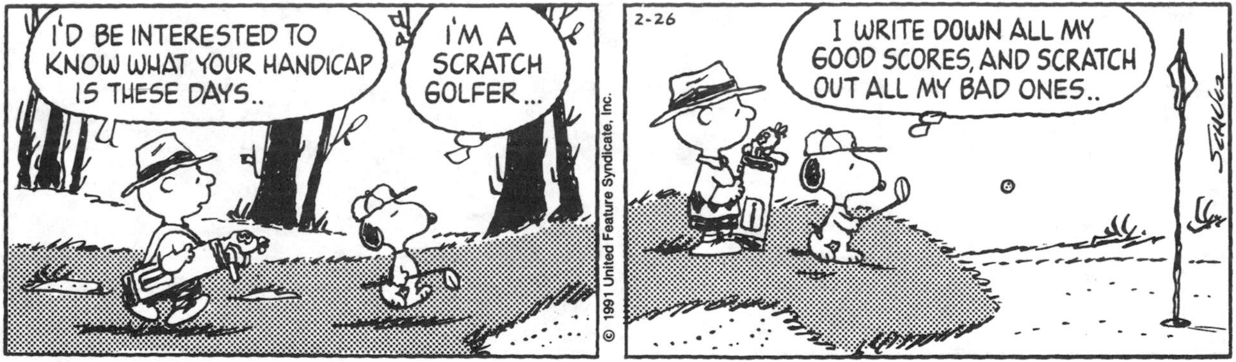
I'D BE INTERESTED TO KNOW WHAT YOUR HANDICAP IS THESE DAYS..
I'M A SCRATCH GOLFER...
© 1991 United Feature Syndicate, Inc.
2-26
I WRITE DOWN ALL MY GOOD SCORES, AND SCRATCH OUT ALL MY BAD ONES..
SCHULZ

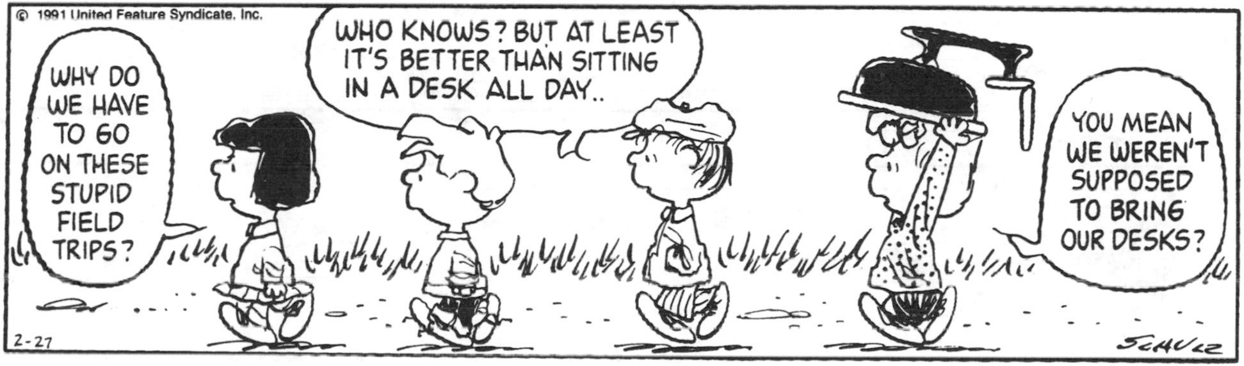
© 1991 United Feature Syndicate, Inc.
WHY DO WE HAVE TO GO ON THESE STUPID FIELD TRIPS?
WHO KNOWS? BUT AT LEAST IT'S BETTER THAN SITTING IN A DESK ALL DAY..
YOU MEAN WE WEREN'T SUPPOSED TO BRING OUR DESKS?
2-27
SCHULZ

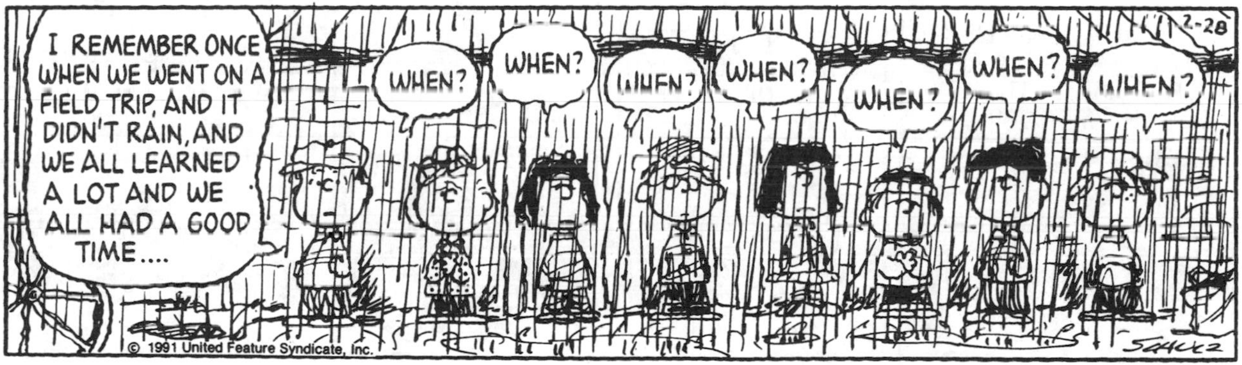
2-28
I REMEMBER ONCE WHEN WE WENT ON A FIELD TRIP, AND IT DIDN'T RAIN, AND WE ALL LEARNED A LOT AND WE ALL HAD A GOOD TIME....
WHEN?
WHEN?
WHEN?
WHEN?
WHEN?
WHEN?
WHEN?
© 1991 United Feature Syndicate, Inc.
SCHULZ

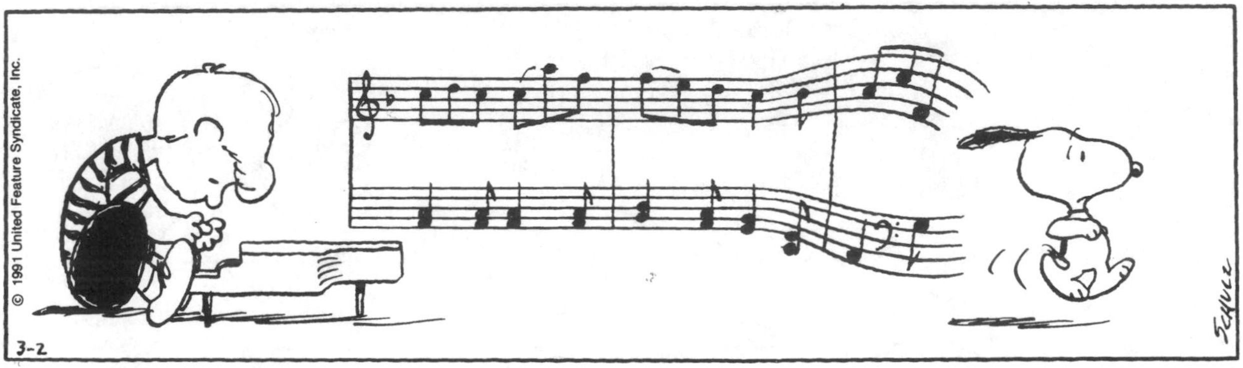
© 1991 United Feature Syndicate, Inc.
3-2
SCHULZ

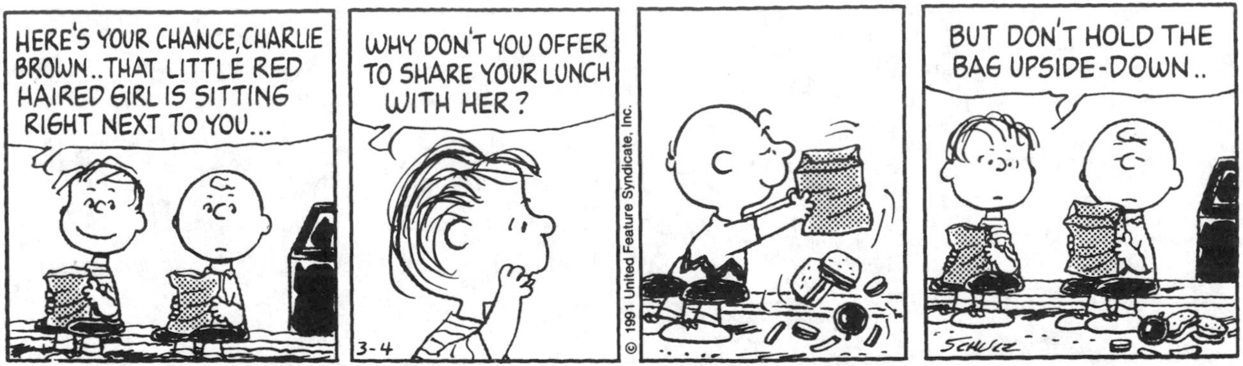
HERE'S YOUR CHANCE, CHARLIE BROWN..THAT LITTLE RED HAIRED GIRL IS SITTING RIGHT NEXT TO YOU...
WHY DON'T YOU OFFER TO SHARE YOUR LUNCH WITH HER?
3-4
© 1991 United Feature Syndicate, Inc.
BUT DON'T HOLD THE BAG UPSIDE-DOWN..
SCHULZ

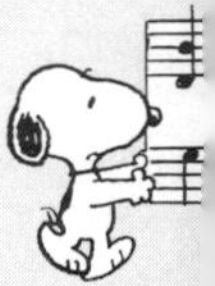

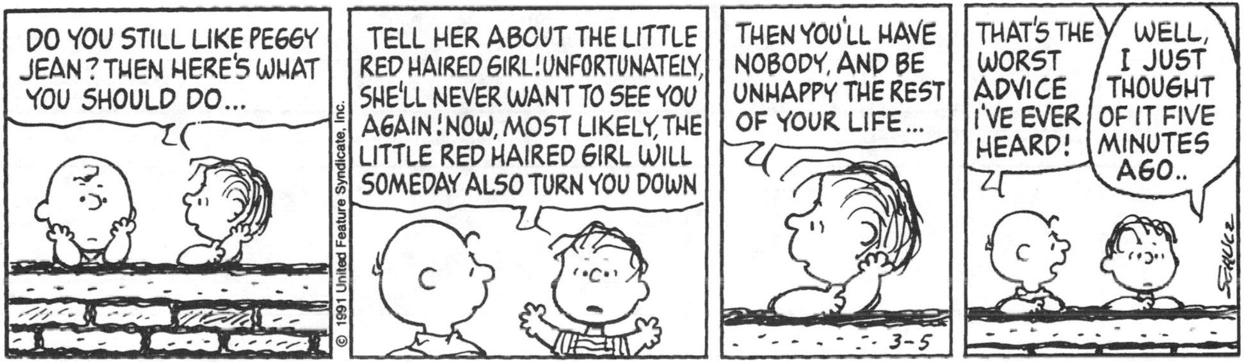
DO YOU STILL LIKE PEGGY JEAN? THEN HERE'S WHAT YOU SHOULD DO...
TELL HER ABOUT THE LITTLE RED HAIRED GIRL! UNFORTUNATELY, SHE'LL NEVER WANT TO SEE YOU AGAIN! NOW, MOST LIKELY, THE LITTLE RED HAIRED GIRL WILL SOMEDAY ALSO TURN YOU DOWN
THEN YOU'LL HAVE NOBODY, AND BE UNHAPPY THE REST OF YOUR LIFE...
THAT'S THE WORST ADVICE I'VE EVER HEARD!
WELL, I JUST THOUGHT OF IT FIVE MINUTES AGO..
© 1991 United Feature Syndicate, Inc.
3-5
SCHULZ

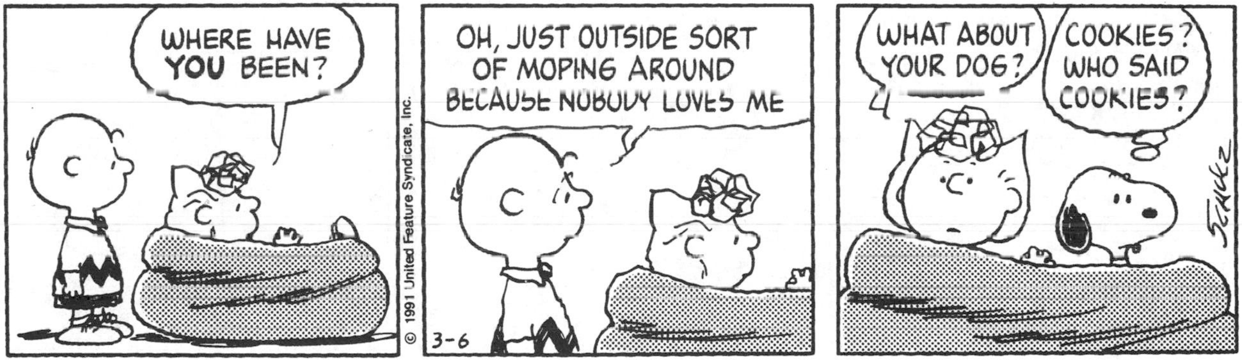
WHERE HAVE **YOU** BEEN?
OH, JUST OUTSIDE SORT OF MOPING AROUND BECAUSE NOBODY LOVES ME
WHAT ABOUT YOUR DOG?
COOKIES? WHO SAID COOKIES?
© 1991 United Feature Syndicate, Inc.
3-6
SCHULZ

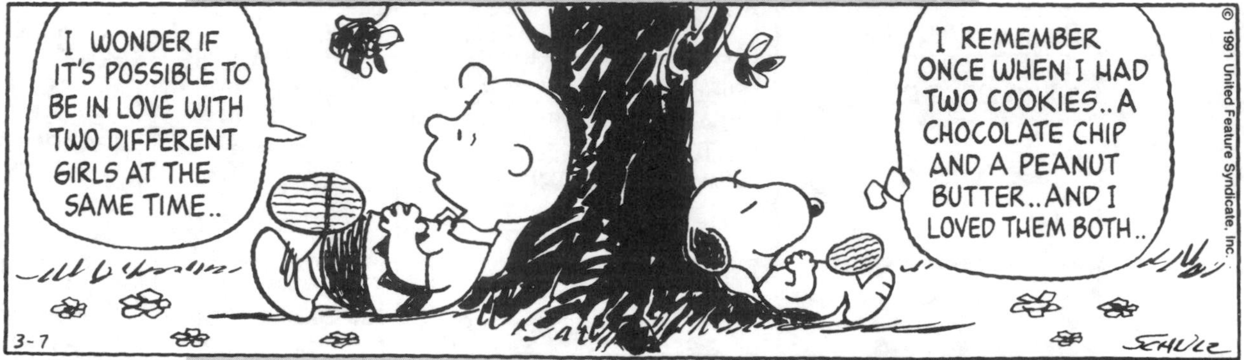
I WONDER IF IT'S POSSIBLE TO BE IN LOVE WITH TWO DIFFERENT GIRLS AT THE SAME TIME..
I REMEMBER ONCE WHEN I HAD TWO COOKIES..A CHOCOLATE CHIP AND A PEANUT BUTTER..AND I LOVED THEM BOTH..
3-7
SCHULZ
© 1991 United Feature Syndicate, Inc.

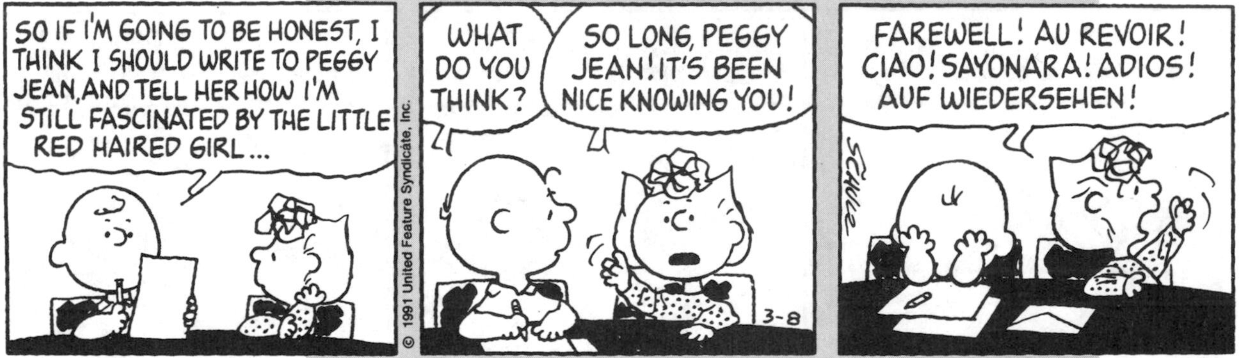
SO IF I'M GOING TO BE HONEST, I THINK I SHOULD WRITE TO PEGGY JEAN, AND TELL HER HOW I'M STILL FASCINATED BY THE LITTLE RED HAIRED GIRL...
© 1991 United Feature Syndicate, Inc.
WHAT DO YOU THINK?
SO LONG, PEGGY JEAN! IT'S BEEN NICE KNOWING YOU!
3-8
FAREWELL! AU REVOIR! CIAO! SAYONARA! ADIOS! AUF WIEDERSEHEN!
SCHULZ

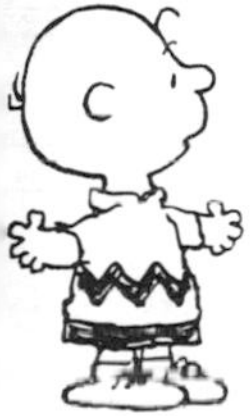

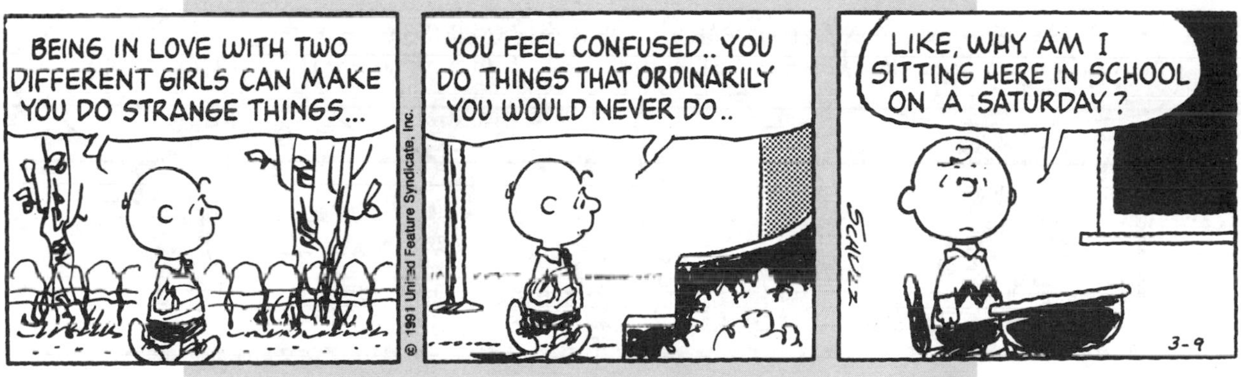
BEING IN LOVE WITH TWO DIFFERENT GIRLS CAN MAKE YOU DO STRANGE THINGS...
© 1991 United Feature Syndicate, Inc.
YOU FEEL CONFUSED..YOU DO THINGS THAT ORDINARILY YOU WOULD NEVER DO..
LIKE, WHY AM I SITTING HERE IN SCHOOL ON A SATURDAY?
SCHULZ
3-9

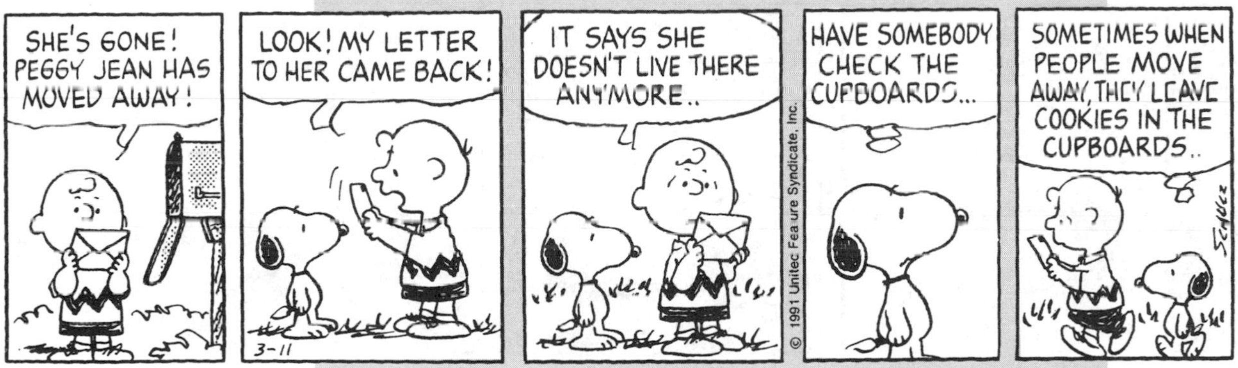
SHE'S GONE! PEGGY JEAN HAS MOVED AWAY!
LOOK! MY LETTER TO HER CAME BACK!
3-11
IT SAYS SHE DOESN'T LIVE THERE ANYMORE..
© 1991 United Feature Syndicate, Inc.
HAVE SOMEBODY CHECK THE CUPBOARDS...
SOMETIMES WHEN PEOPLE MOVE AWAY, THEY LEAVE COOKIES IN THE CUPBOARDS..
SCHULZ

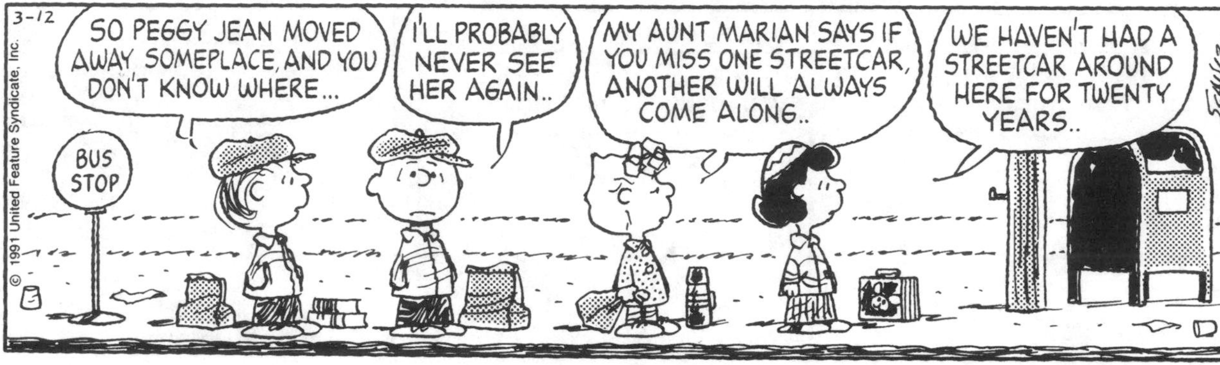
3-12
© 1991 United Feature Syndicate, Inc.
SO PEGGY JEAN MOVED AWAY SOMEPLACE, AND YOU DON'T KNOW WHERE...
I'LL PROBABLY NEVER SEE HER AGAIN..
MY AUNT MARIAN SAYS IF YOU MISS ONE STREETCAR, ANOTHER WILL ALWAYS COME ALONG..
WE HAVEN'T HAD A STREETCAR AROUND HERE FOR TWENTY YEARS..
BUS STOP
SCHULZ

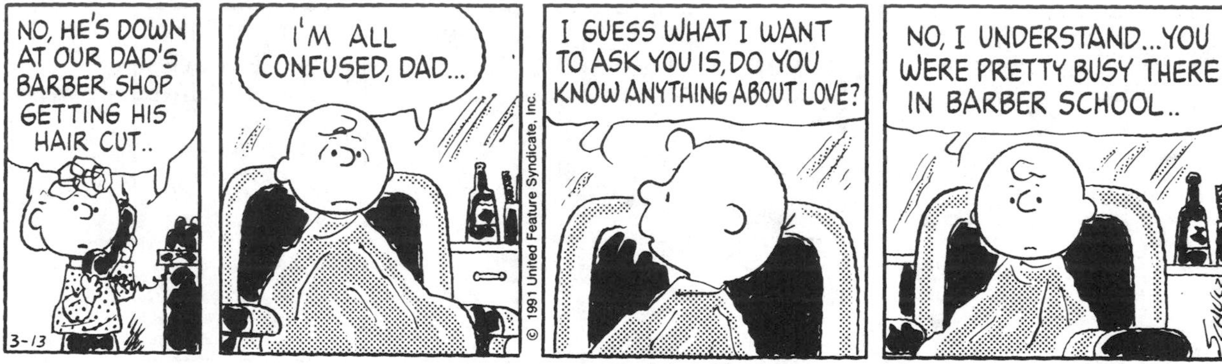
NO, HE'S DOWN AT OUR DAD'S BARBER SHOP GETTING HIS HAIR CUT..
3-13
I'M ALL CONFUSED, DAD...
© 1991 United Feature Syndicate, Inc.
I GUESS WHAT I WANT TO ASK YOU IS, DO YOU KNOW ANYTHING ABOUT LOVE?
NO, I UNDERSTAND...YOU WERE PRETTY BUSY THERE IN BARBER SCHOOL..
SCHULZ

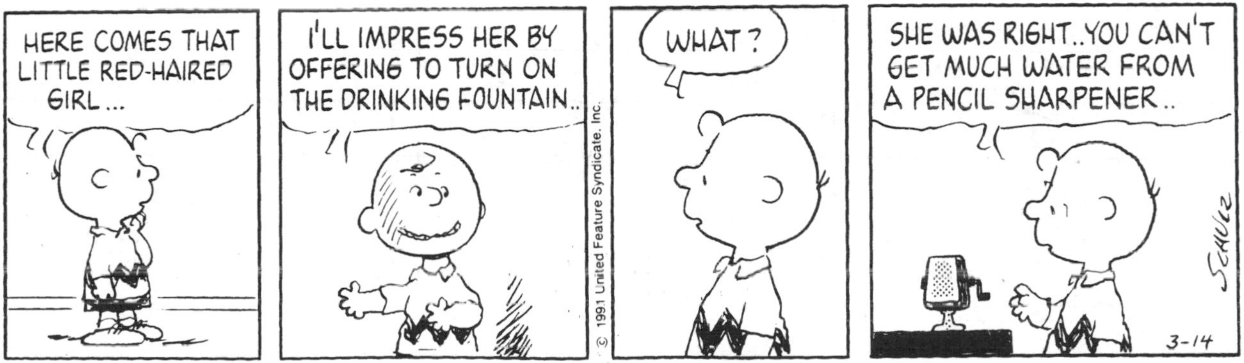
HERE COMES THAT LITTLE RED-HAIRED GIRL...
I'LL IMPRESS HER BY OFFERING TO TURN ON THE DRINKING FOUNTAIN..
WHAT?
SHE WAS RIGHT..YOU CAN'T GET MUCH WATER FROM A PENCIL SHARPENER..
© 1991 United Feature Syndicate, Inc.
SCHULZ
3-14

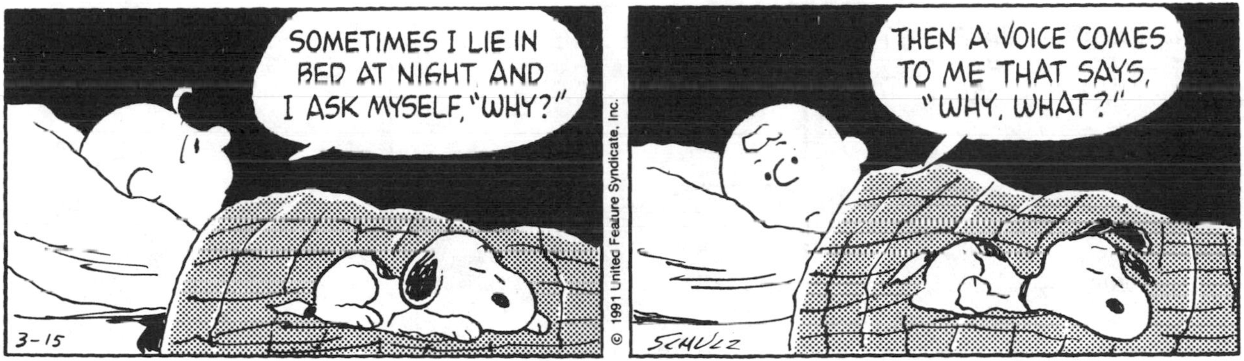
SOMETIMES I LIE IN BED AT NIGHT AND I ASK MYSELF, "WHY?"
THEN A VOICE COMES TO ME THAT SAYS, "WHY, WHAT?"
© 1991 United Feature Syndicate, Inc.
3-15
SCHULZ

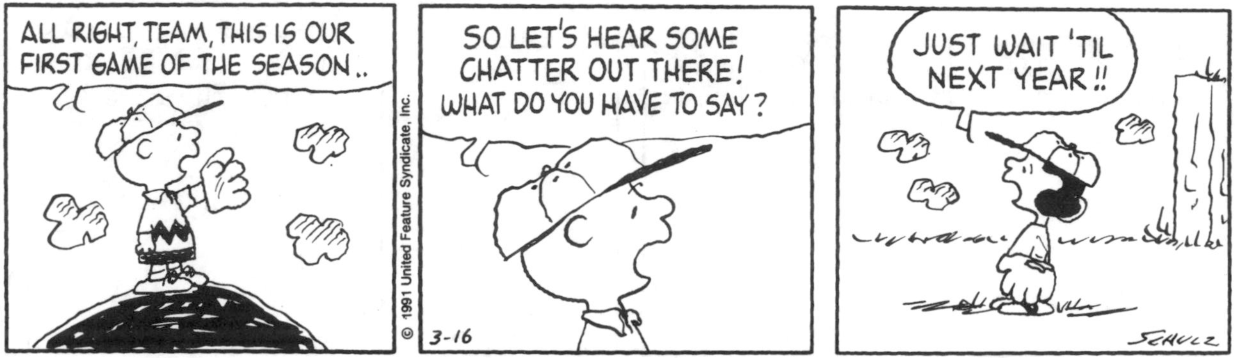
ALL RIGHT, TEAM, THIS IS OUR FIRST GAME OF THE SEASON..
© 1991 United Feature Syndicate, Inc.
SO LET'S HEAR SOME CHATTER OUT THERE! WHAT DO YOU HAVE TO SAY?
3-16
JUST WAIT 'TIL NEXT YEAR!!
SCHULZ

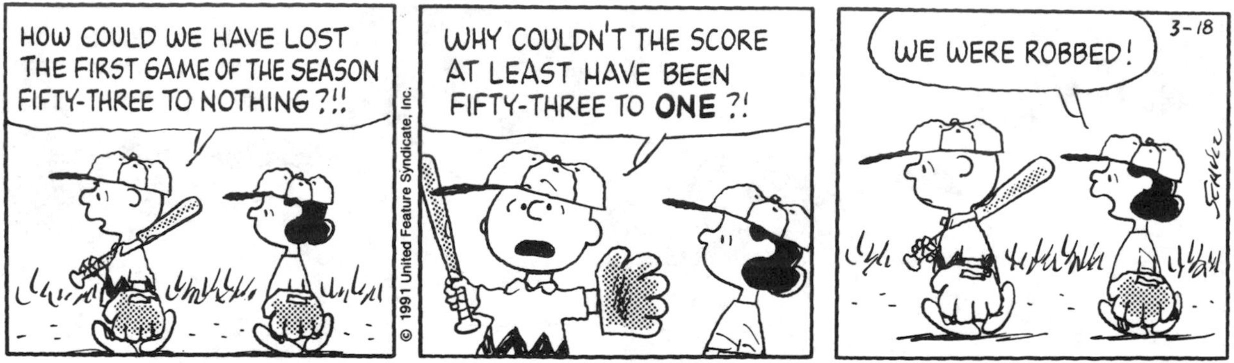
HOW COULD WE HAVE LOST THE FIRST GAME OF THE SEASON FIFTY-THREE TO NOTHING?!!
© 1991 United Feature Syndicate, Inc.
WHY COULDN'T THE SCORE AT LEAST HAVE BEEN FIFTY-THREE TO ONE?!
WE WERE ROBBED!
3-18
SCHULZ

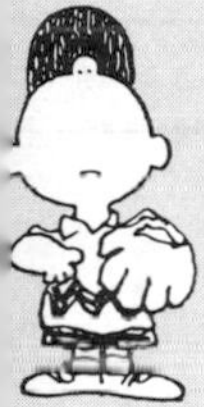

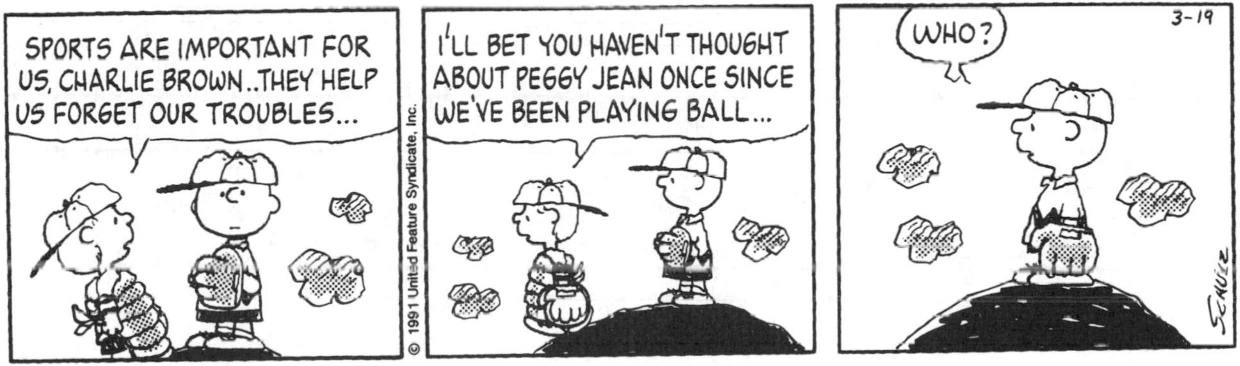
SPORTS ARE IMPORTANT FOR US, CHARLIE BROWN..THEY HELP US FORGET OUR TROUBLES...
© 1991 United Feature Syndicate, Inc.
I'LL BET YOU HAVEN'T THOUGHT ABOUT PEGGY JEAN ONCE SINCE WE'VE BEEN PLAYING BALL...
3-19
WHO?
SCHULZ

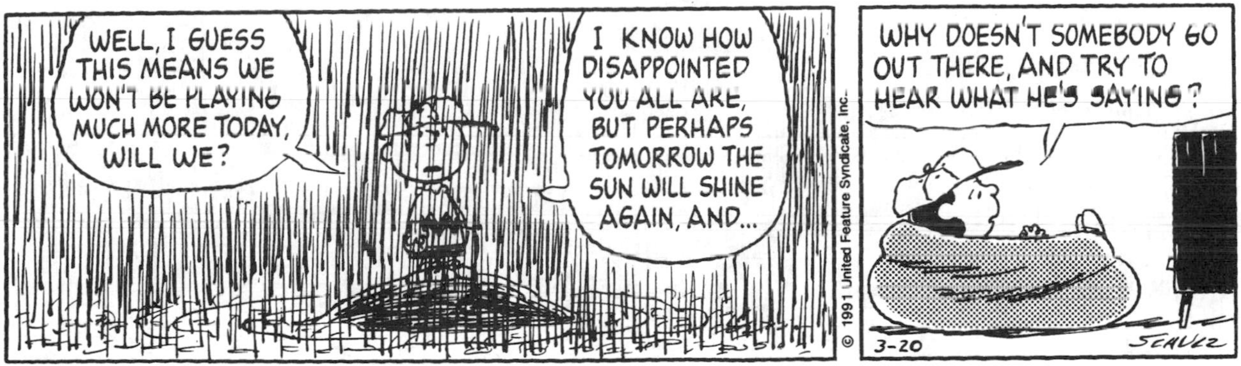
WELL, I GUESS THIS MEANS WE WON'T BE PLAYING MUCH MORE TODAY, WILL WE?
I KNOW HOW DISAPPOINTED YOU ALL ARE, BUT PERHAPS TOMORROW THE SUN WILL SHINE AGAIN, AND...
© 1991 United Feature Syndicate, Inc.
WHY DOESN'T SOMEBODY GO OUT THERE, AND TRY TO HEAR WHAT HE'S SAYING?
3-20
SCHULZ

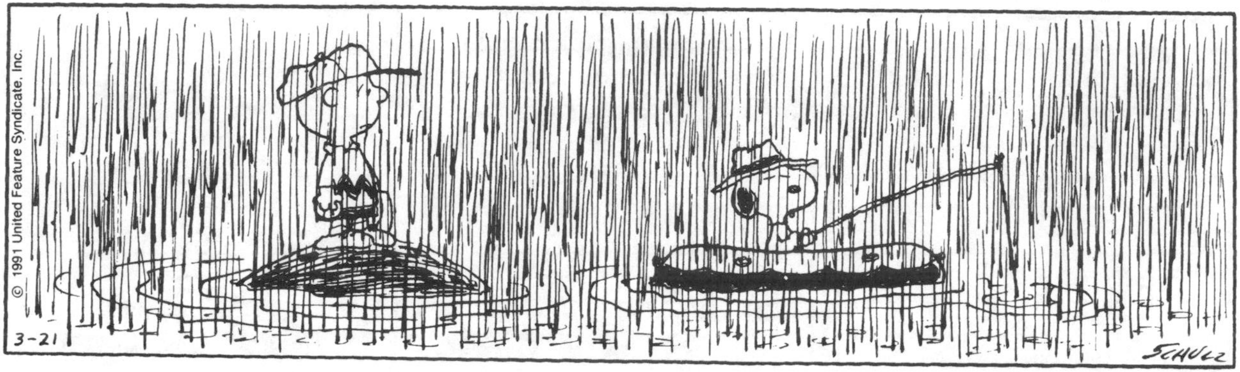
© 1991 United Feature Syndicate, Inc.
3-21
SCHULZ

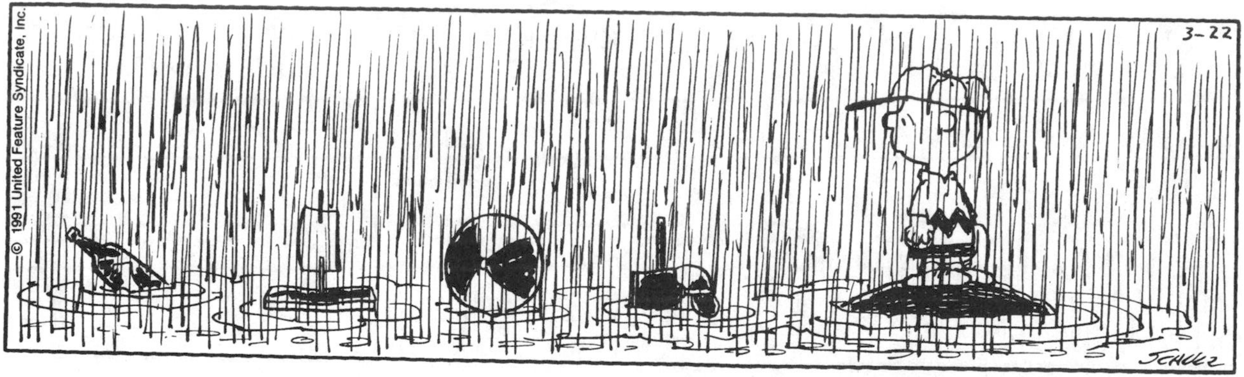
© 1991 United Feature Syndicate, Inc.
3-22
SCHULZ

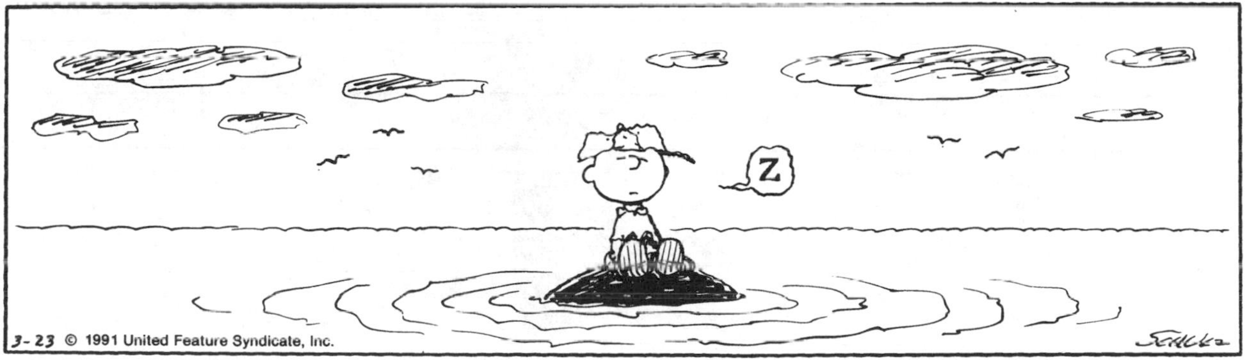
Z
3-23 © 1991 United Feature Syndicate, Inc.
SCHULZ

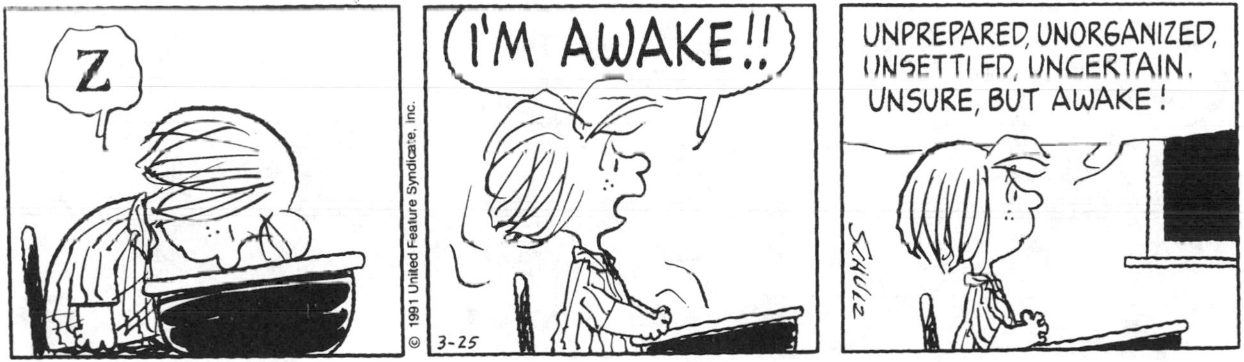
Z
© 1991 United Feature Syndicate, Inc.
3-25
I'M AWAKE!!
UNPREPARED, UNORGANIZED, UNSETTLED, UNCERTAIN, UNSURE, BUT AWAKE!
SCHULZ

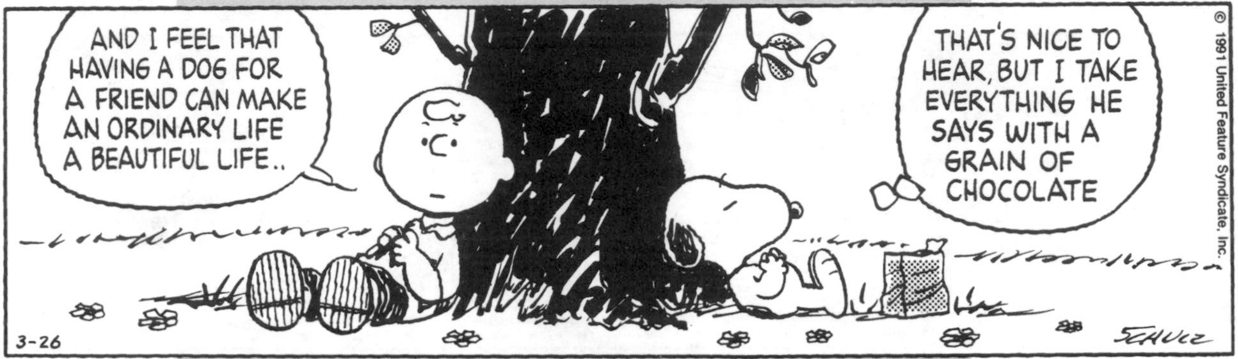
AND I FEEL THAT HAVING A DOG FOR A FRIEND CAN MAKE AN ORDINARY LIFE A BEAUTIFUL LIFE..
THAT'S NICE TO HEAR, BUT I TAKE EVERYTHING HE SAYS WITH A GRAIN OF CHOCOLATE
© 1991 United Feature Syndicate, Inc.
3-26
SCHULZ

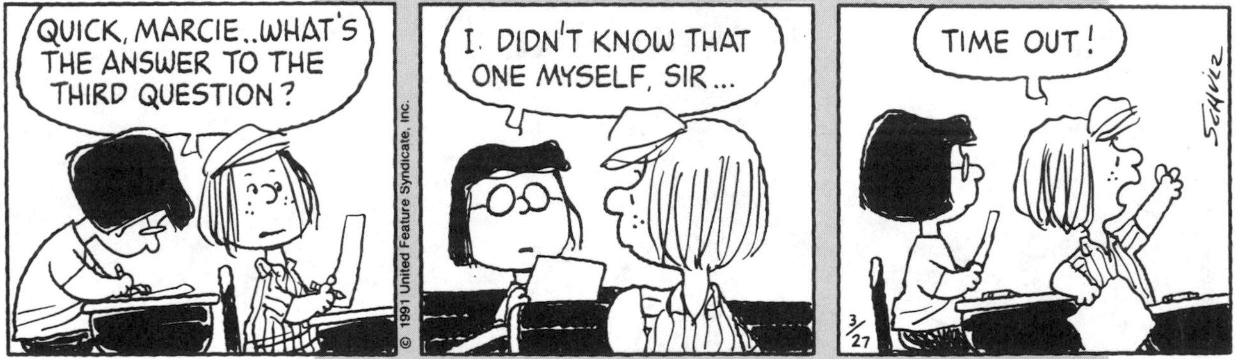
QUICK, MARCIE..WHAT'S THE ANSWER TO THE THIRD QUESTION?
© 1991 United Feature Syndicate, Inc.
I. DIDN'T KNOW THAT ONE MYSELF, SIR...
TIME OUT!
SCHULZ
3/27

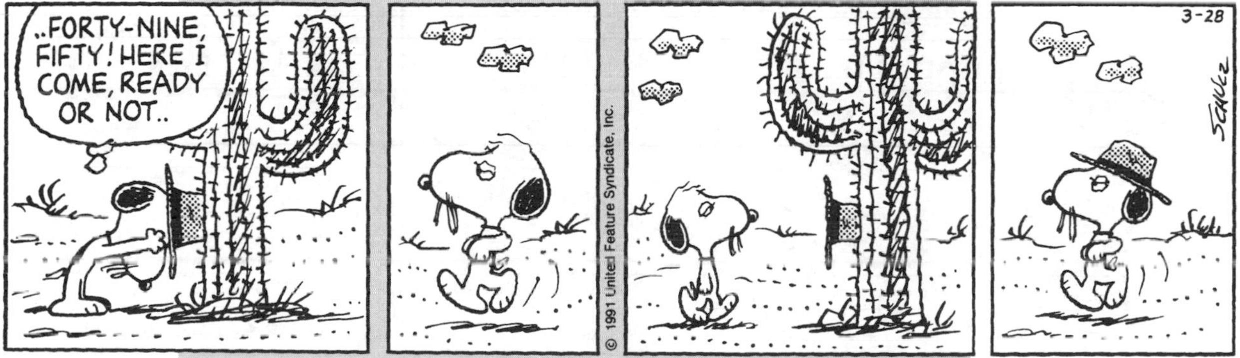
..FORTY-NINE, FIFTY! HERE I COME, READY OR NOT..
© 1991 United Feature Syndicate, Inc.
3-28
SCHULZ

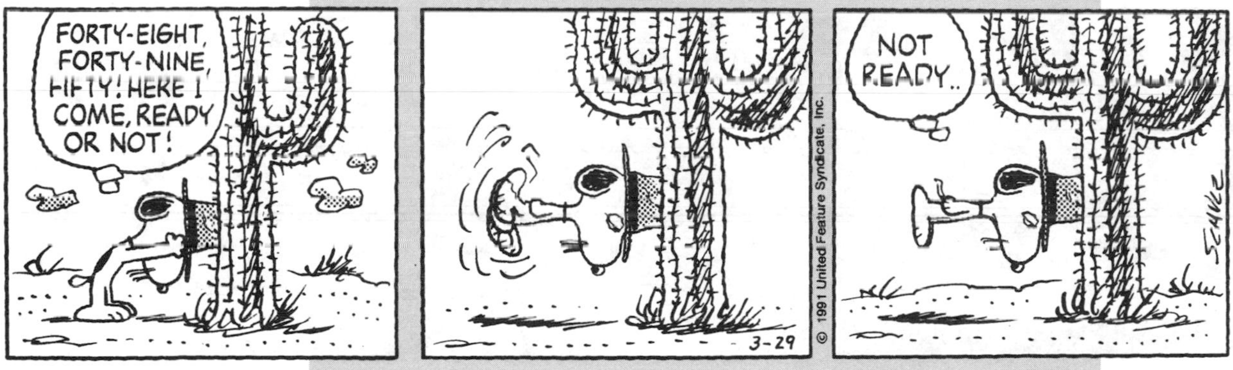
FORTY-EIGHT, FORTY-NINE, FIFTY! HERE I COME, READY OR NOT!
3-29
© 1991 United Feature Syndicate, Inc.
NOT READY..
SCHULZ

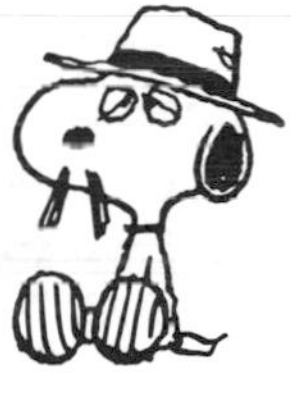

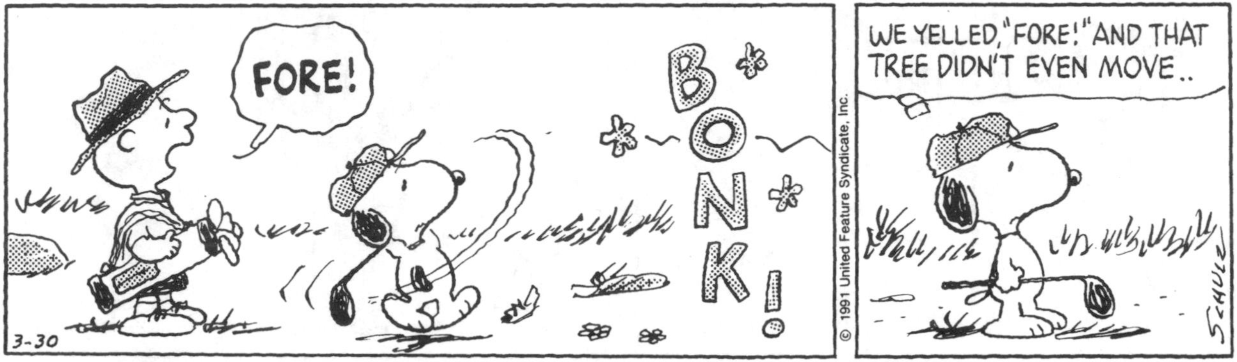
3-30
FORE!
BONK!
© 1991 United Feature Syndicate, Inc.
WE YELLED, "FORE!" AND THAT TREE DIDN'T EVEN MOVE..
SCHULZ

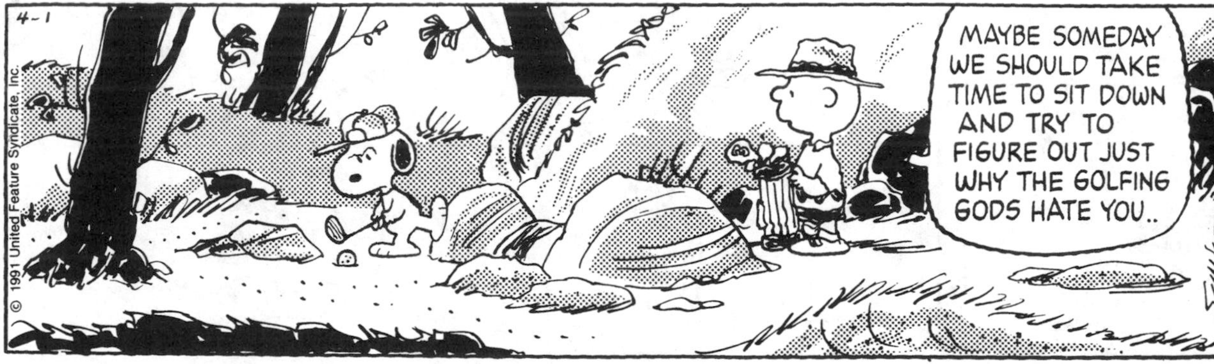
4-1
© 1991 United Feature Syndicate, Inc.
MAYBE SOMEDAY WE SHOULD TAKE TIME TO SIT DOWN AND TRY TO FIGURE OUT JUST WHY THE GOLFING GODS HATE YOU..
SCHULZ

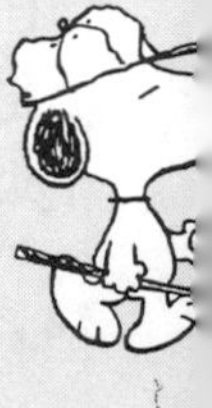

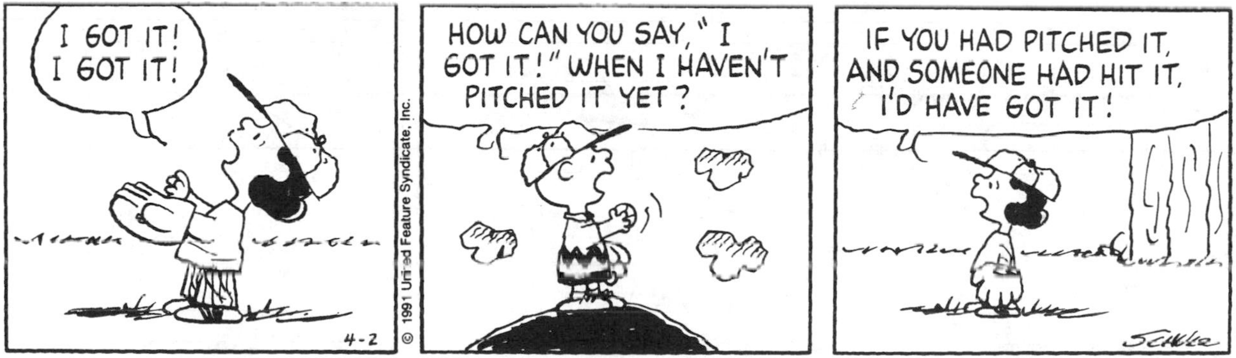
I GOT IT! I GOT IT!
HOW CAN YOU SAY, "I GOT IT!" WHEN I HAVEN'T PITCHED IT YET?
IF YOU HAD PITCHED IT, AND SOMEONE HAD HIT IT, I'D HAVE GOT IT!
4-2
© 1991 United Feature Syndicate, Inc.
SCHULZ

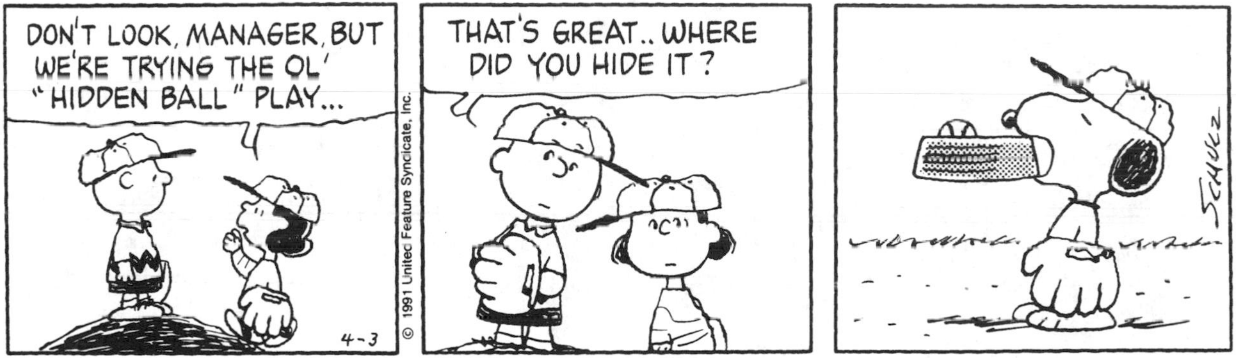
DON'T LOOK, MANAGER, BUT WE'RE TRYING THE OL' "HIDDEN BALL" PLAY...
THAT'S GREAT.. WHERE DID YOU HIDE IT?
4-3
© 1991 United Feature Syndicate, Inc.
SCHULZ

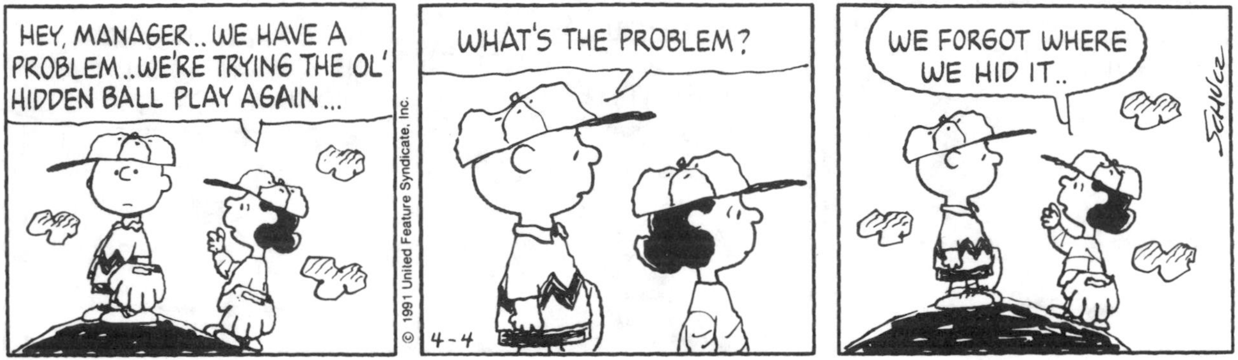
HEY, MANAGER.. WE HAVE A PROBLEM..WE'RE TRYING THE OL' HIDDEN BALL PLAY AGAIN...
© 1991 United Feature Syndicate, Inc.
WHAT'S THE PROBLEM?
4-4
WE FORGOT WHERE WE HID IT..
SCHULZ

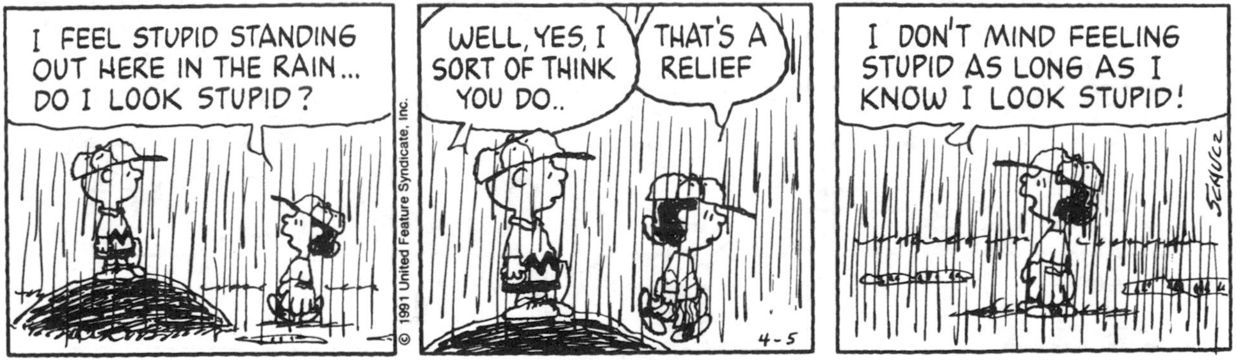
I FEEL STUPID STANDING OUT HERE IN THE RAIN... DO I LOOK STUPID?
© 1991 United Feature Syndicate, Inc.
WELL, YES, I SORT OF THINK YOU DO..
THAT'S A RELIEF
4-5
I DON'T MIND FEELING STUPID AS LONG AS I KNOW I LOOK STUPID!
SCHULZ

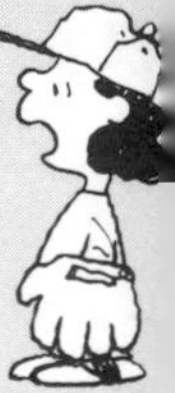

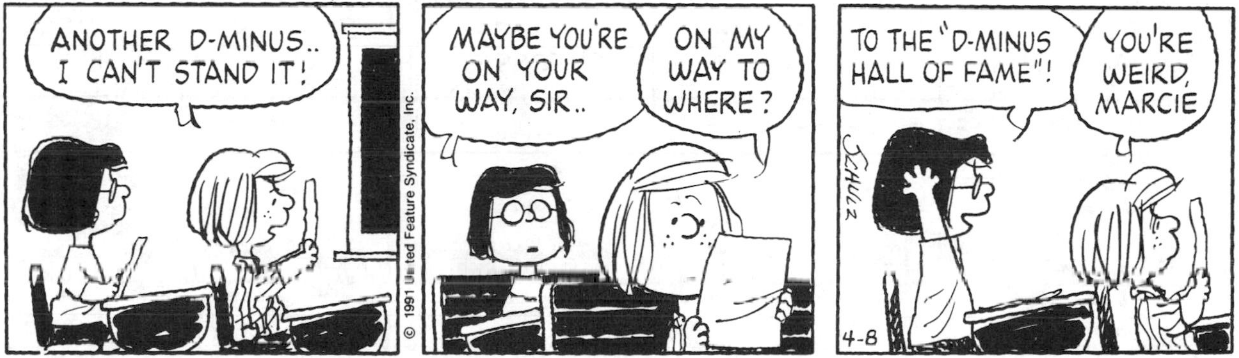
ANOTHER D-MINUS.. I CAN'T STAND IT!
© 1991 United Feature Syndicate, Inc.
MAYBE YOU'RE ON YOUR WAY, SIR..
ON MY WAY TO WHERE?
TO THE "D-MINUS HALL OF FAME"!
YOU'RE WEIRD, MARCIE
SCHULZ
4-8

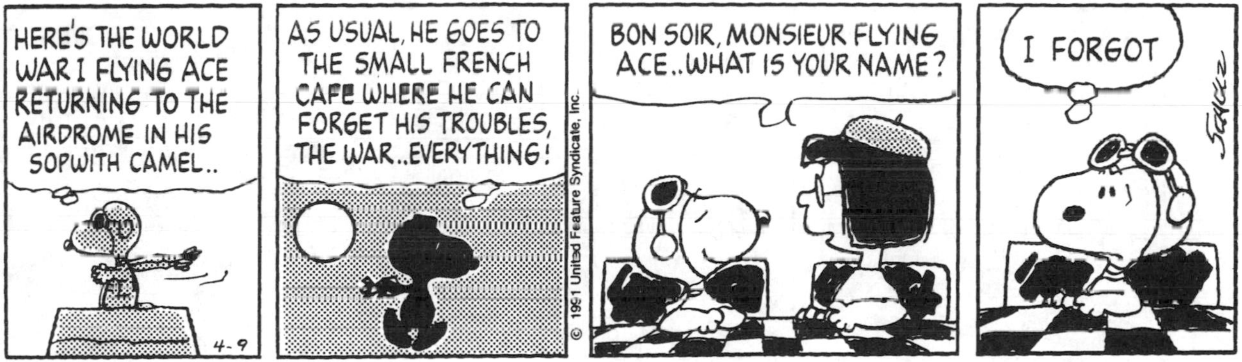
HERE'S THE WORLD WAR I FLYING ACE RETURNING TO THE AIRDROME IN HIS SOPWITH CAMEL..
4-9
AS USUAL, HE GOES TO THE SMALL FRENCH CAFE WHERE HE CAN FORGET HIS TROUBLES, THE WAR..EVERYTHING!
© 1991 United Feature Syndicate, Inc.
BON SOIR, MONSIEUR FLYING ACE..WHAT IS YOUR NAME?
I FORGOT
SCHULZ

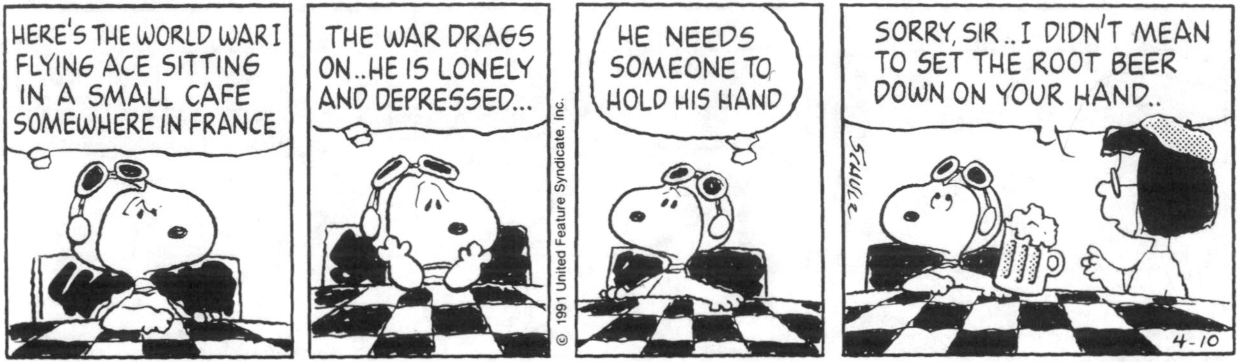
HERE'S THE WORLD WAR I FLYING ACE SITTING IN A SMALL CAFE SOMEWHERE IN FRANCE
THE WAR DRAGS ON..HE IS LONELY AND DEPRESSED...
© 1991 United Feature Syndicate, Inc.
HE NEEDS SOMEONE TO HOLD HIS HAND
SORRY, SIR..I DIDN'T MEAN TO SET THE ROOT BEER DOWN ON YOUR HAND..
SCHULZ
4-10

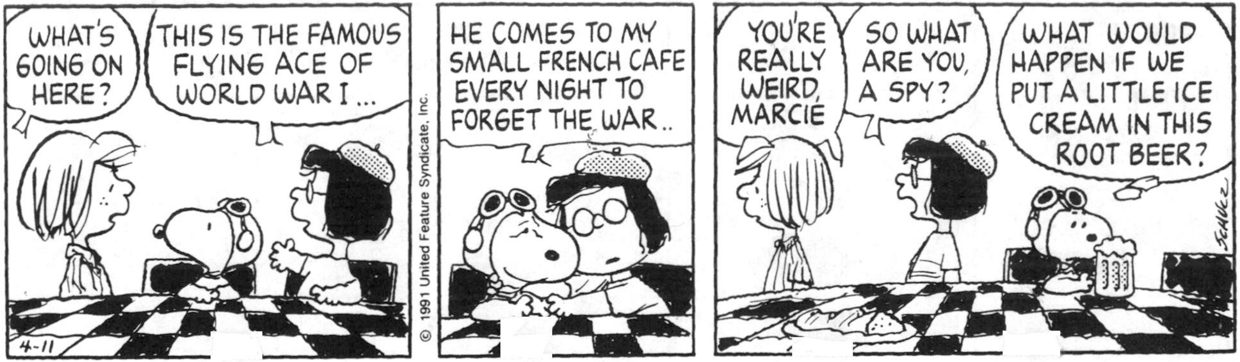
WHAT'S GOING ON HERE?
THIS IS THE FAMOUS FLYING ACE OF WORLD WAR I ...
4-11
© 1991 United Feature Syndicate, Inc.
HE COMES TO MY SMALL FRENCH CAFE EVERY NIGHT TO FORGET THE WAR..
YOU'RE REALLY WEIRD, MARCIE
SO WHAT ARE YOU, A SPY?
WHAT WOULD HAPPEN IF WE PUT A LITTLE ICE CREAM IN THIS ROOT BEER?
SCHULZ

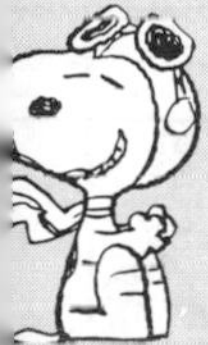

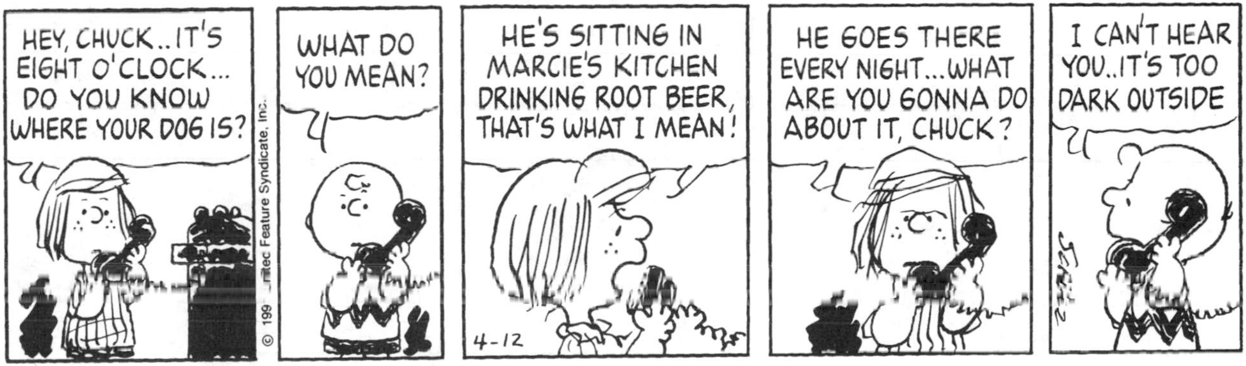
HEY, CHUCK..IT'S EIGHT O'CLOCK... DO YOU KNOW WHERE YOUR DOG IS?
WHAT DO YOU MEAN?
HE'S SITTING IN MARCIE'S KITCHEN DRINKING ROOT BEER, THAT'S WHAT I MEAN!
HE GOES THERE EVERY NIGHT...WHAT ARE YOU GONNA DO ABOUT IT, CHUCK?
I CAN'T HEAR YOU..IT'S TOO DARK OUTSIDE
4-12

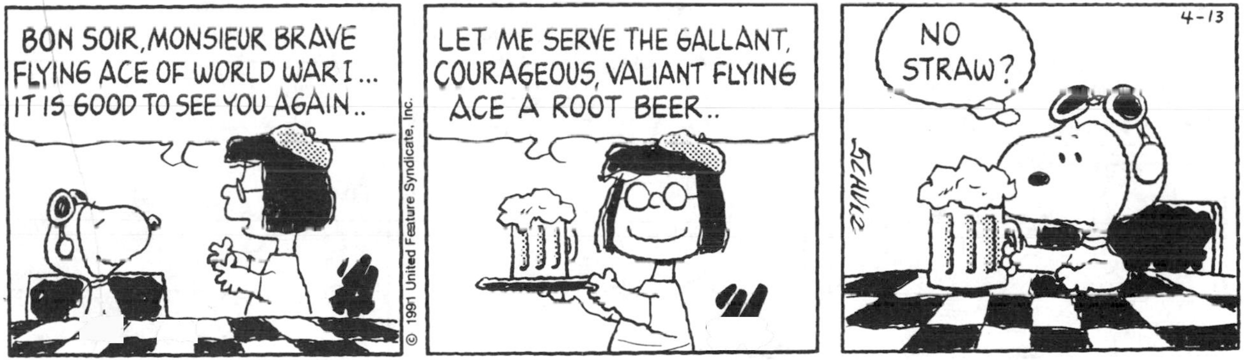
BON SOIR, MONSIEUR BRAVE FLYING ACE OF WORLD WAR I... IT IS GOOD TO SEE YOU AGAIN..
© 1991 United Feature Syndicate, Inc.
LET ME SERVE THE GALLANT, COURAGEOUS, VALIANT FLYING ACE A ROOT BEER..
NO STRAW?
4-13

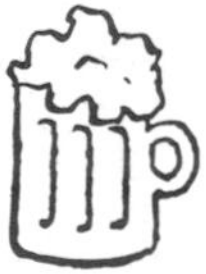

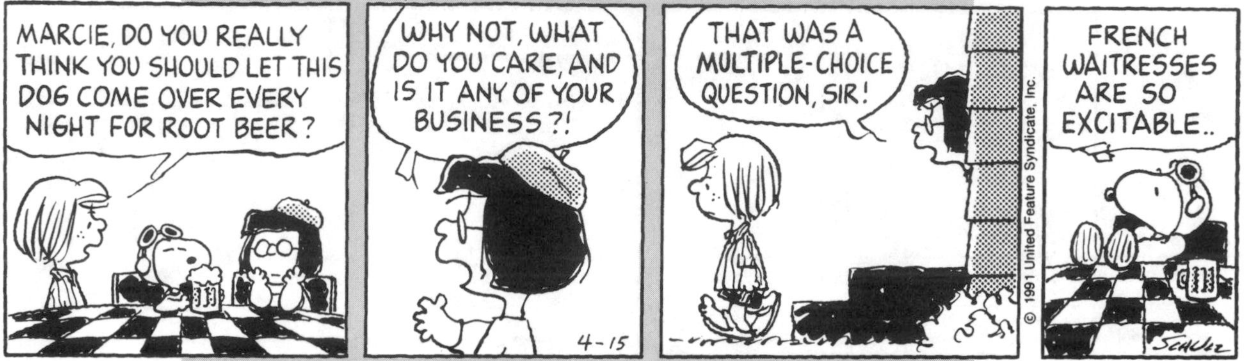

MARCIE, DO YOU REALLY THINK YOU SHOULD LET THIS DOG COME OVER EVERY NIGHT FOR ROOT BEER?
WHY NOT, WHAT DO YOU CARE, AND IS IT ANY OF YOUR BUSINESS?!
4-15
THAT WAS A MULTIPLE-CHOICE QUESTION, SIR!
© 1991 United Feature Syndicate, Inc.
FRENCH WAITRESSES ARE SO EXCITABLE..
SCHULZ

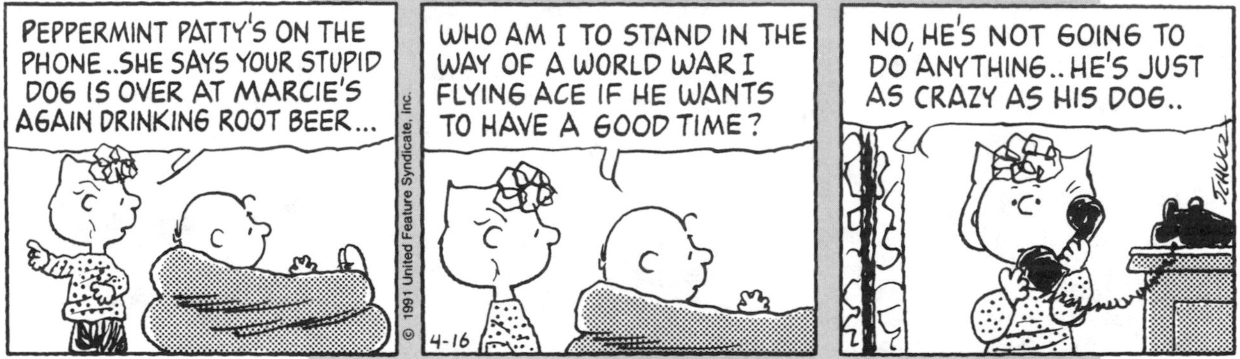

PEPPERMINT PATTY'S ON THE PHONE..SHE SAYS YOUR STUPID DOG IS OVER AT MARCIE'S AGAIN DRINKING ROOT BEER...
© 1991 United Feature Syndicate, Inc.
WHO AM I TO STAND IN THE WAY OF A WORLD WAR I FLYING ACE IF HE WANTS TO HAVE A GOOD TIME?
4-16
NO, HE'S NOT GOING TO DO ANYTHING.. HE'S JUST AS CRAZY AS HIS DOG..
SCHULZ

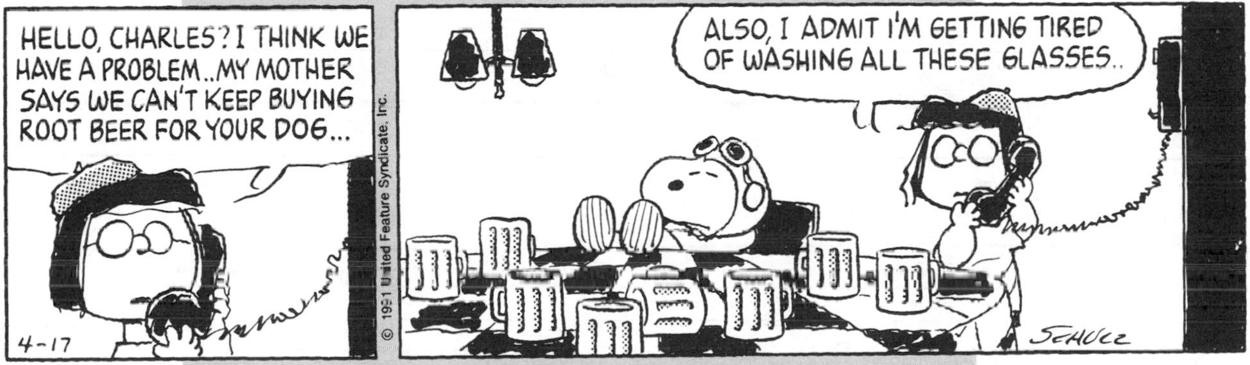
HELLO, CHARLES? I THINK WE HAVE A PROBLEM..MY MOTHER SAYS WE CAN'T KEEP BUYING ROOT BEER FOR YOUR DOG...
4-17
© 1991 United Feature Syndicate, Inc.
ALSO, I ADMIT I'M GETTING TIRED OF WASHING ALL THESE GLASSES..
SCHULZ

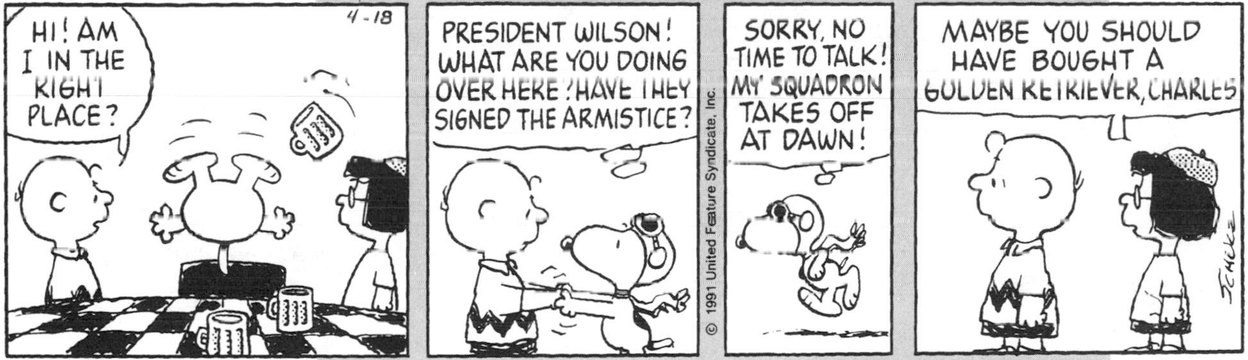
4-18
HI! AM I IN THE RIGHT PLACE?
PRESIDENT WILSON! WHAT ARE YOU DOING OVER HERE? HAVE THEY SIGNED THE ARMISTICE?
© 1991 United Feature Syndicate, Inc.
SORRY, NO TIME TO TALK! MY SQUADRON TAKES OFF AT DAWN!
MAYBE YOU SHOULD HAVE BOUGHT A GOLDEN RETRIEVER, CHARLES
SCHULZ

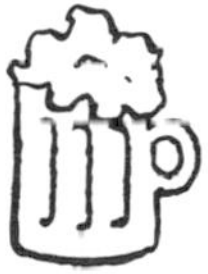

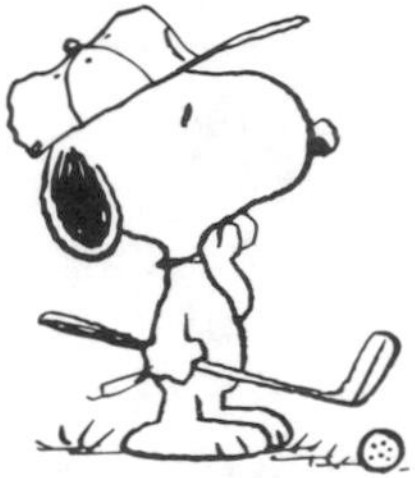

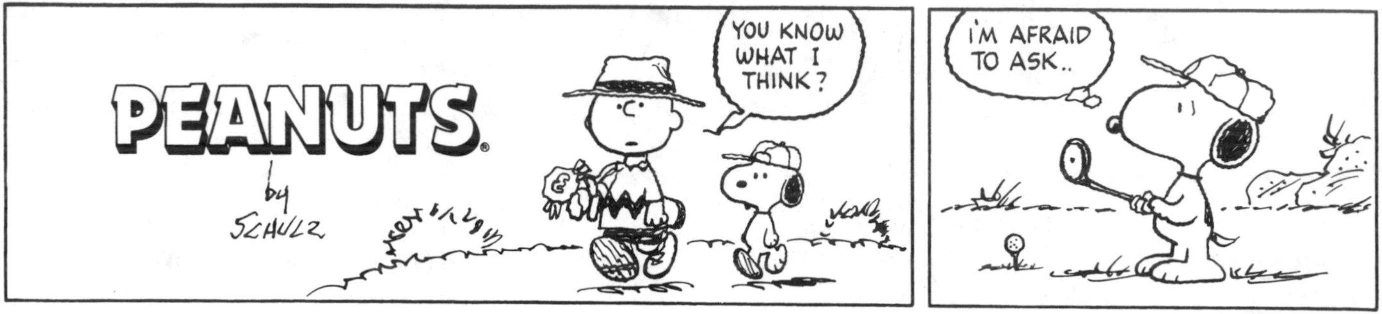
PEANUTS
by SCHULZ
YOU KNOW WHAT I THINK?
I'M AFRAID TO ASK..

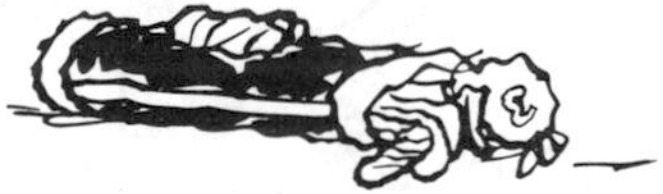

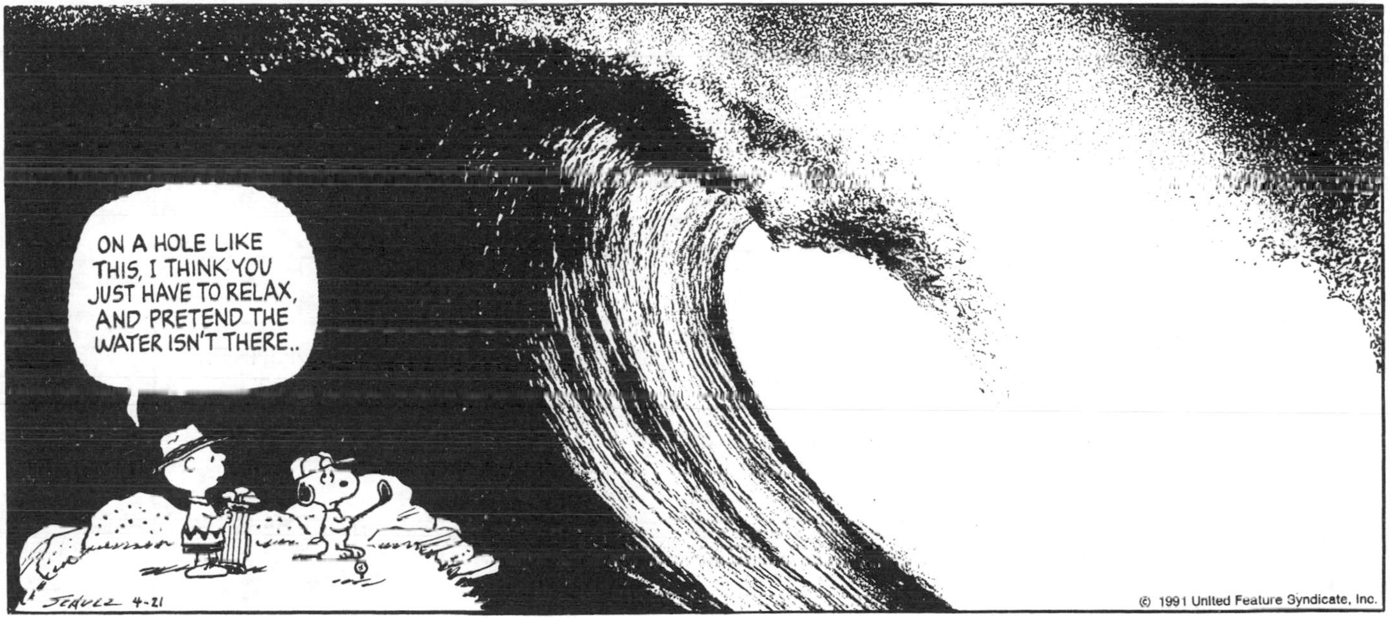
ON A HOLE LIKE THIS, I THINK YOU JUST HAVE TO RELAX, AND PRETEND THE WATER ISN'T THERE..
© 1991 United Feature Syndicate, Inc.

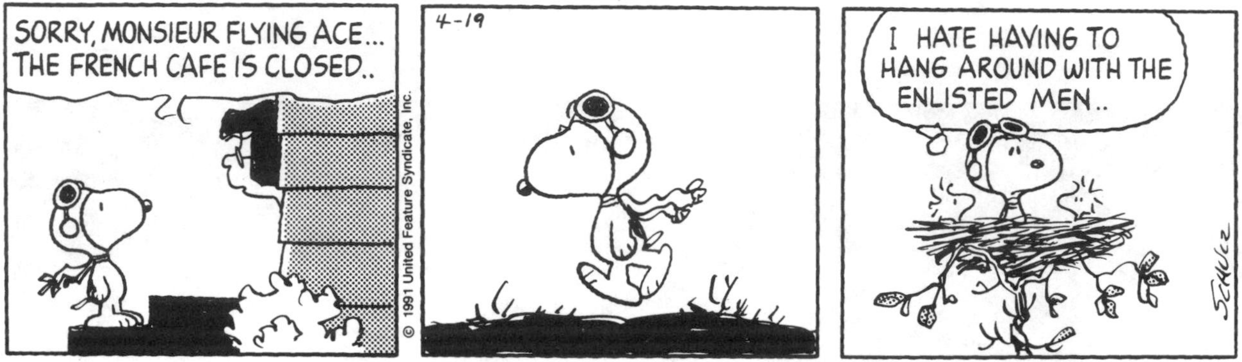
SORRY, MONSIEUR FLYING ACE... THE FRENCH CAFE IS CLOSED..
© 1991 United Feature Syndicate, Inc.
4-19
I HATE HAVING TO HANG AROUND WITH THE ENLISTED MEN..

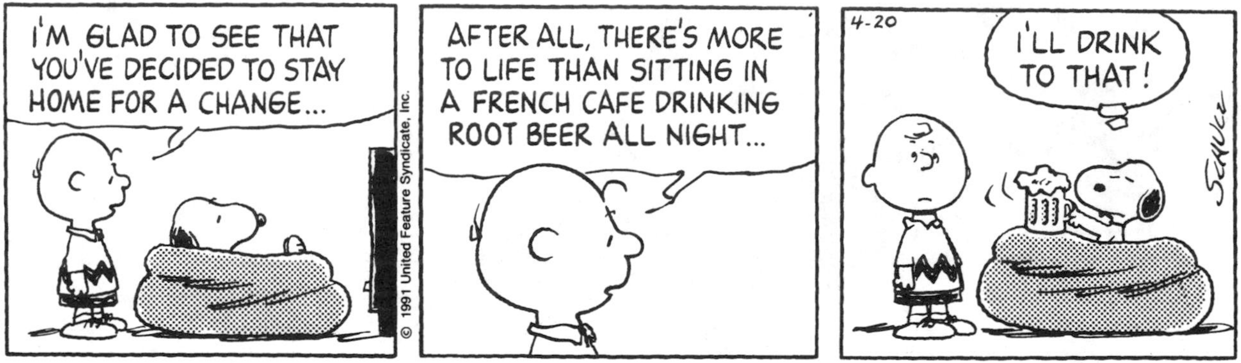
I'M GLAD TO SEE THAT YOU'VE DECIDED TO STAY HOME FOR A CHANGE...
© 1991 United Feature Syndicate, Inc.
AFTER ALL, THERE'S MORE TO LIFE THAN SITTING IN A FRENCH CAFE DRINKING ROOT BEER ALL NIGHT...
4-20
I'LL DRINK TO THAT!

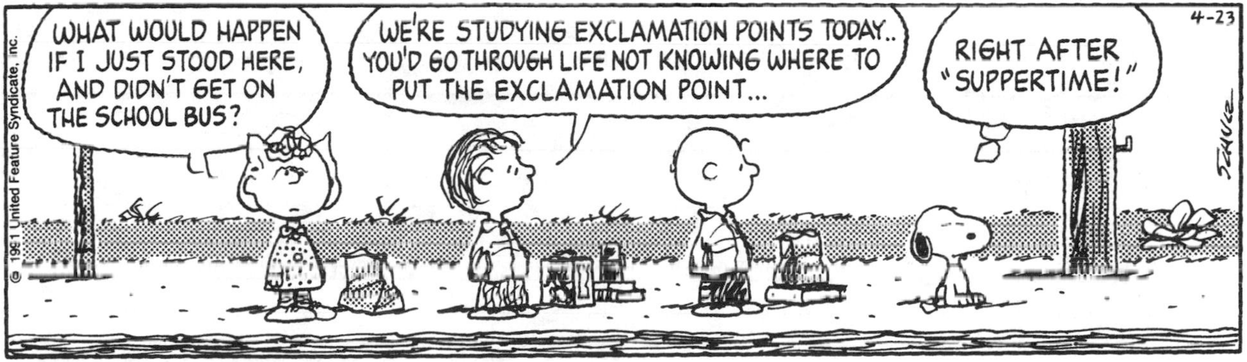
© 1991 United Feature Syndicate, Inc.
4-23
WHAT WOULD HAPPEN IF I JUST STOOD HERE, AND DIDN'T GET ON THE SCHOOL BUS?
WE'RE STUDYING EXCLAMATION POINTS TODAY.. YOU'D GO THROUGH LIFE NOT KNOWING WHERE TO PUT THE EXCLAMATION POINT...
RIGHT AFTER "SUPPERTIME!"
SCHULZ

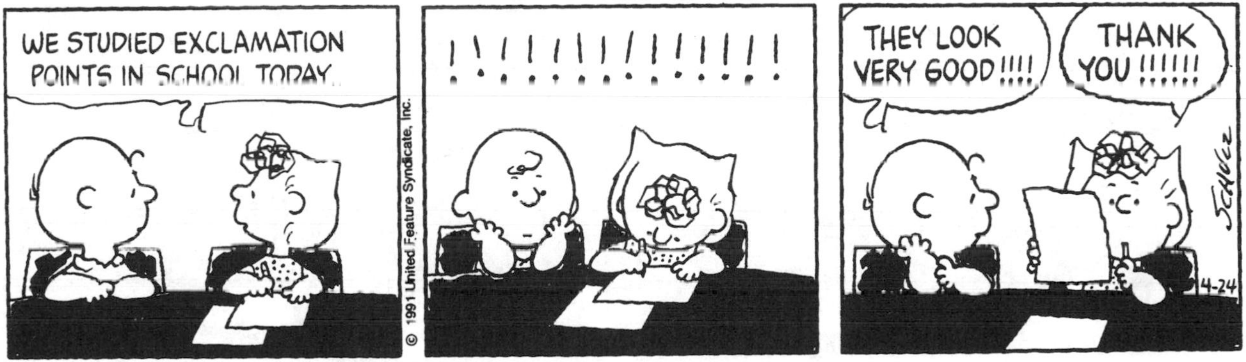
WE STUDIED EXCLAMATION POINTS IN SCHOOL TODAY..
© 1991 United Feature Syndicate, Inc.
!!!!!!!!!!!!!!!
THEY LOOK VERY GOOD!!!!
THANK YOU!!!!!!
SCHULZ
4-24

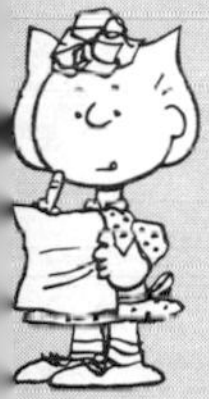

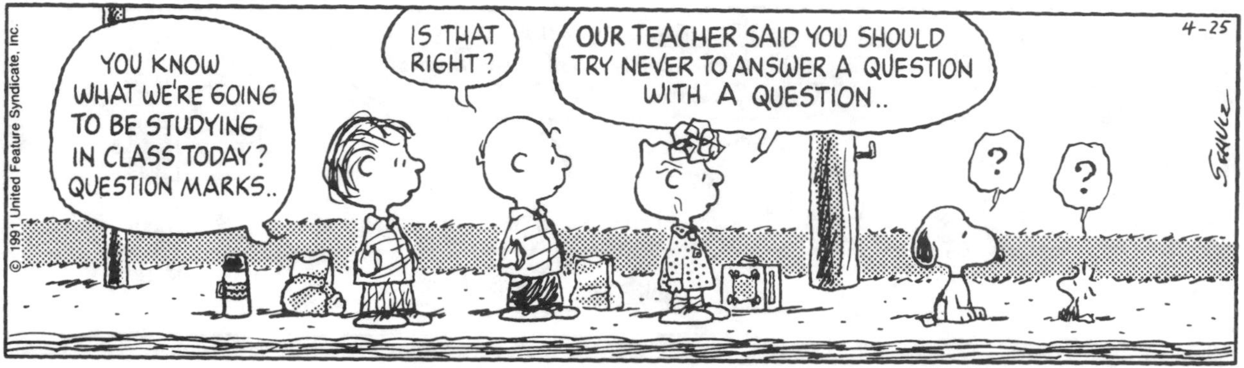
© 1991 United Feature Syndicate, Inc.
4-25
YOU KNOW WHAT WE'RE GOING TO BE STUDYING IN CLASS TODAY? QUESTION MARKS..
IS THAT RIGHT?
OUR TEACHER SAID YOU SHOULD TRY NEVER TO ANSWER A QUESTION WITH A QUESTION..
?
?
SCHULZ

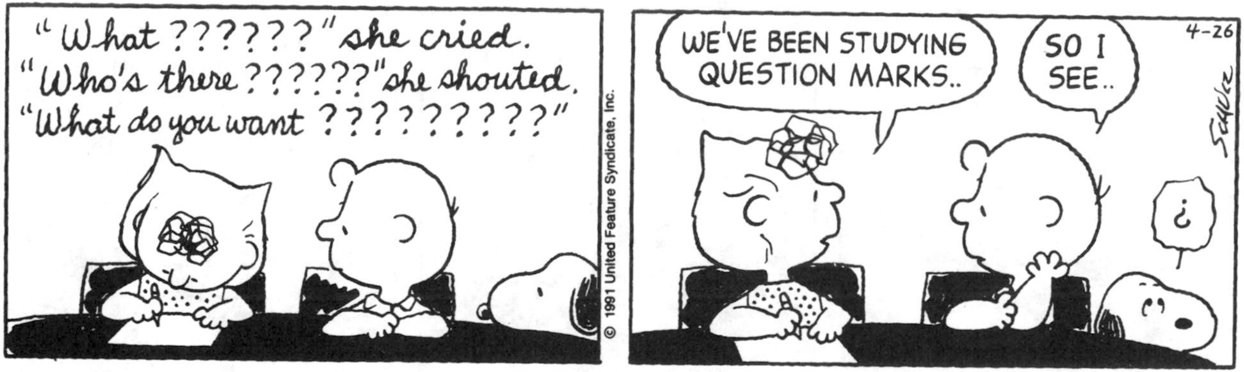
"What ??????" she cried.
"Who's there ??????" she shouted.
"What do you want ??????????"
© 1991 United Feature Syndicate, Inc.
4-26
WE'VE BEEN STUDYING QUESTION MARKS..
SO I SEE..
¿
SCHULZ

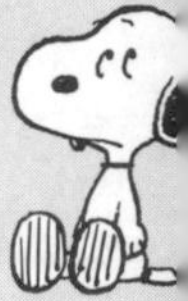

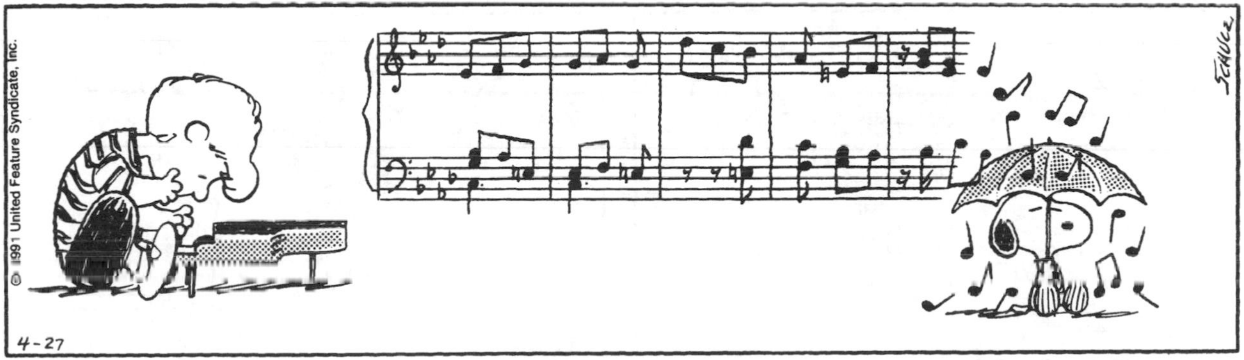
© 1991 United Feature Syndicate, Inc.
SCHULZ
4-27

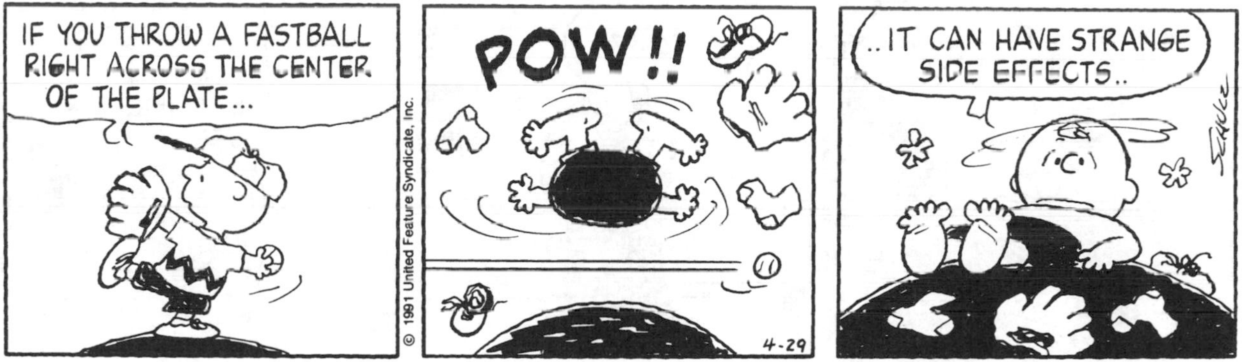
IF YOU THROW A FASTBALL RIGHT ACROSS THE CENTER OF THE PLATE...
© 1991 United Feature Syndicate, Inc.
POW!!
4-29
..IT CAN HAVE STRANGE SIDE EFFECTS..
SCHULZ

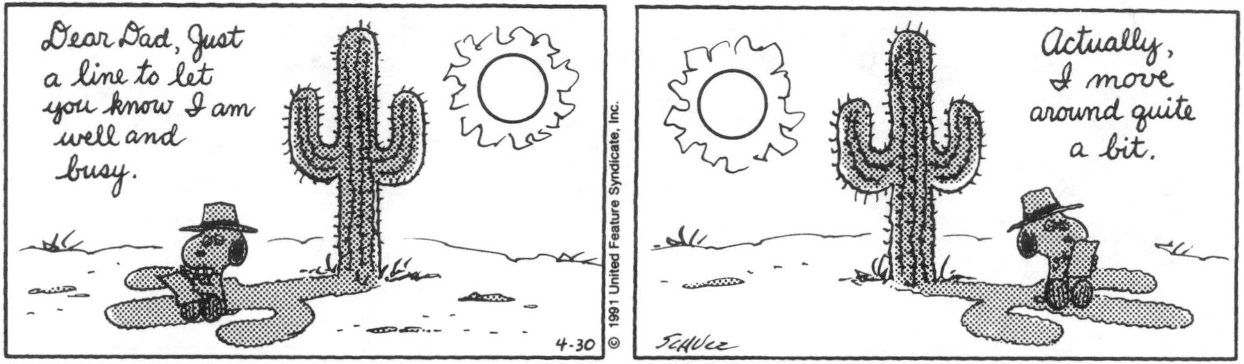
Dear Dad, Just a line to let you know I am well and busy.
Actually, I move around quite a bit.
© 1991 United Feature Syndicate, Inc.
4-30
SCHULZ

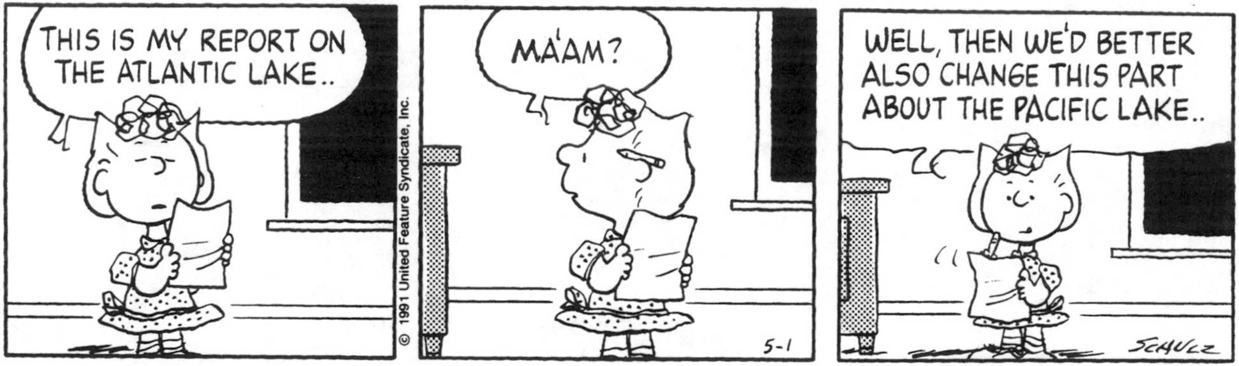
THIS IS MY REPORT ON THE ATLANTIC LAKE..
MA'AM?
WELL, THEN WE'D BETTER ALSO CHANGE THIS PART ABOUT THE PACIFIC LAKE..
© 1991 United Feature Syndicate, Inc.
5-1
SCHULZ

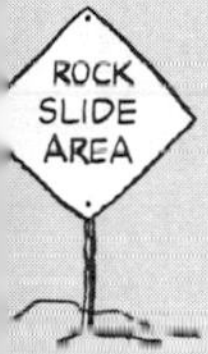
ROCK
SLIDE
AREA

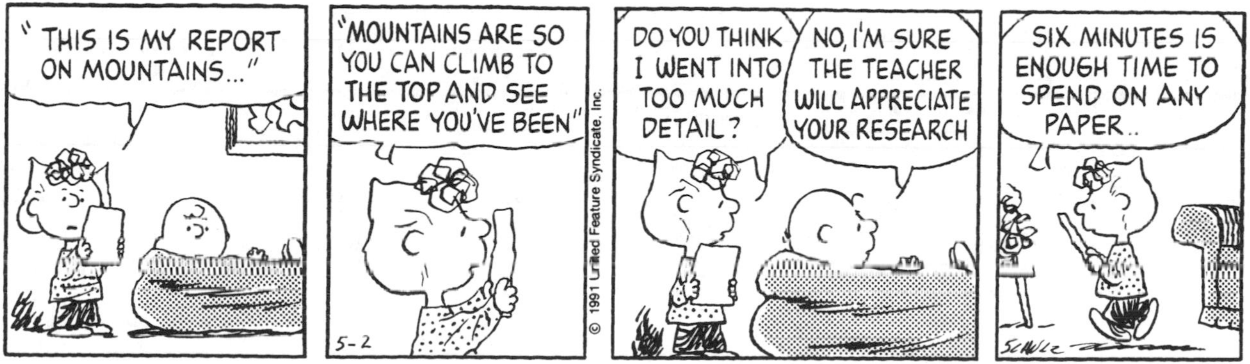
" THIS IS MY REPORT ON MOUNTAINS..."
"MOUNTAINS ARE SO YOU CAN CLIMB TO THE TOP AND SEE WHERE YOU'VE BEEN"
5-2
© 1991 United Feature Syndicate, Inc.
DO YOU THINK I WENT INTO TOO MUCH DETAIL?
NO, I'M SURE THE TEACHER WILL APPRECIATE YOUR RESEARCH
SIX MINUTES IS ENOUGH TIME TO SPEND ON ANY PAPER..
SCHULZ

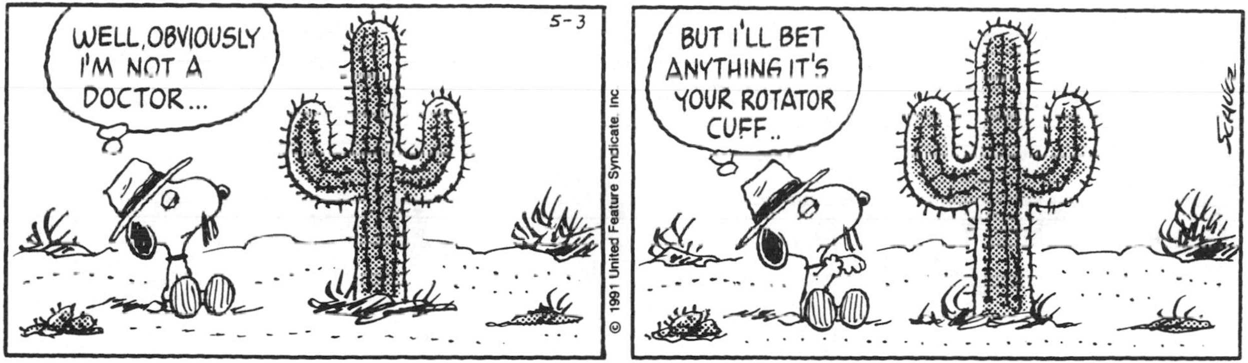
WELL, OBVIOUSLY I'M NOT A DOCTOR...
5-3
© 1991 United Feature Syndicate, Inc
BUT I'LL BET ANYTHING IT'S YOUR ROTATOR CUFF..
SCHULZ

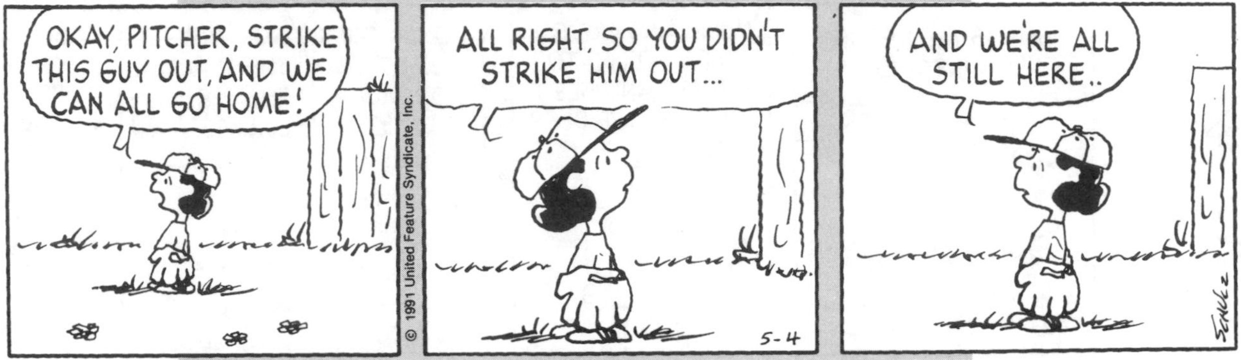
OKAY, PITCHER, STRIKE THIS GUY OUT, AND WE CAN ALL GO HOME!
© 1991 United Feature Syndicate, Inc.
ALL RIGHT, SO YOU DIDN'T STRIKE HIM OUT...
5-4
AND WE'RE ALL STILL HERE..
SCHULZ

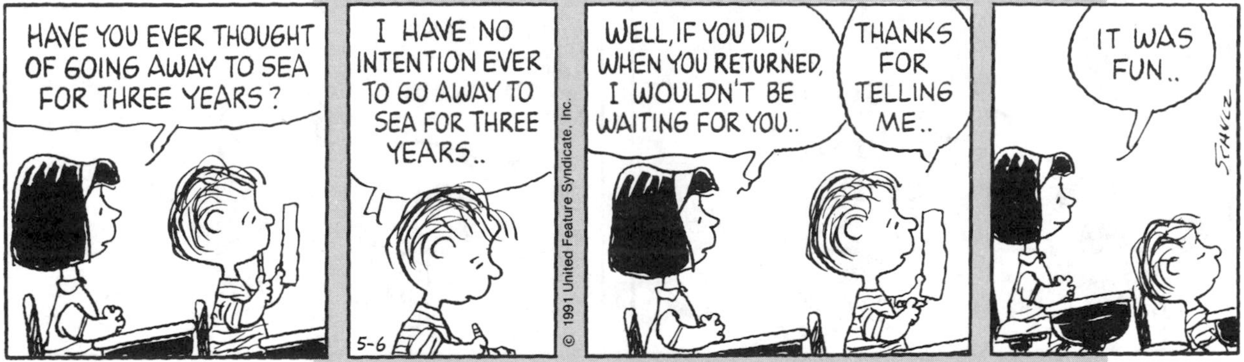
HAVE YOU EVER THOUGHT OF GOING AWAY TO SEA FOR THREE YEARS?
I HAVE NO INTENTION EVER TO GO AWAY TO SEA FOR THREE YEARS..
5-6
© 1991 United Feature Syndicate, Inc.
WELL, IF YOU DID, WHEN YOU RETURNED, I WOULDN'T BE WAITING FOR YOU..
THANKS FOR TELLING ME..
IT WAS FUN..
SCHULZ

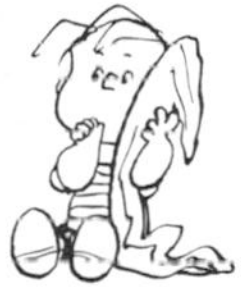

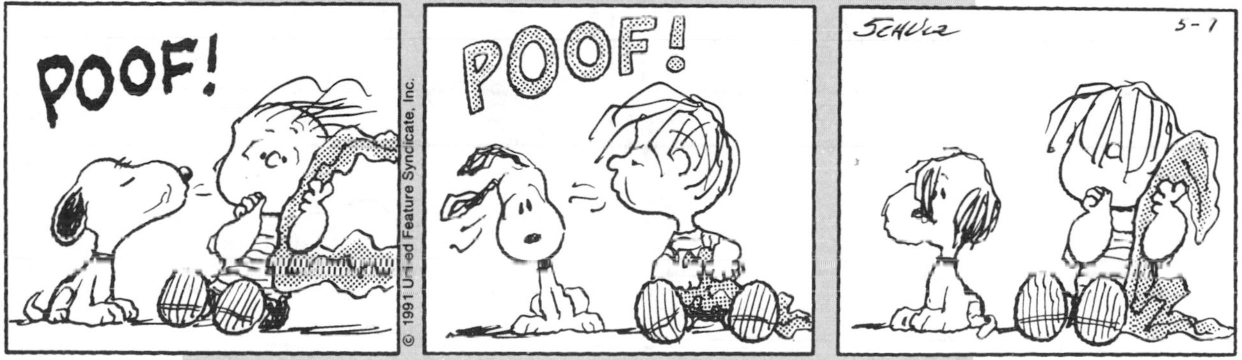
POOF!
© 1991 United Feature Syndicate, Inc.
POOF!
SCHULZ
5-7

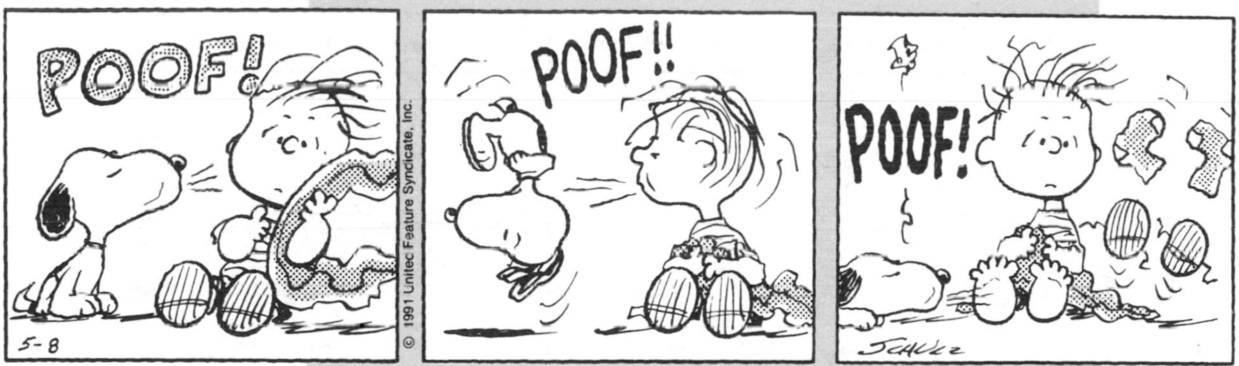
POOF!
5-8
© 1991 United Feature Syndicate, Inc.
POOF!!
POOF!
SCHULZ

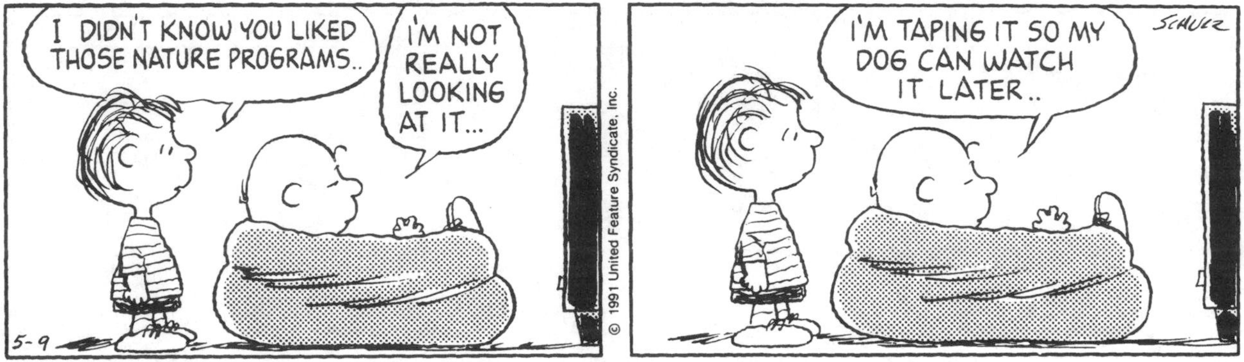
I DIDN'T KNOW YOU LIKED THOSE NATURE PROGRAMS..
I'M NOT REALLY LOOKING AT IT...
© 1991 United Feature Syndicate, Inc.
I'M TAPING IT SO MY DOG CAN WATCH IT LATER..

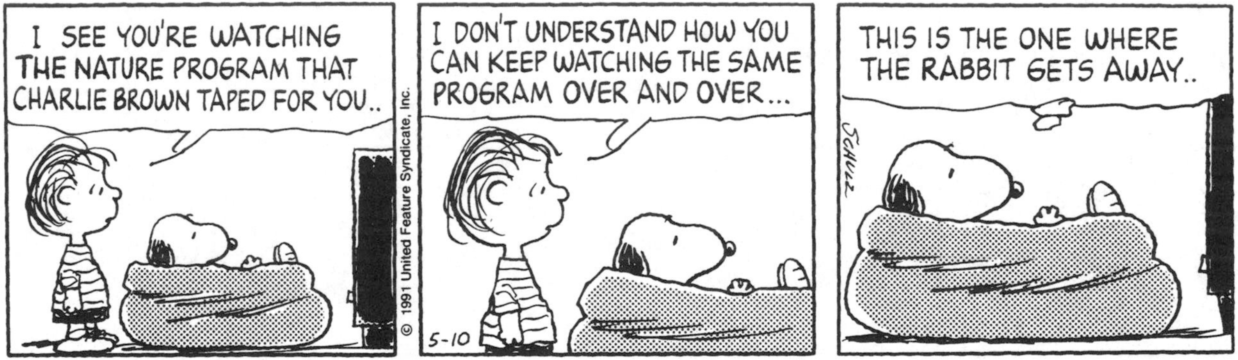
I SEE YOU'RE WATCHING THE NATURE PROGRAM THAT CHARLIE BROWN TAPED FOR YOU..
© 1991 United Feature Syndicate, Inc.
I DON'T UNDERSTAND HOW YOU CAN KEEP WATCHING THE SAME PROGRAM OVER AND OVER...
THIS IS THE ONE WHERE THE RABBIT GETS AWAY..

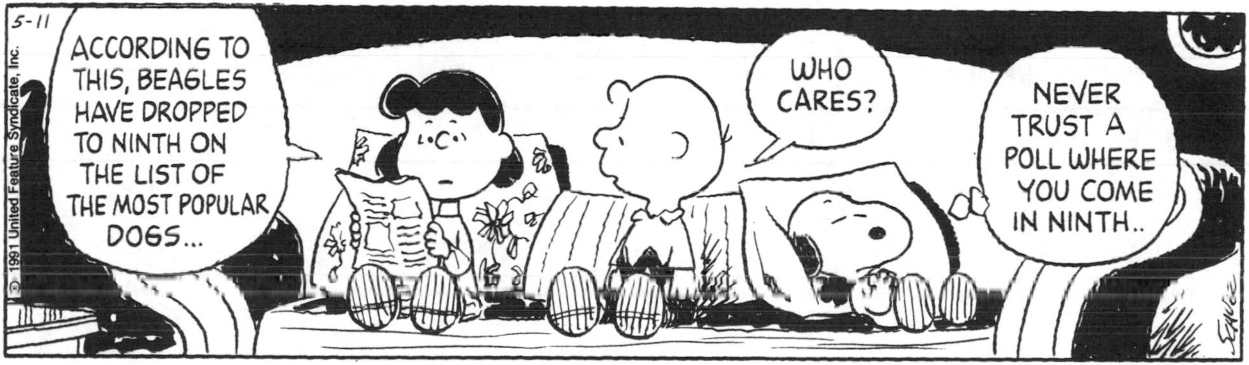
5-11
© 1991 United Feature Syndicate, Inc.
ACCORDING TO THIS, BEAGLES HAVE DROPPED TO NINTH ON THE LIST OF THE MOST POPULAR DOGS...
WHO CARES?
NEVER TRUST A POLL WHERE YOU COME IN NINTH..
SCHULZ

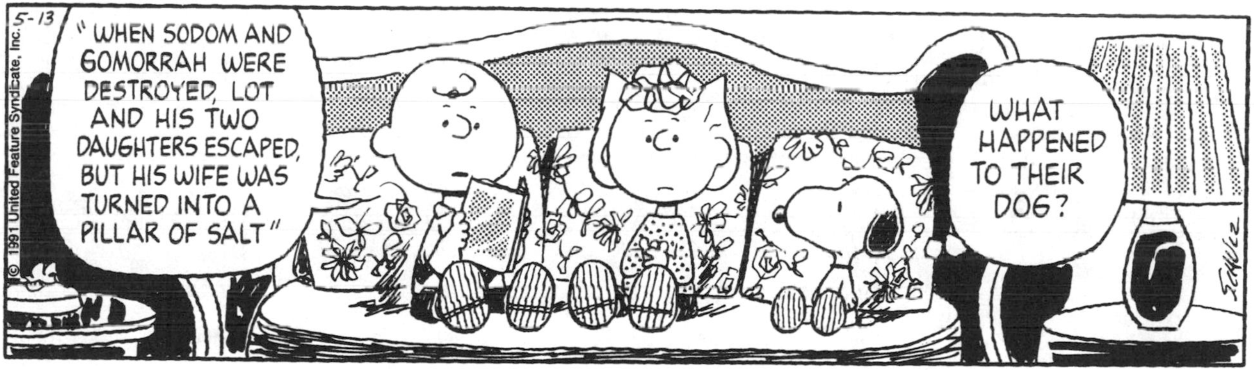
5-13
© 1991 United Feature Syndicate, Inc.
"WHEN SODOM AND GOMORRAH WERE DESTROYED, LOT AND HIS TWO DAUGHTERS ESCAPED, BUT HIS WIFE WAS TURNED INTO A PILLAR OF SALT"
WHAT HAPPENED TO THEIR DOG?
SCHULZ

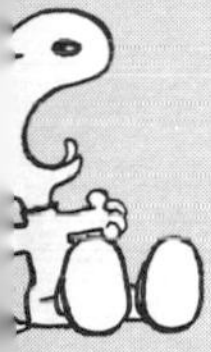

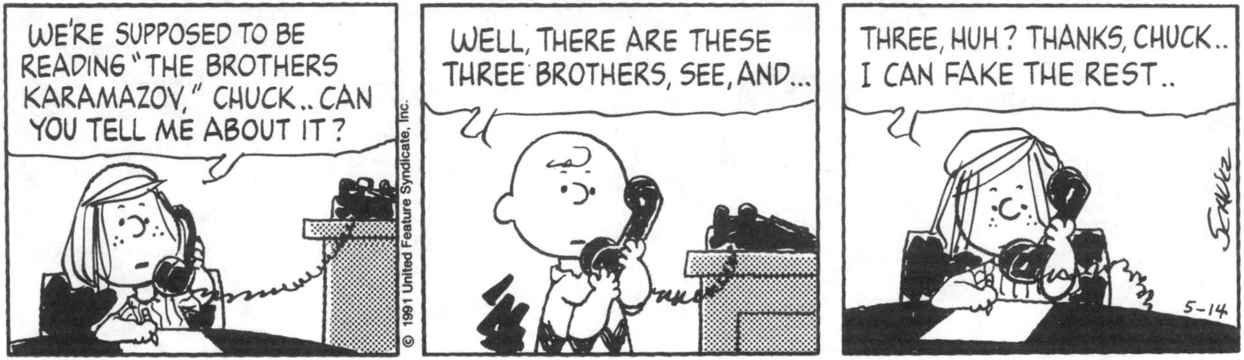
WE'RE SUPPOSED TO BE READING "THE BROTHERS KARAMAZOV," CHUCK.. CAN YOU TELL ME ABOUT IT?
© 1991 United Feature Syndicate, Inc.
WELL, THERE ARE THESE THREE BROTHERS, SEE, AND...
THREE, HUH? THANKS, CHUCK.. I CAN FAKE THE REST..
5-14

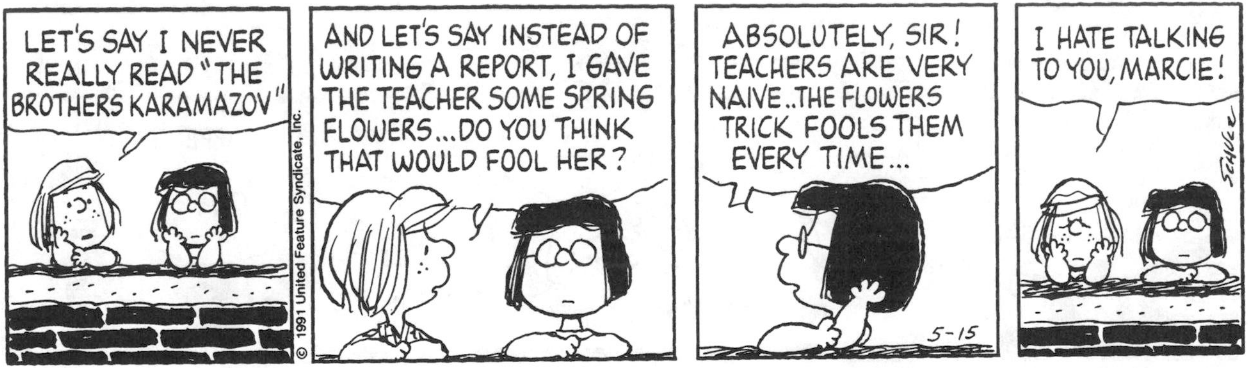
LET'S SAY I NEVER REALLY READ "THE BROTHERS KARAMAZOV"
© 1991 United Feature Syndicate, Inc.
AND LET'S SAY INSTEAD OF WRITING A REPORT, I GAVE THE TEACHER SOME SPRING FLOWERS...DO YOU THINK THAT WOULD FOOL HER?
ABSOLUTELY, SIR! TEACHERS ARE VERY NAIVE..THE FLOWERS TRICK FOOLS THEM EVERY TIME...
5-15
I HATE TALKING TO YOU, MARCIE!

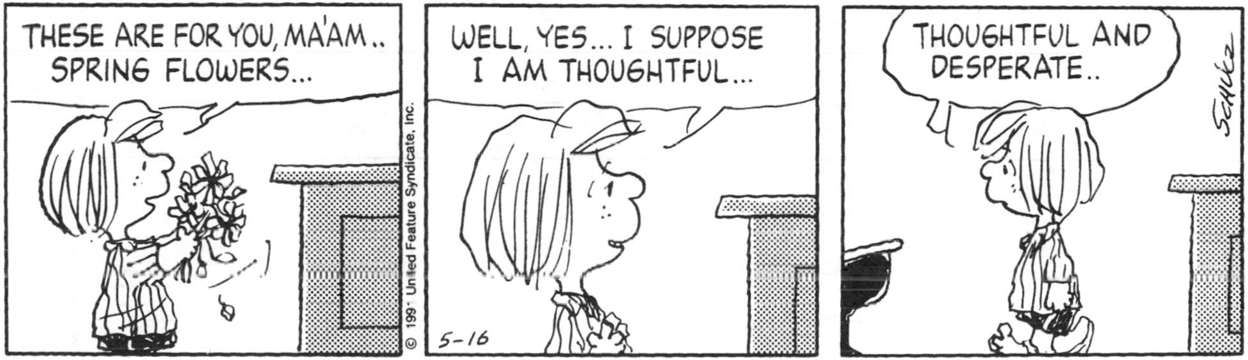
THESE ARE FOR YOU, MA'AM.. SPRING FLOWERS...
WELL, YES... I SUPPOSE I AM THOUGHTFUL...
THOUGHTFUL AND DESPERATE..
© 1991 United Feature Syndicate, Inc.
5-16
SCHULZ

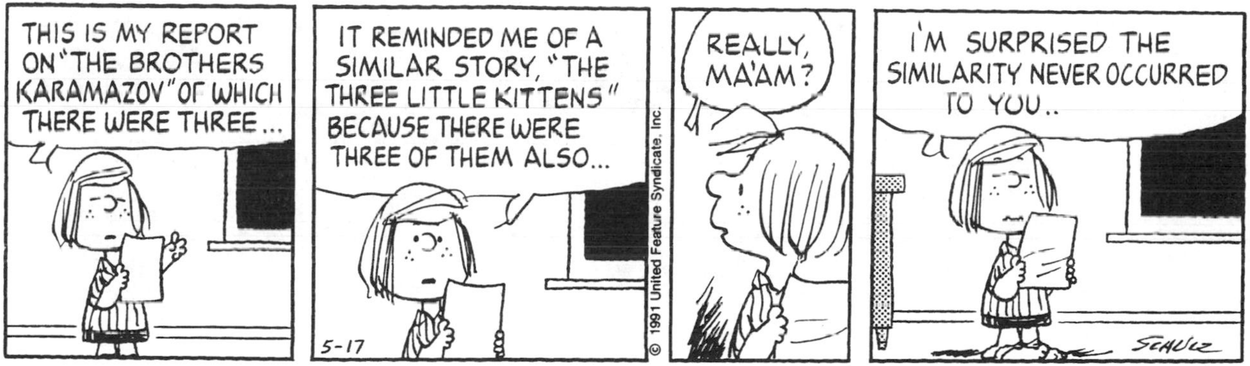
THIS IS MY REPORT ON "THE BROTHERS KARAMAZOV" OF WHICH THERE WERE THREE...
IT REMINDED ME OF A SIMILAR STORY, "THE THREE LITTLE KITTENS" BECAUSE THERE WERE THREE OF THEM ALSO...
REALLY, MA'AM?
I'M SURPRISED THE SIMILARITY NEVER OCCURRED TO YOU..
© 1991 United Feature Syndicate, Inc.
5-17
SCHULZ

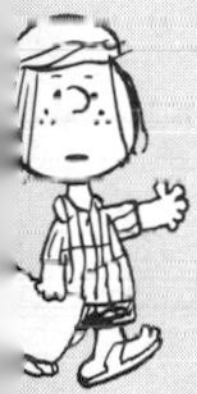

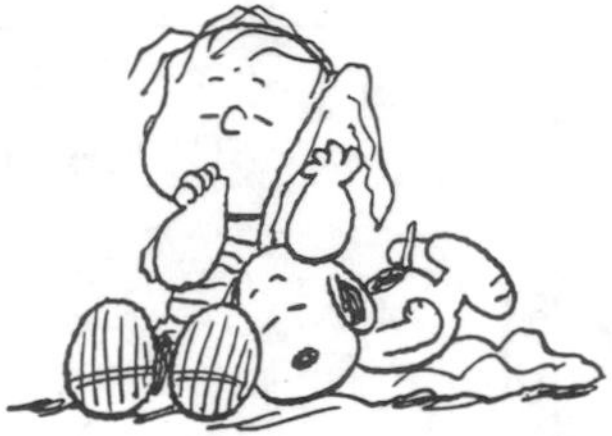

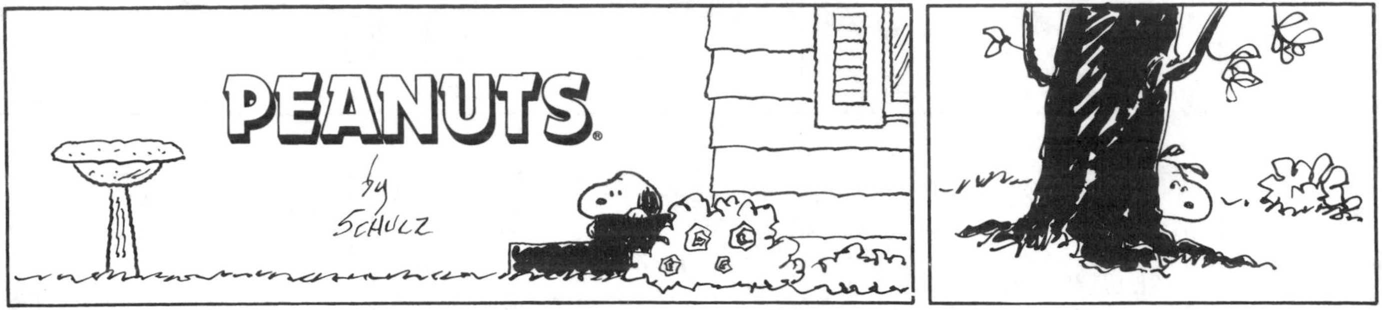
PEANUTS®
by SCHULZ

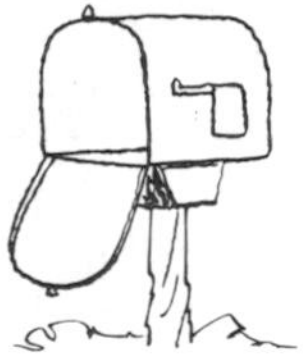

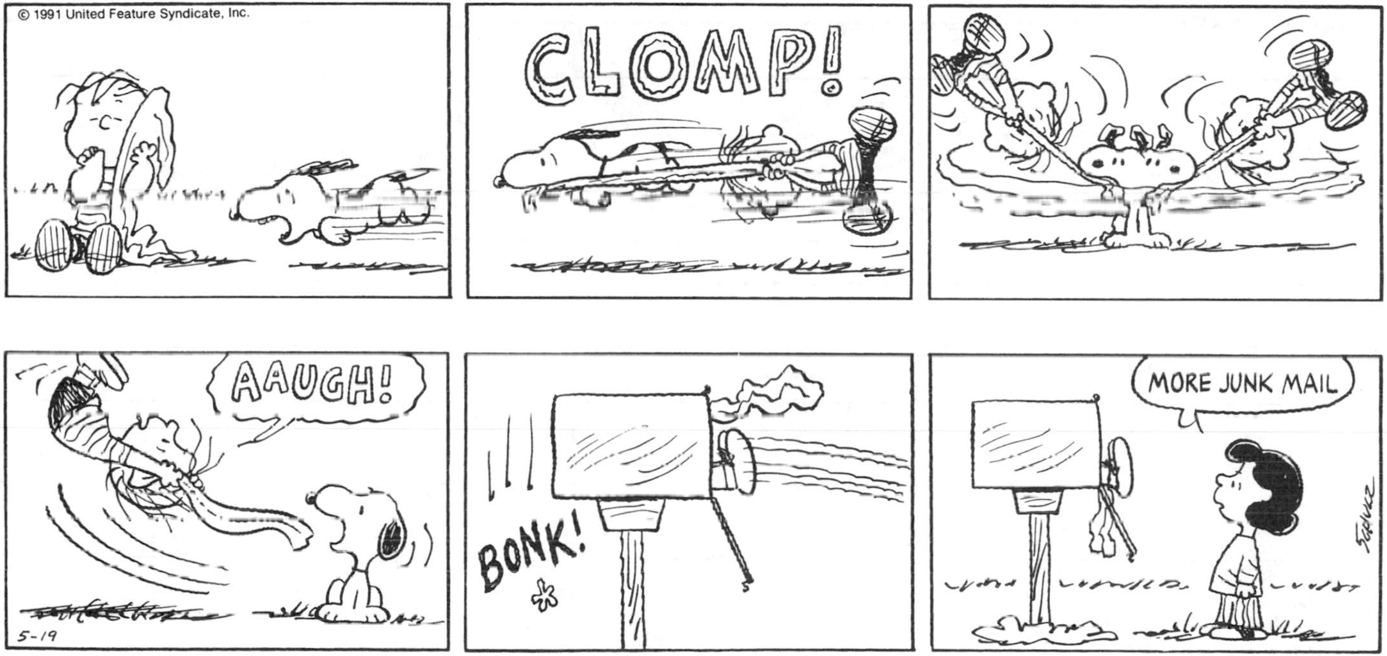
© 1991 United Feature Syndicate, Inc.
CLOMP!
AAUGH!
5-19
BONK!
MORE JUNK MAIL

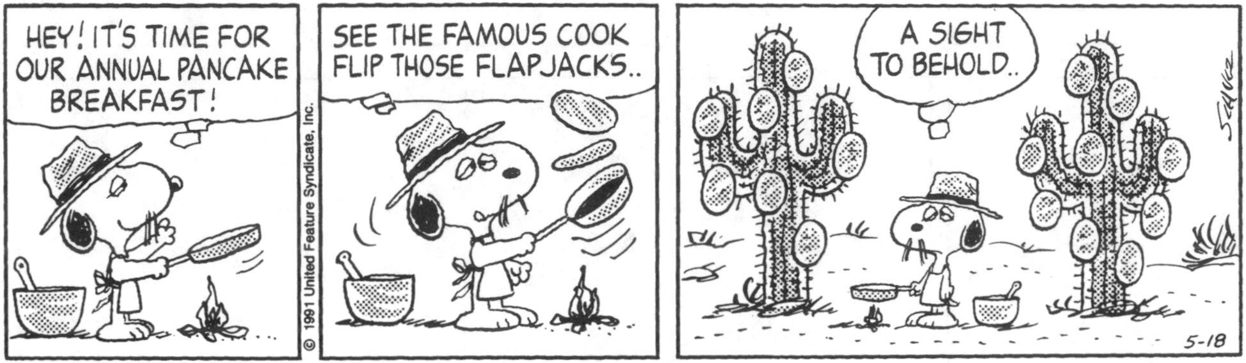
HEY! IT'S TIME FOR OUR ANNUAL PANCAKE BREAKFAST!
SEE THE FAMOUS COOK FLIP THOSE FLAPJACKS..
A SIGHT TO BEHOLD..
© 1991 United Feature Syndicate, Inc.
5-18

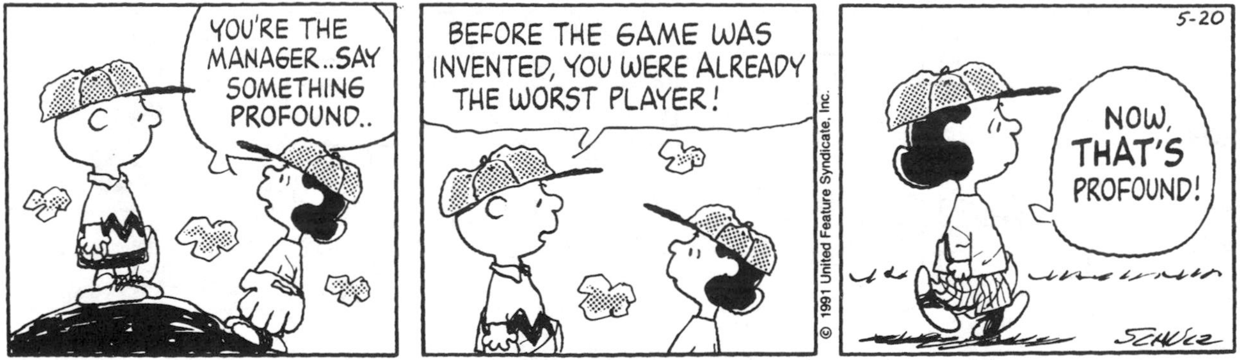
YOU'RE THE MANAGER..SAY SOMETHING PROFOUND..
BEFORE THE GAME WAS INVENTED, YOU WERE ALREADY THE WORST PLAYER!
NOW, THAT'S PROFOUND!
© 1991 United Feature Syndicate, Inc.
5-20

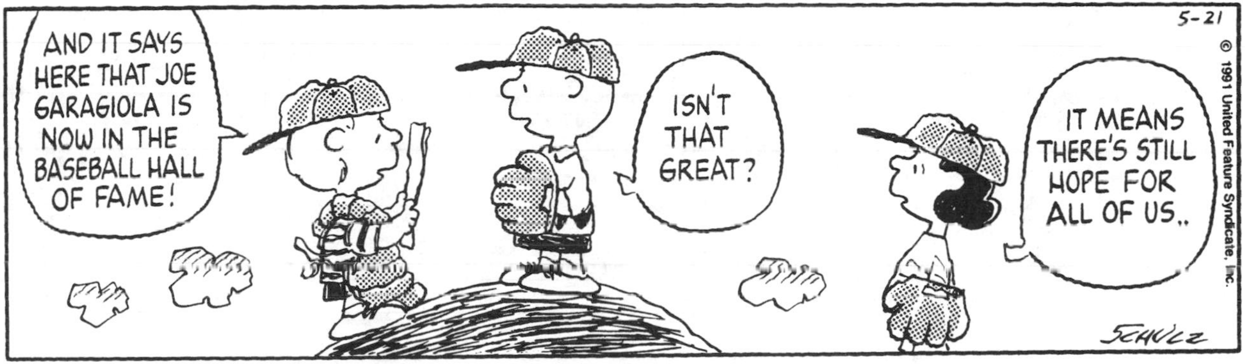
5-21
© 1991 United Feature Syndicate, Inc.
AND IT SAYS HERE THAT JOE GARAGIOLA IS NOW IN THE BASEBALL HALL OF FAME!
ISN'T THAT GREAT?
IT MEANS THERE'S STILL HOPE FOR ALL OF US..
SCHULZ

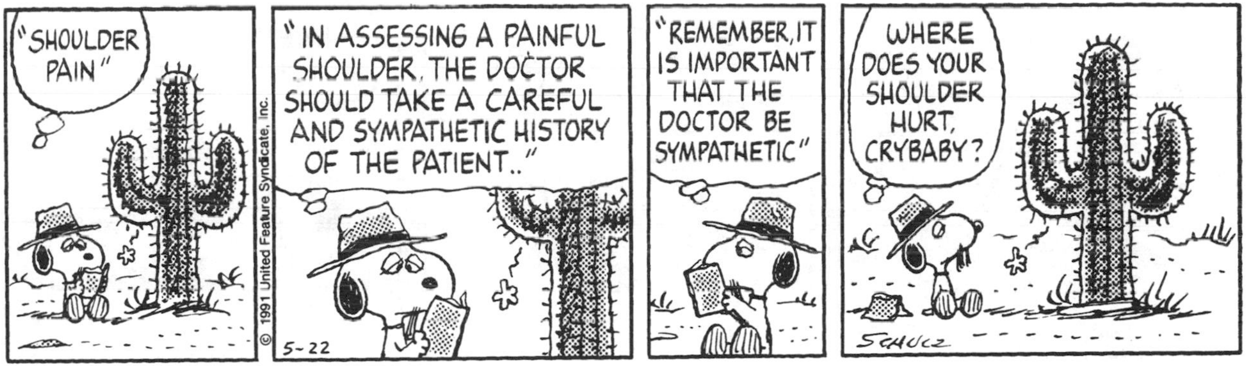
"SHOULDER PAIN"
© 1991 United Feature Syndicate, Inc.
5-22
"IN ASSESSING A PAINFUL SHOULDER, THE DOCTOR SHOULD TAKE A CAREFUL AND SYMPATHETIC HISTORY OF THE PATIENT.."
"REMEMBER, IT IS IMPORTANT THAT THE DOCTOR BE SYMPATHETIC"
WHERE DOES YOUR SHOULDER HURT, CRYBABY?
SCHULZ

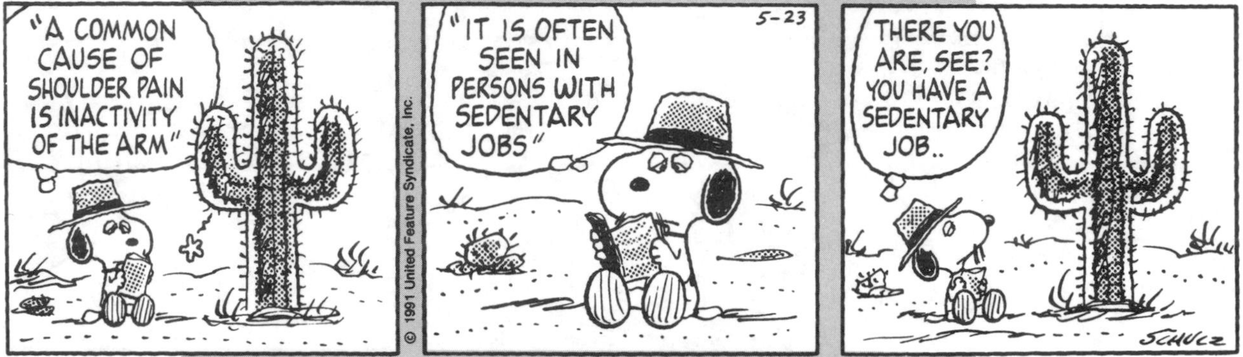
"A COMMON CAUSE OF SHOULDER PAIN IS INACTIVITY OF THE ARM"
© 1991 United Feature Syndicate, Inc.
"IT IS OFTEN SEEN IN PERSONS WITH SEDENTARY JOBS"
5-23
THERE YOU ARE, SEE? YOU HAVE A SEDENTARY JOB..
SCHULZ

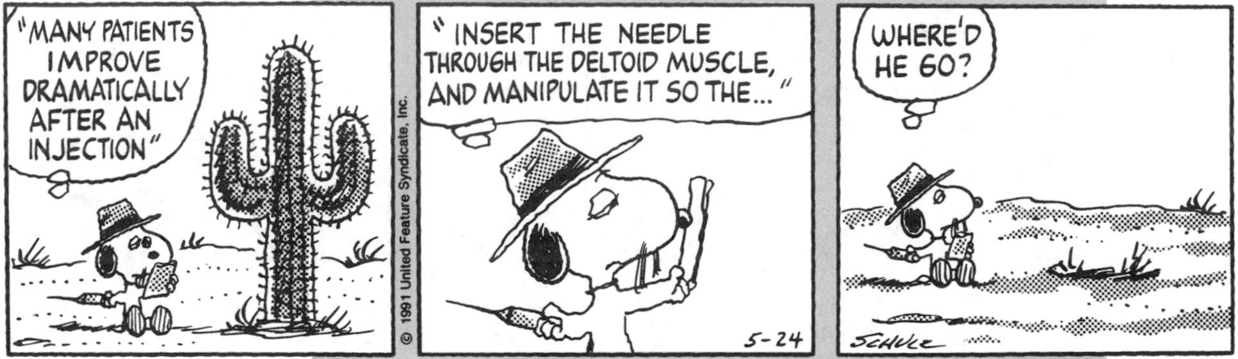
"MANY PATIENTS IMPROVE DRAMATICALLY AFTER AN INJECTION"
© 1991 United Feature Syndicate, Inc.
"INSERT THE NEEDLE THROUGH THE DELTOID MUSCLE, AND MANIPULATE IT SO THE..."
5-24
WHERE'D HE GO?
SCHULZ

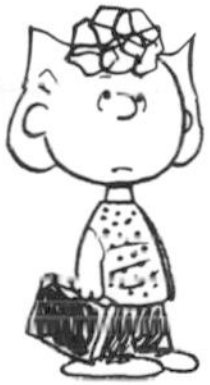

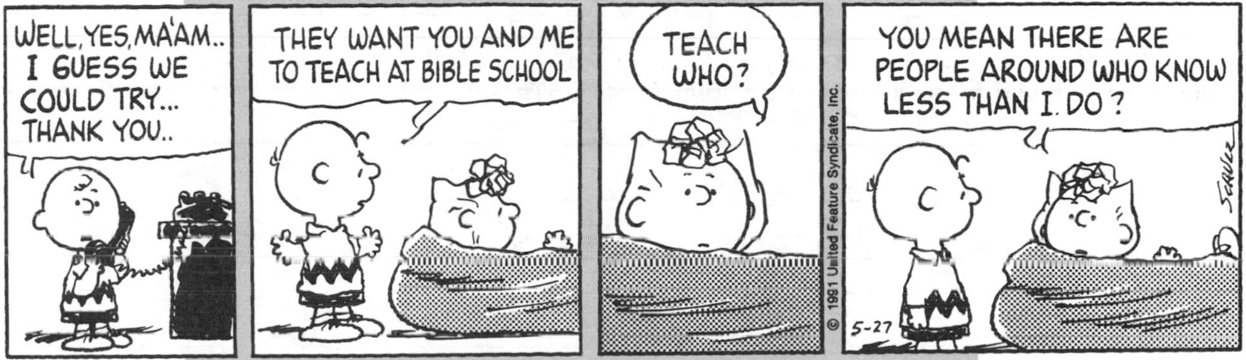

WELL, YES, MA'AM.. I GUESS WE COULD TRY... THANK YOU..
THEY WANT YOU AND ME TO TEACH AT BIBLE SCHOOL
TEACH WHO?
YOU MEAN THERE ARE PEOPLE AROUND WHO KNOW LESS THAN I DO?
© 1991 United Feature Syndicate, Inc.
5-27
SCHULZ

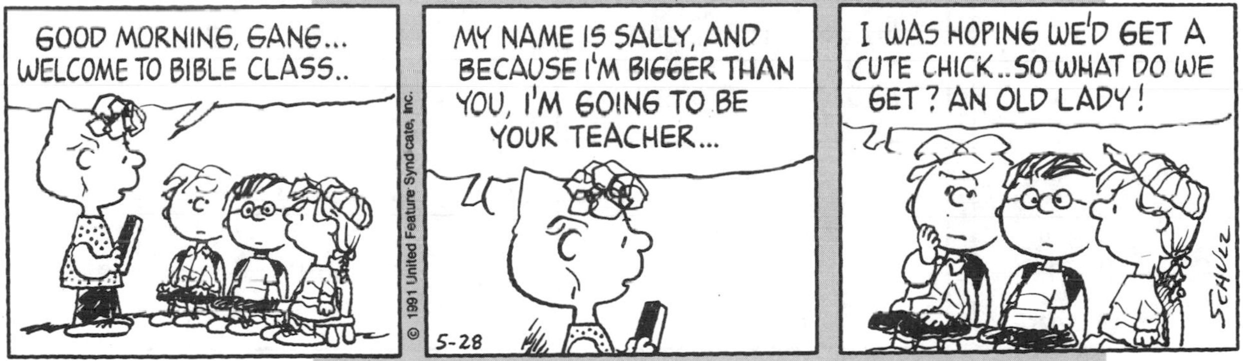

GOOD MORNING, GANG... WELCOME TO BIBLE CLASS..
MY NAME IS SALLY, AND BECAUSE I'M BIGGER THAN YOU, I'M GOING TO BE YOUR TEACHER...
I WAS HOPING WE'D GET A CUTE CHICK..SO WHAT DO WE GET? AN OLD LADY!
© 1991 United Feature Syndicate, Inc.
5-28
SCHULZ

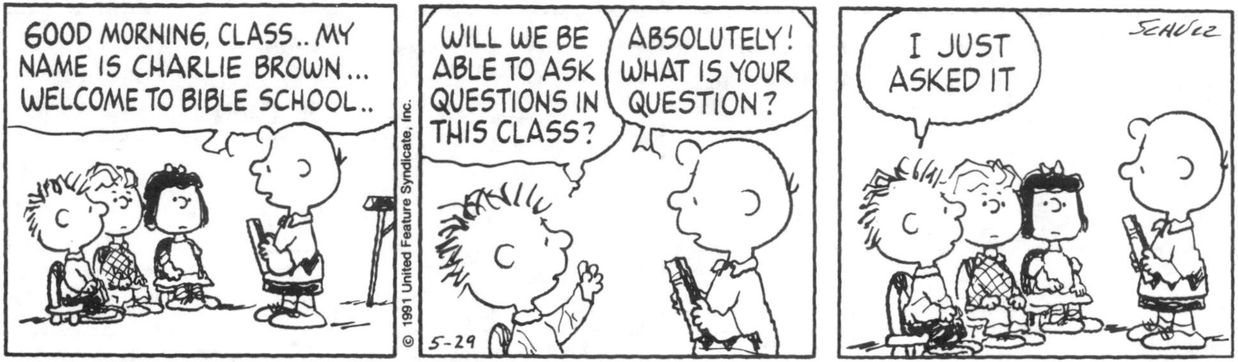
GOOD MORNING, CLASS.. MY NAME IS CHARLIE BROWN... WELCOME TO BIBLE SCHOOL..
WILL WE BE ABLE TO ASK QUESTIONS IN THIS CLASS?
ABSOLUTELY! WHAT IS YOUR QUESTION?
I JUST ASKED IT
5-29
SCHULZ

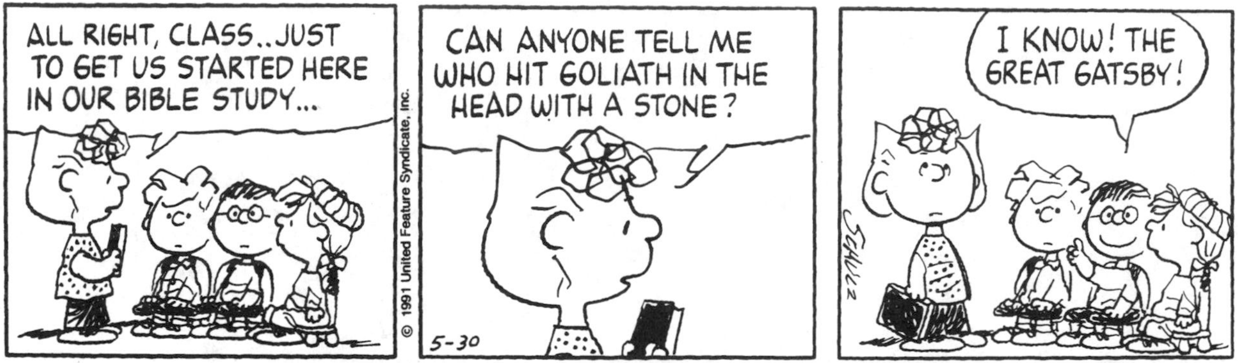
ALL RIGHT, CLASS..JUST TO GET US STARTED HERE IN OUR BIBLE STUDY...
CAN ANYONE TELL ME WHO HIT GOLIATH IN THE HEAD WITH A STONE?
I KNOW! THE GREAT GATSBY!
5-30
SCHULZ

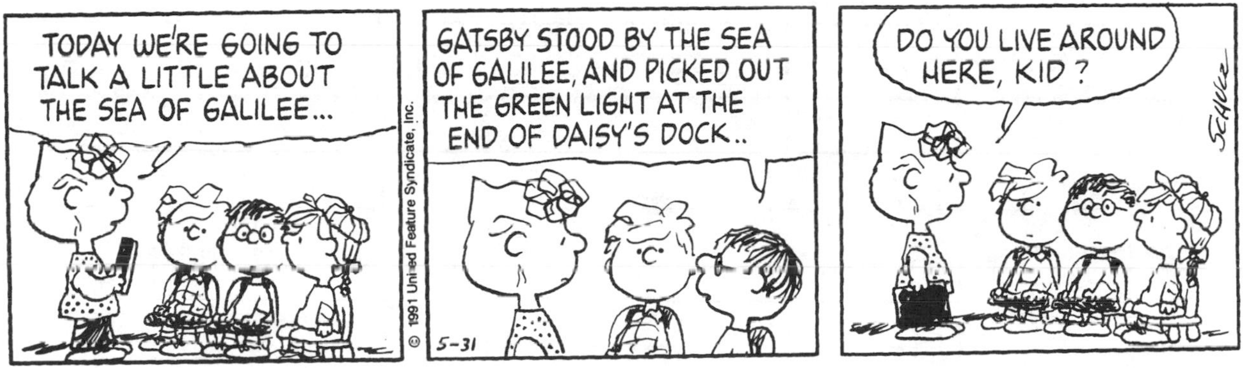
TODAY WE'RE GOING TO TALK A LITTLE ABOUT THE SEA OF GALILEE...
© 1991 United Feature Syndicate, Inc.
GATSBY STOOD BY THE SEA OF GALILEE, AND PICKED OUT THE GREEN LIGHT AT THE END OF DAISY'S DOCK..
5-31
DO YOU LIVE AROUND HERE, KID ?
SCHULZ

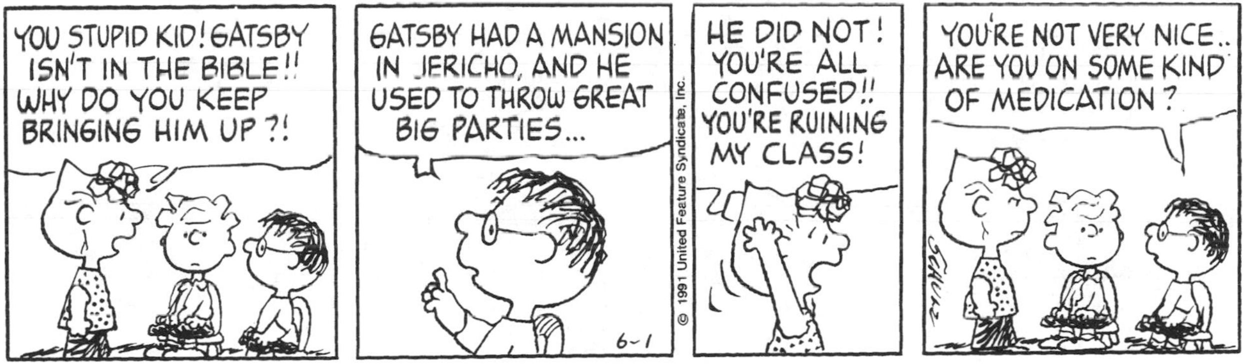
YOU STUPID KID! GATSBY ISN'T IN THE BIBLE!! WHY DO YOU KEEP BRINGING HIM UP ?!
GATSBY HAD A MANSION IN JERICHO, AND HE USED TO THROW GREAT BIG PARTIES...
6-1
© 1991 United Feature Syndicate, Inc.
HE DID NOT ! YOU'RE ALL CONFUSED!! YOU'RE RUINING MY CLASS!
YOU'RE NOT VERY NICE.. ARE YOU ON SOME KIND OF MEDICATION ?
SCHULZ

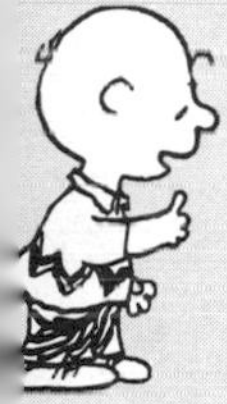

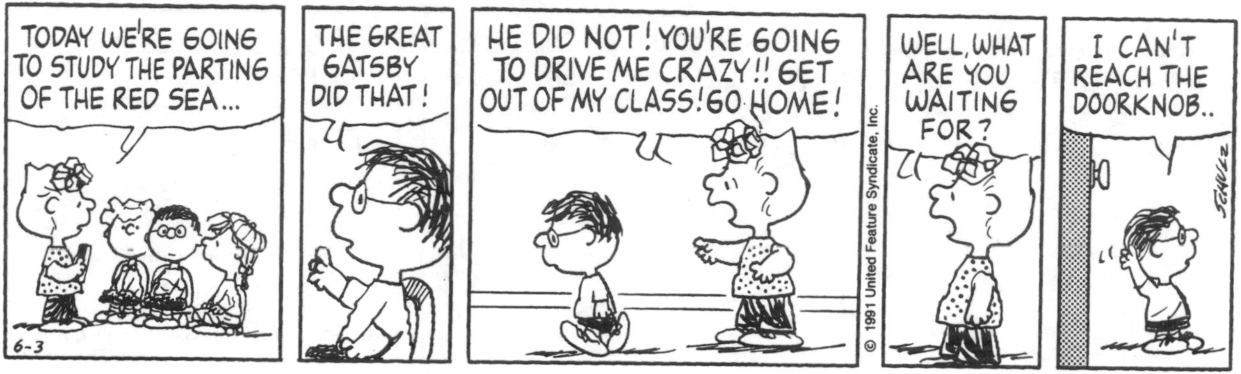
TODAY WE'RE GOING TO STUDY THE PARTING OF THE RED SEA...
6-3
THE GREAT GATSBY DID THAT!
HE DID NOT! YOU'RE GOING TO DRIVE ME CRAZY!! GET OUT OF MY CLASS! GO HOME!
© 1991 United Feature Syndicate, Inc.
WELL, WHAT ARE YOU WAITING FOR?
I CAN'T REACH THE DOORKNOB..
SCHULZ

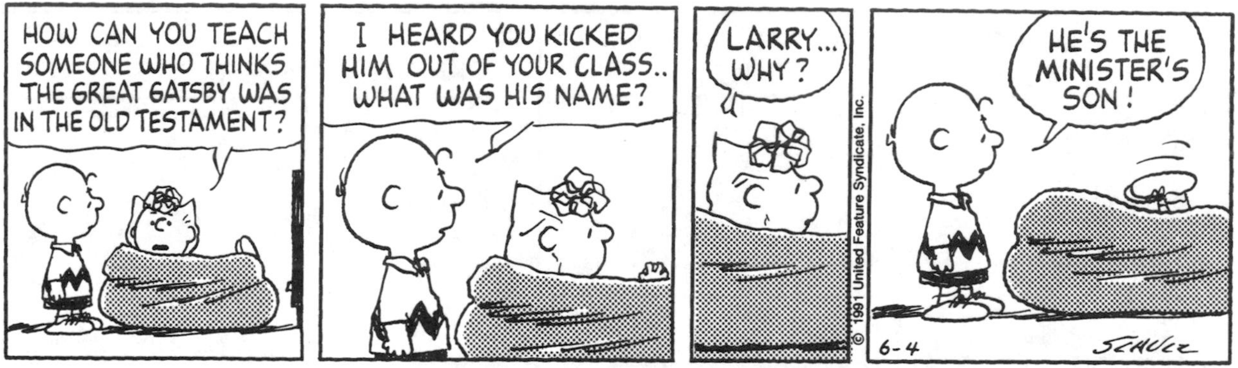
HOW CAN YOU TEACH SOMEONE WHO THINKS THE GREAT GATSBY WAS IN THE OLD TESTAMENT?
I HEARD YOU KICKED HIM OUT OF YOUR CLASS.. WHAT WAS HIS NAME?
LARRY... WHY?
© 1991 United Feature Syndicate, Inc.
HE'S THE MINISTER'S SON!
6-4
SCHULZ

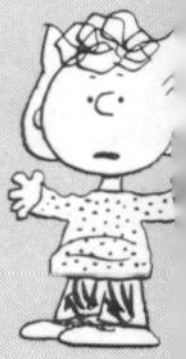

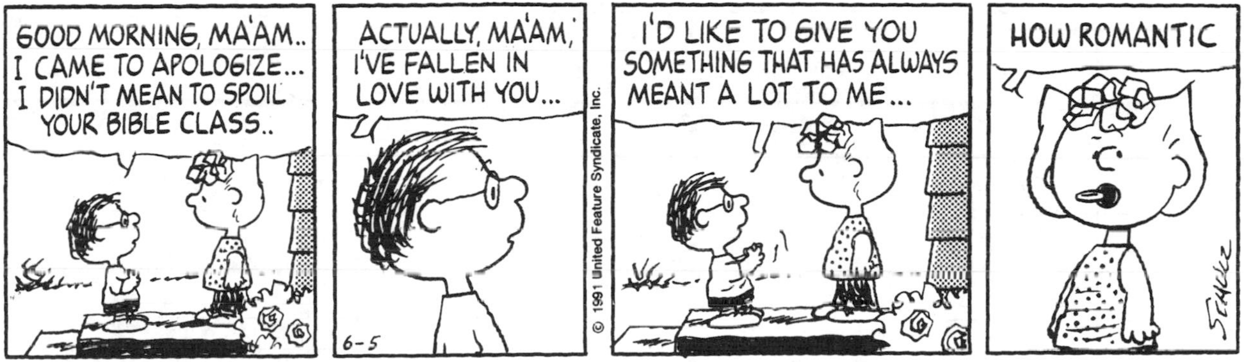
GOOD MORNING, MA'AM.. I CAME TO APOLOGIZE... I DIDN'T MEAN TO SPOIL YOUR BIBLE CLASS..
ACTUALLY, MA'AM, I'VE FALLEN IN LOVE WITH YOU...
6-5
© 1991 United Feature Syndicate, Inc.
I'D LIKE TO GIVE YOU SOMETHING THAT HAS ALWAYS MEANT A LOT TO ME...
HOW ROMANTIC
SCHULZ

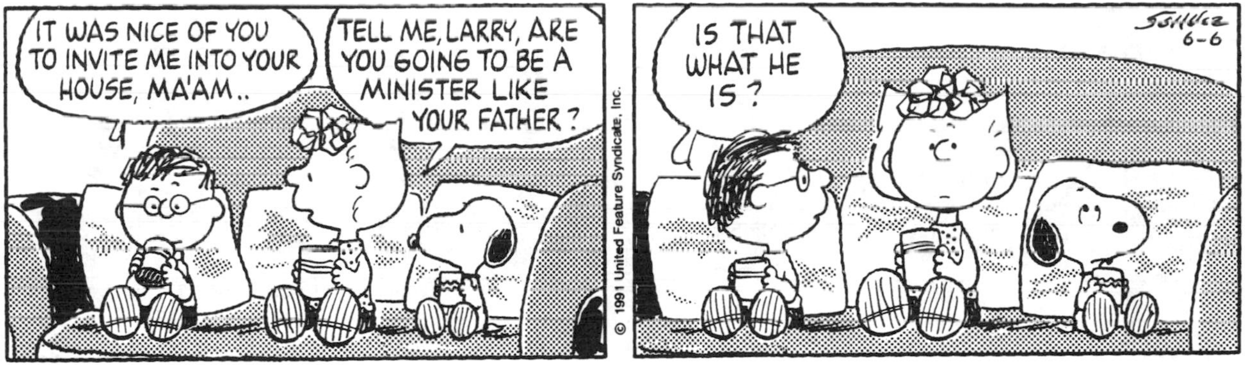
IT WAS NICE OF YOU TO INVITE ME INTO YOUR HOUSE, MA'AM..
TELL ME, LARRY, ARE YOU GOING TO BE A MINISTER LIKE YOUR FATHER?
© 1991 United Feature Syndicate, Inc.
SCHULZ
6-6
IS THAT WHAT HE IS?

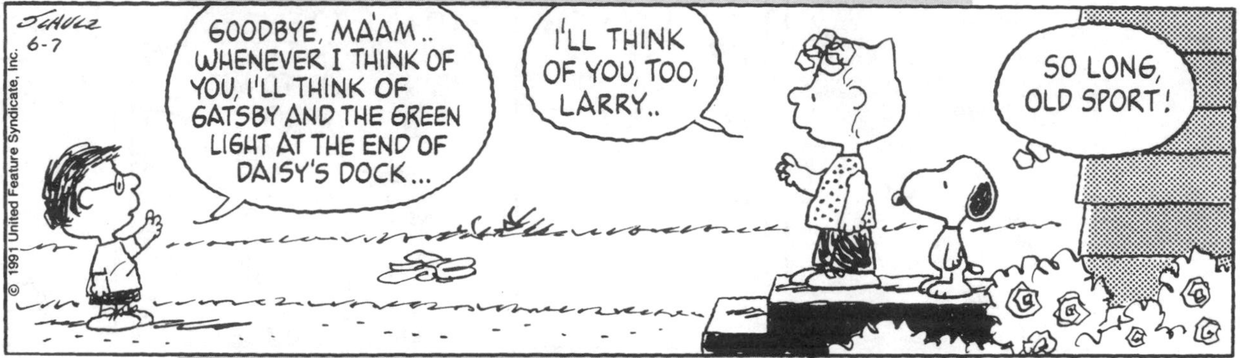
SCHULZ 6-7
© 1991 United Feature Syndicate, Inc.
GOODBYE, MA'AM.. WHENEVER I THINK OF YOU, I'LL THINK OF GATSBY AND THE GREEN LIGHT AT THE END OF DAISY'S DOCK...
I'LL THINK OF YOU, TOO, LARRY..
SO LONG, OLD SPORT!

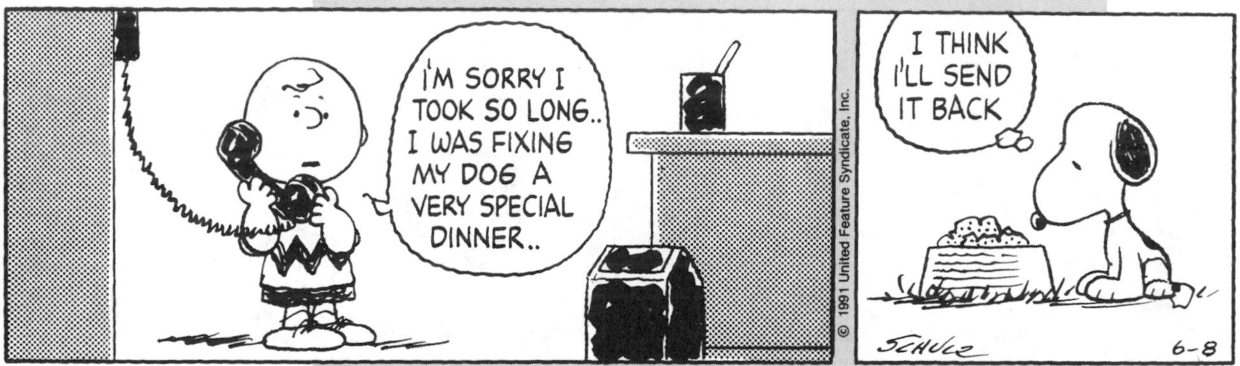
I'M SORRY I TOOK SO LONG.. I WAS FIXING MY DOG A VERY SPECIAL DINNER..
© 1991 United Feature Syndicate, Inc.
I THINK I'LL SEND IT BACK
SCHULZ 6-8

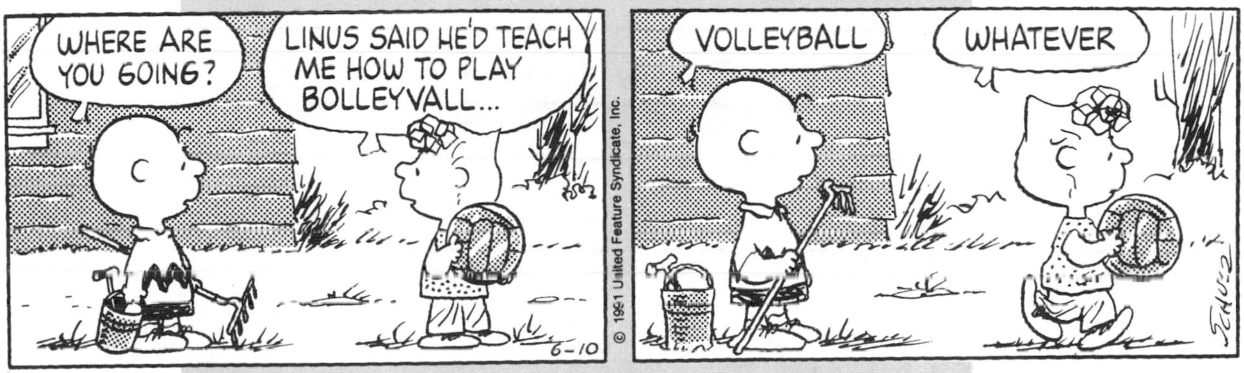
WHERE ARE YOU GOING?
LINUS SAID HE'D TEACH ME HOW TO PLAY BOLLEYVALL...
6-10
© 1991 United Feature Syndicate, Inc.
VOLLEYBALL
WHATEVER
SCHULZ

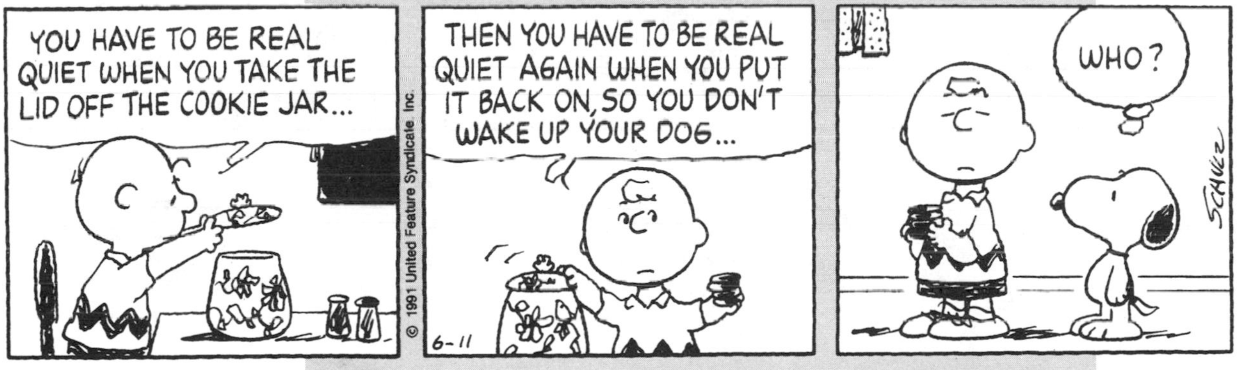
YOU HAVE TO BE REAL QUIET WHEN YOU TAKE THE LID OFF THE COOKIE JAR...
© 1991 United Feature Syndicate, Inc.
THEN YOU HAVE TO BE REAL QUIET AGAIN WHEN YOU PUT IT BACK ON, SO YOU DON'T WAKE UP YOUR DOG...
6-11
WHO?
SCHULZ

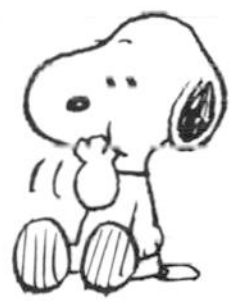

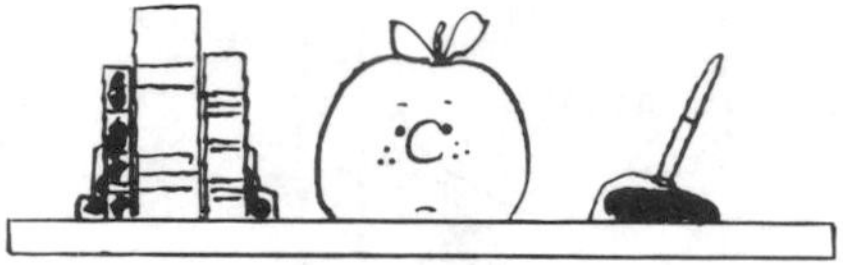

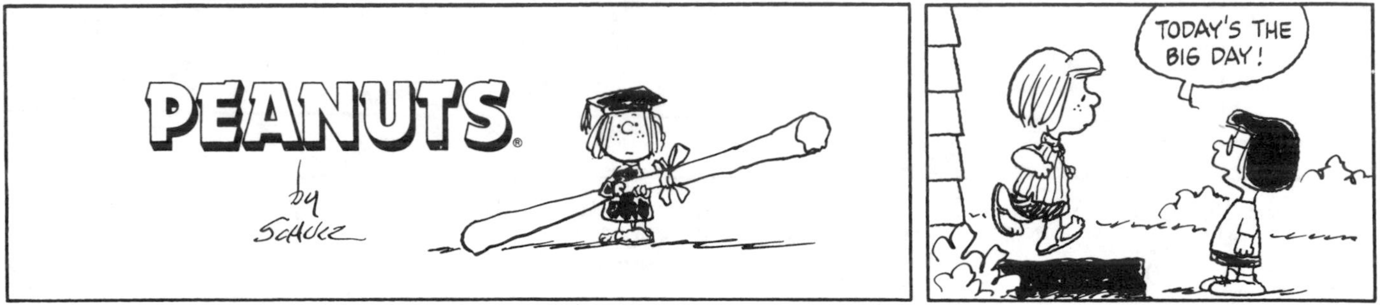
PEANUTS®
by SCHULZ
TODAY'S THE BIG DAY!

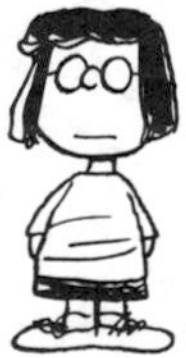

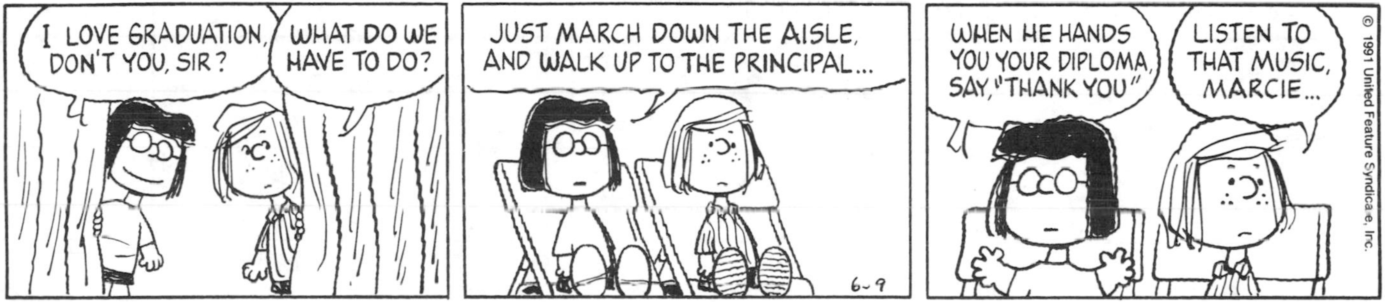
I LOVE GRADUATION, DON'T YOU, SIR?
WHAT DO WE HAVE TO DO?
JUST MARCH DOWN THE AISLE, AND WALK UP TO THE PRINCIPAL...
6-9
WHEN HE HANDS YOU YOUR DIPLOMA, SAY, "THANK YOU"
LISTEN TO THAT MUSIC, MARCIE...
© 1991 United Feature Syndicate, Inc.

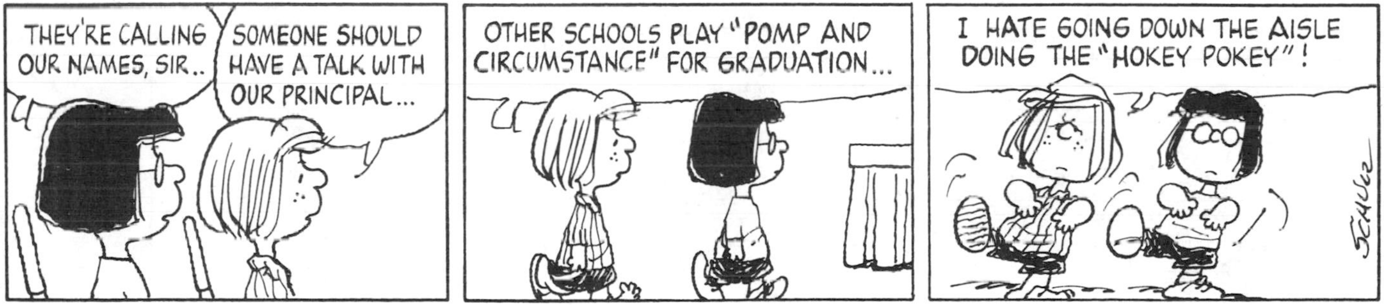
THEY'RE CALLING OUR NAMES, SIR..
SOMEONE SHOULD HAVE A TALK WITH OUR PRINCIPAL...
OTHER SCHOOLS PLAY "POMP AND CIRCUMSTANCE" FOR GRADUATION...
I HATE GOING DOWN THE AISLE DOING THE "HOKEY POKEY"!
SCHULZ

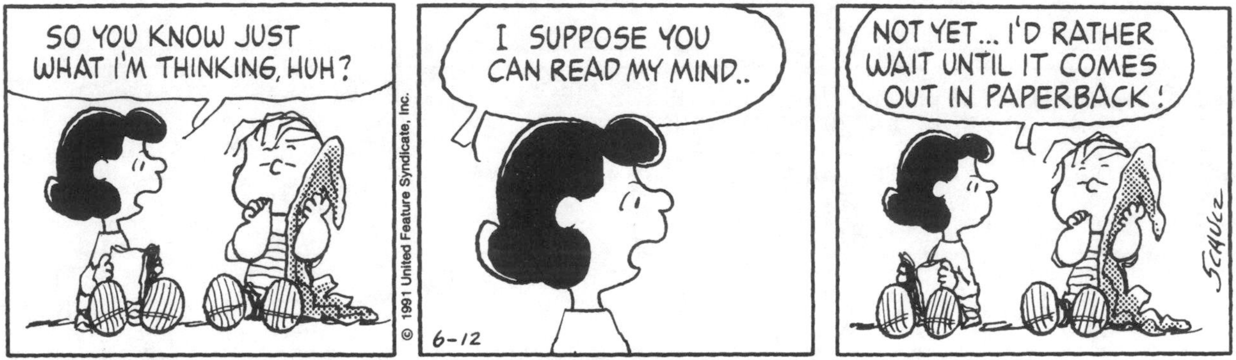
SO YOU KNOW JUST WHAT I'M THINKING, HUH?
I SUPPOSE YOU CAN READ MY MIND..
NOT YET... I'D RATHER WAIT UNTIL IT COMES OUT IN PAPERBACK!
© 1991 United Feature Syndicate, Inc.
6-12
SCHULZ

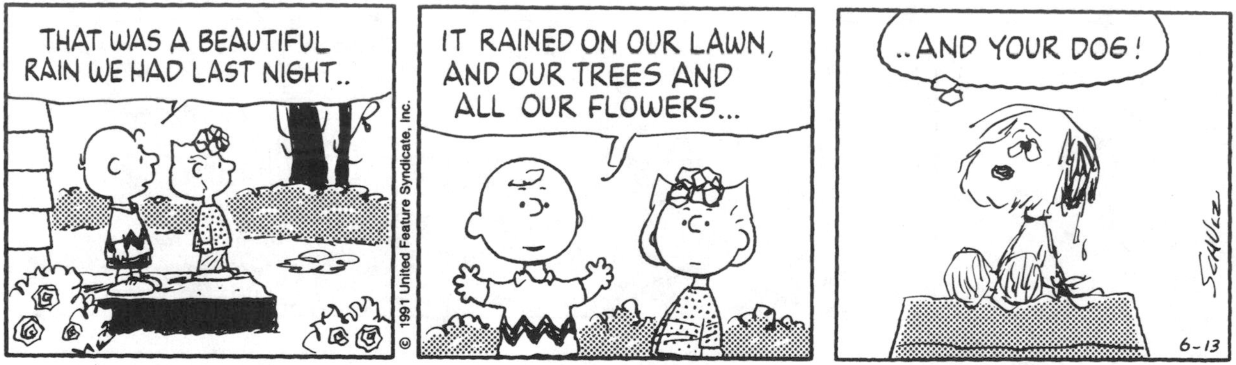
THAT WAS A BEAUTIFUL RAIN WE HAD LAST NIGHT..
IT RAINED ON OUR LAWN, AND OUR TREES AND ALL OUR FLOWERS...
..AND YOUR DOG!
© 1991 United Feature Syndicate, Inc.
6-13
SCHULZ

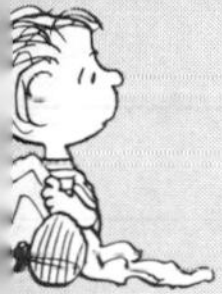

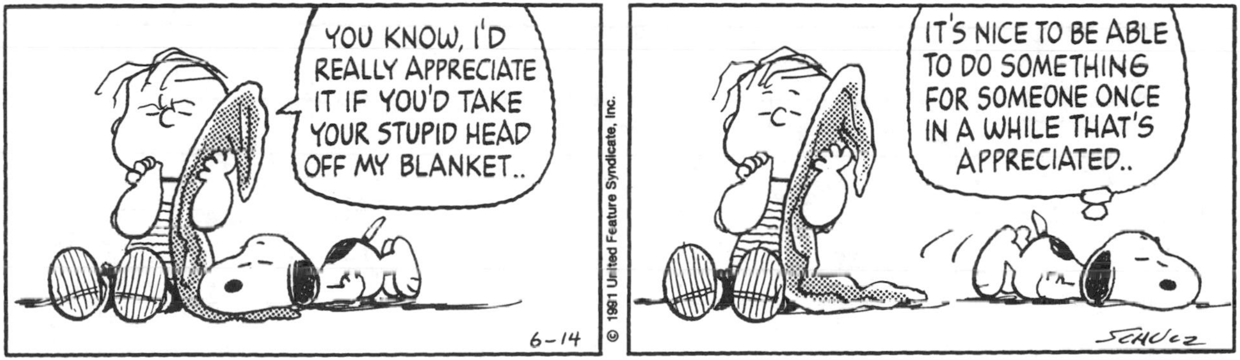
YOU KNOW, I'D REALLY APPRECIATE IT IF YOU'D TAKE YOUR STUPID HEAD OFF MY BLANKET..
6-14
© 1991 United Feature Syndicate, Inc.
IT'S NICE TO BE ABLE TO DO SOMETHING FOR SOMEONE ONCE IN A WHILE THAT'S APPRECIATED..
SCHULZ

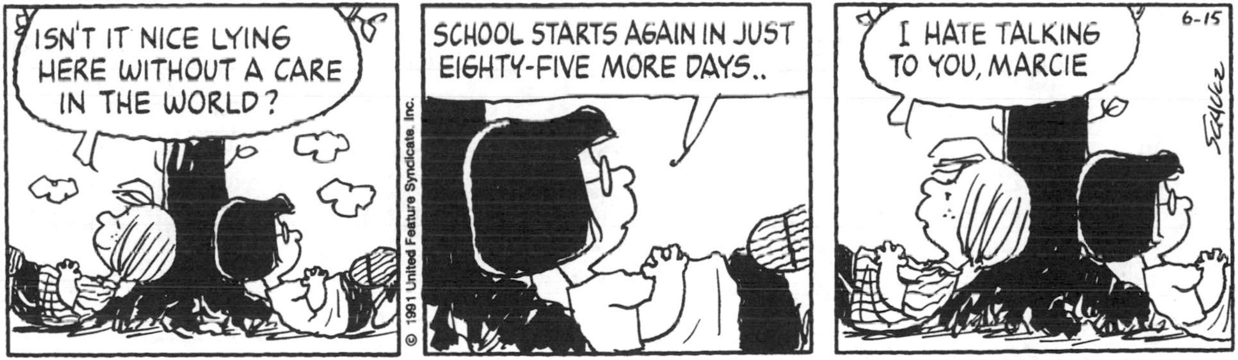
ISN'T IT NICE LYING HERE WITHOUT A CARE IN THE WORLD?
© 1991 United Feature Syndicate, Inc.
SCHOOL STARTS AGAIN IN JUST EIGHTY-FIVE MORE DAYS..
6-15
I HATE TALKING TO YOU, MARCIE
SCHULZ

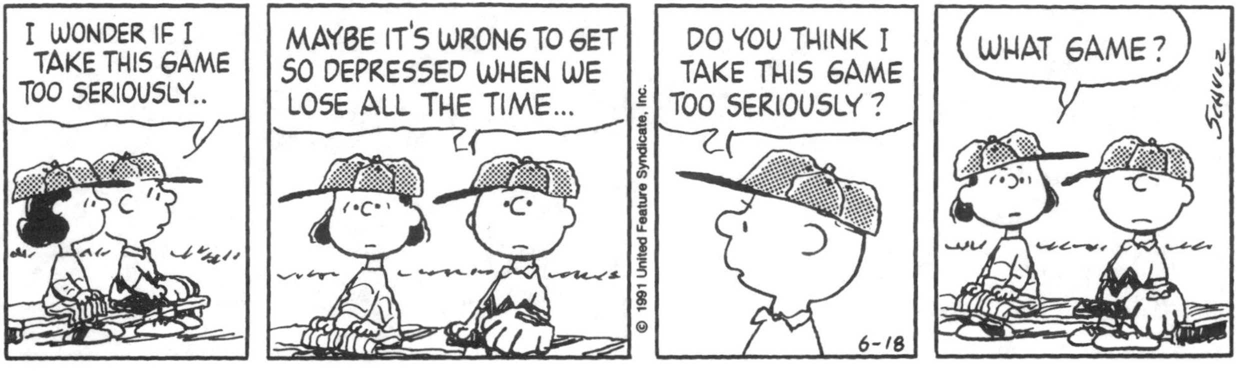
I WONDER IF I TAKE THIS GAME TOO SERIOUSLY..
MAYBE IT'S WRONG TO GET SO DEPRESSED WHEN WE LOSE ALL THE TIME...
© 1991 United Feature Syndicate, Inc.
DO YOU THINK I TAKE THIS GAME TOO SERIOUSLY?
6-18
WHAT GAME?
SCHULZ

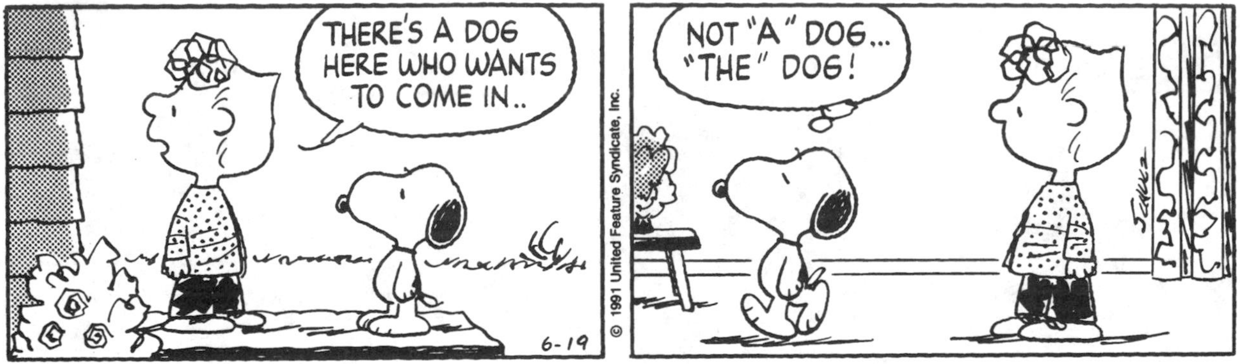
THERE'S A DOG HERE WHO WANTS TO COME IN..
6-19
© 1991 United Feature Syndicate, Inc.
NOT "A" DOG... "THE" DOG!
SCHULZ

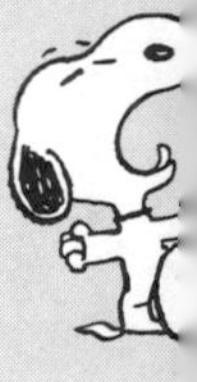

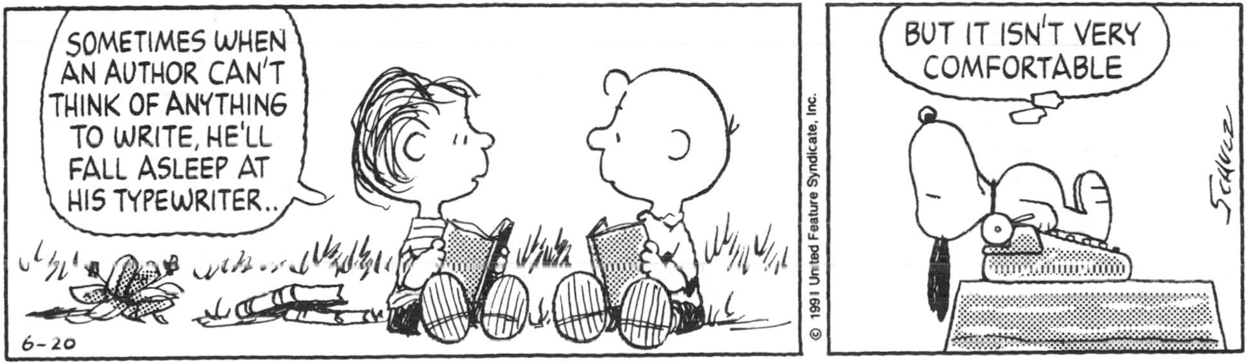
SOMETIMES WHEN AN AUTHOR CAN'T THINK OF ANYTHING TO WRITE, HE'LL FALL ASLEEP AT HIS TYPEWRITER..
6-20
© 1991 United Feature Syndicate, Inc.
BUT IT ISN'T VERY COMFORTABLE
SCHULZ

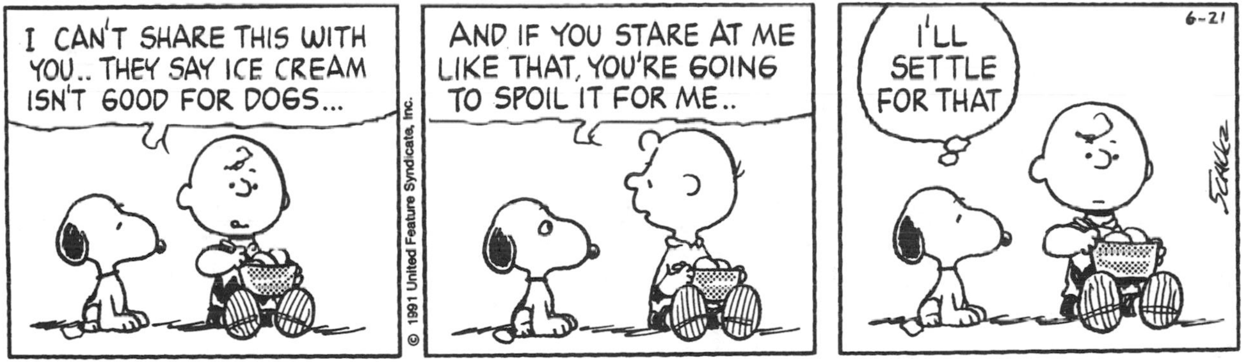
I CAN'T SHARE THIS WITH YOU.. THEY SAY ICE CREAM ISN'T GOOD FOR DOGS...
© 1991 United Feature Syndicate, Inc.
AND IF YOU STARE AT ME LIKE THAT, YOU'RE GOING TO SPOIL IT FOR ME..
6-21
I'LL SETTLE FOR THAT
SCHULZ

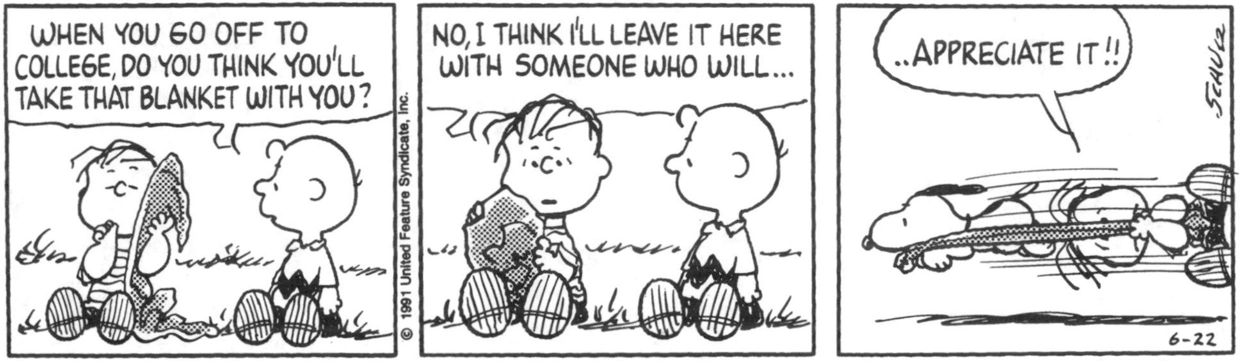
WHEN YOU GO OFF TO COLLEGE, DO YOU THINK YOU'LL TAKE THAT BLANKET WITH YOU?
© 1991 United Feature Syndicate, Inc.
NO, I THINK I'LL LEAVE IT HERE WITH SOMEONE WHO WILL...
..APPRECIATE IT!!
SCHULZ
6-22

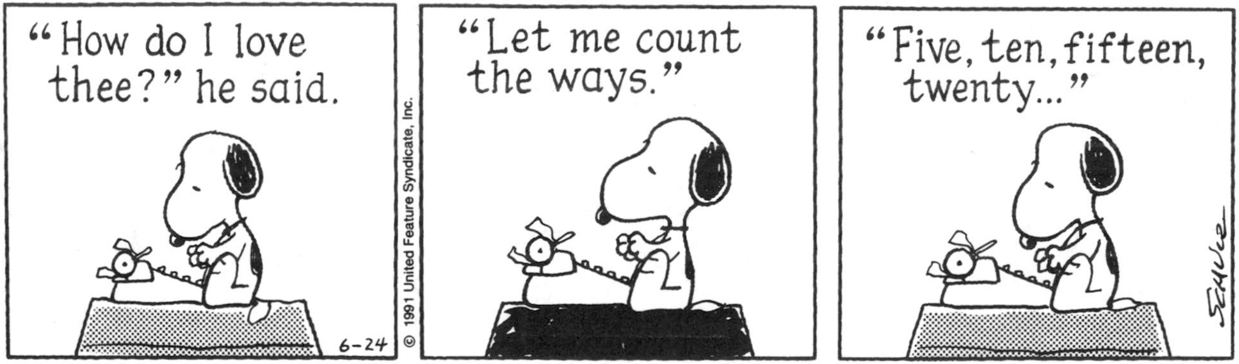
"How do I love thee?" he said.
6-24
© 1991 United Feature Syndicate, Inc.
"Let me count the ways."
"Five, ten, fifteen, twenty..."
SCHULZ

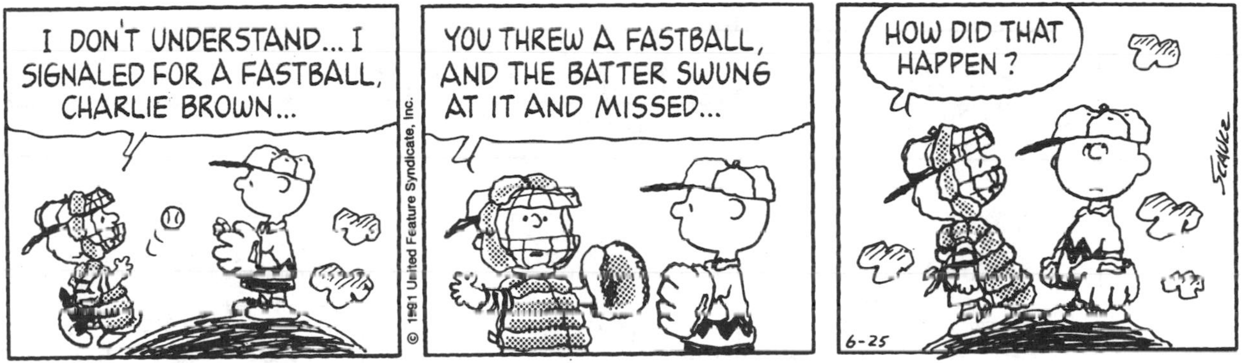
I DON'T UNDERSTAND... I SIGNALED FOR A FASTBALL, CHARLIE BROWN...
© 1991 United Feature Syndicate, Inc.
YOU THREW A FASTBALL, AND THE BATTER SWUNG AT IT AND MISSED...
HOW DID THAT HAPPEN ?
6-25

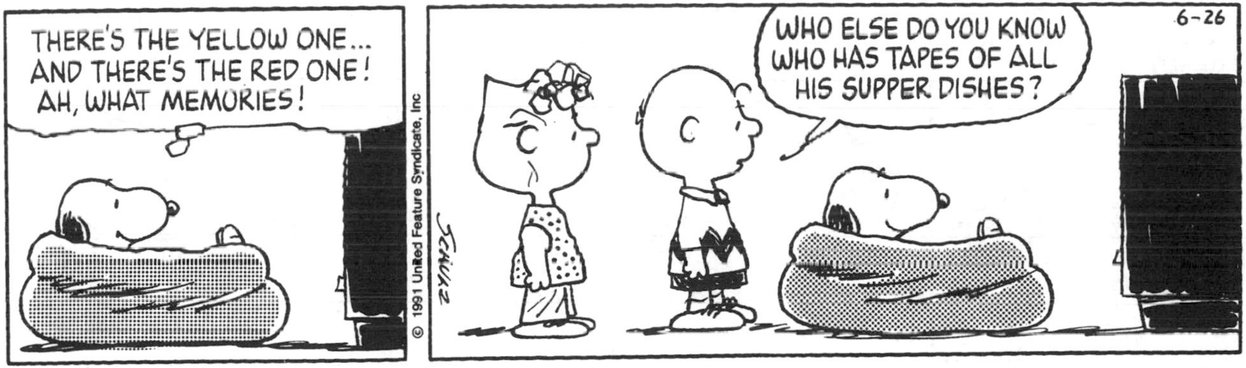
THERE'S THE YELLOW ONE... AND THERE'S THE RED ONE! AH, WHAT MEMORIES!
© 1991 United Feature Syndicate, Inc.
6-26
WHO ELSE DO YOU KNOW WHO HAS TAPES OF ALL HIS SUPPER DISHES ?

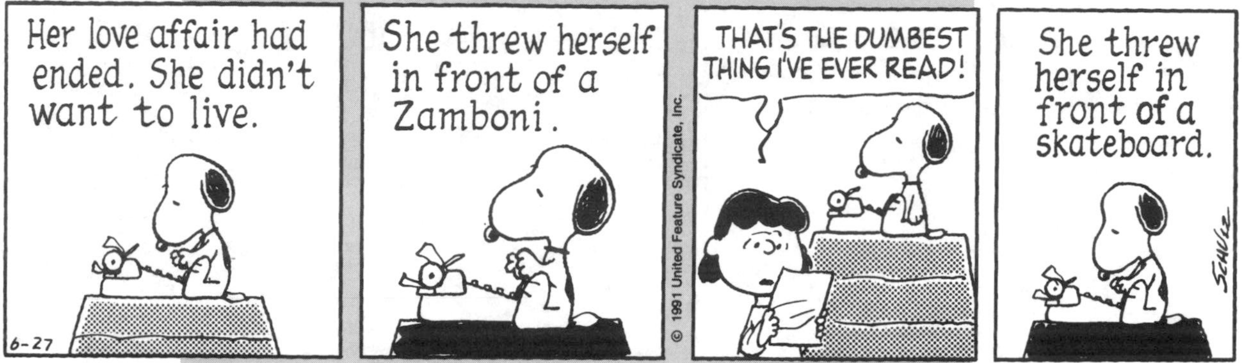
Her love affair had ended. She didn't want to live.
She threw herself in front of a Zamboni.
© 1991 United Feature Syndicate, Inc.
THAT'S THE DUMBEST THING I'VE EVER READ!
She threw herself in front of a skateboard.
6-27
SCHULZ

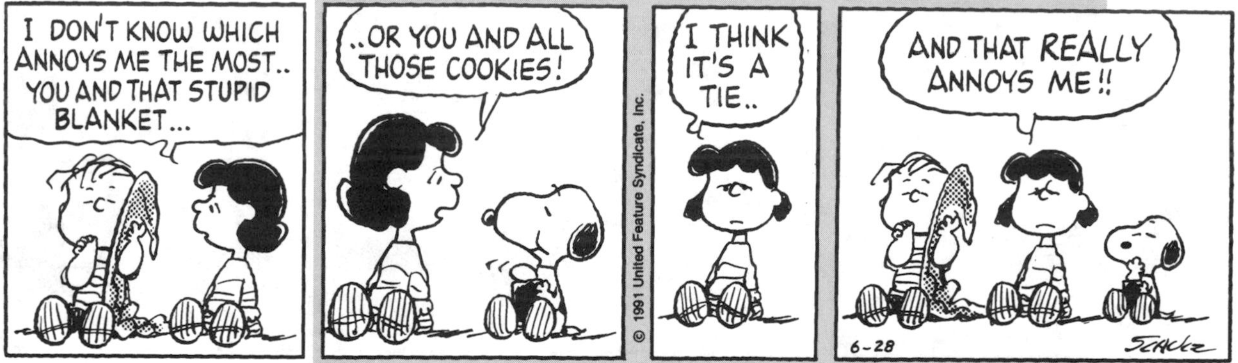
I DON'T KNOW WHICH ANNOYS ME THE MOST.. YOU AND THAT STUPID BLANKET...
..OR YOU AND ALL THOSE COOKIES!
© 1991 United Feature Syndicate, Inc.
I THINK IT'S A TIE..
AND THAT REALLY ANNOYS ME!!
6-28
SCHULZ

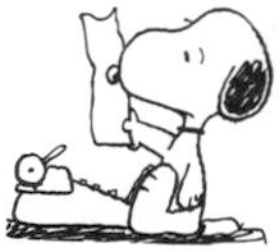

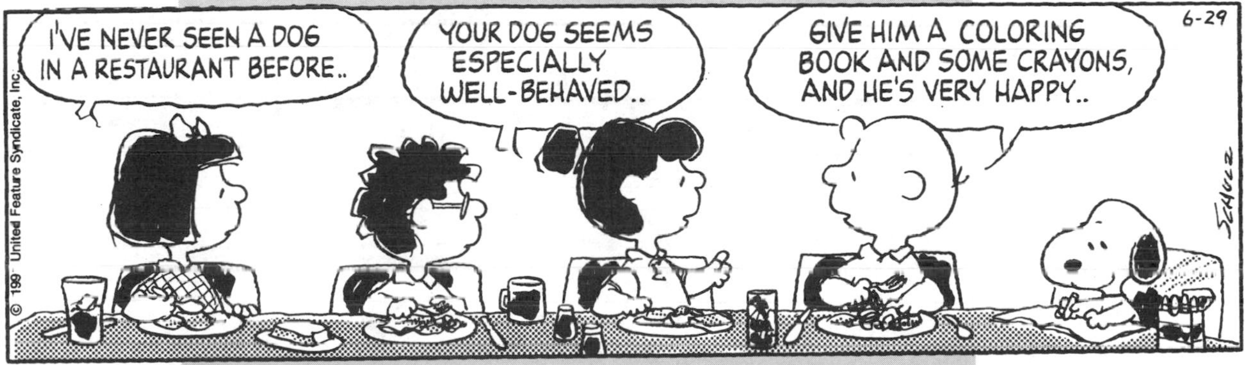
I'VE NEVER SEEN A DOG IN A RESTAURANT BEFORE..
YOUR DOG SEEMS ESPECIALLY WELL-BEHAVED..
GIVE HIM A COLORING BOOK AND SOME CRAYONS, AND HE'S VERY HAPPY..
6-29
SCHULZ
© 1991 United Feature Syndicate, Inc.

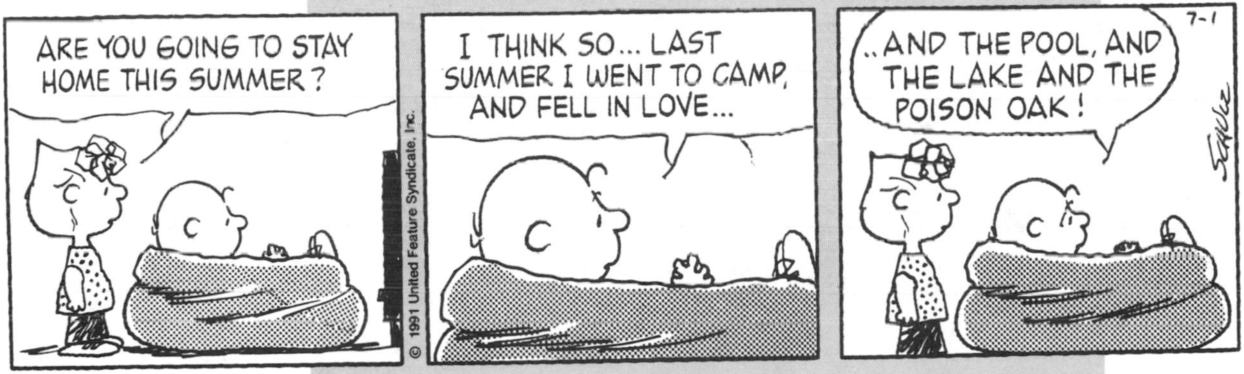
ARE YOU GOING TO STAY HOME THIS SUMMER?
I THINK SO... LAST SUMMER I WENT TO CAMP, AND FELL IN LOVE...
..AND THE POOL, AND THE LAKE AND THE POISON OAK!
7-1
SCHULZ
© 1991 United Feature Syndicate, Inc.

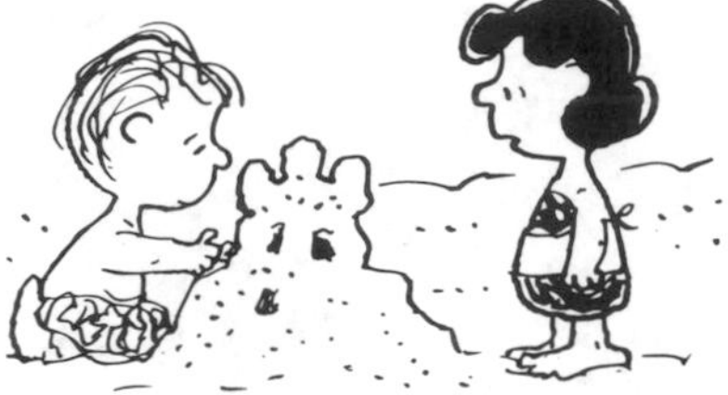

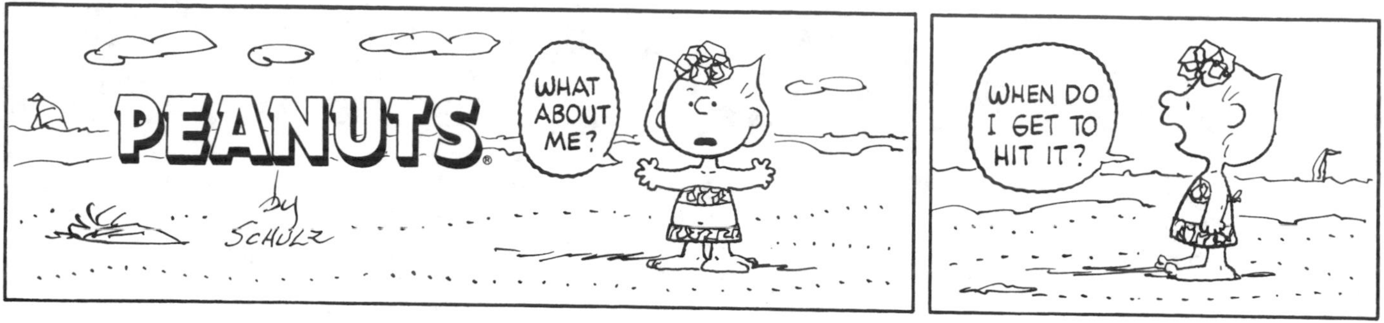

PEANUTS
by SCHULZ
WHAT ABOUT ME?
WHEN DO I GET TO HIT IT?

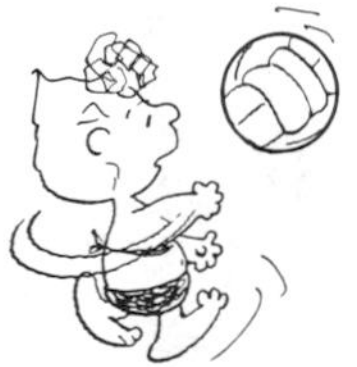

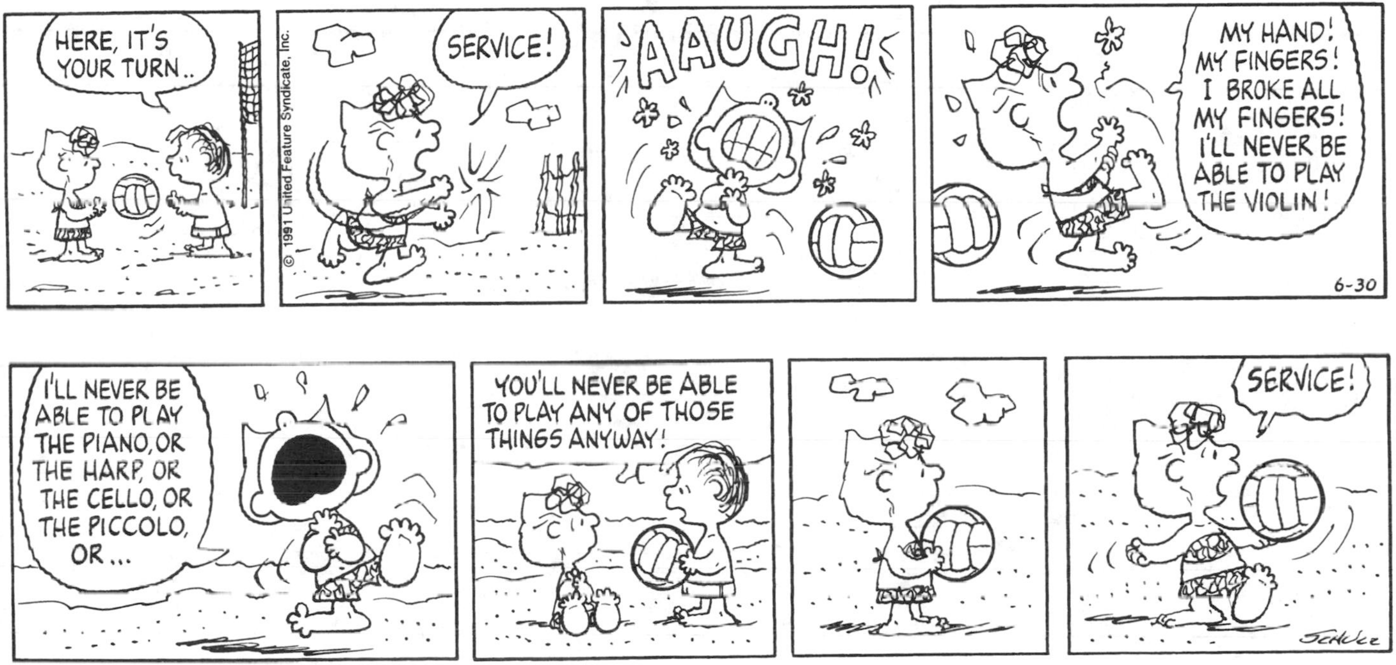
HERE, IT'S YOUR TURN..
© 1991 United Feature Syndicate, Inc.
SERVICE!
AAUGH!
MY HAND! MY FINGERS! I BROKE ALL MY FINGERS! I'LL NEVER BE ABLE TO PLAY THE VIOLIN!
6-30
I'LL NEVER BE ABLE TO PLAY THE PIANO, OR THE HARP, OR THE CELLO, OR THE PICCOLO, OR...
YOU'LL NEVER BE ABLE TO PLAY ANY OF THOSE THINGS ANYWAY!
SERVICE!
SCHULZ

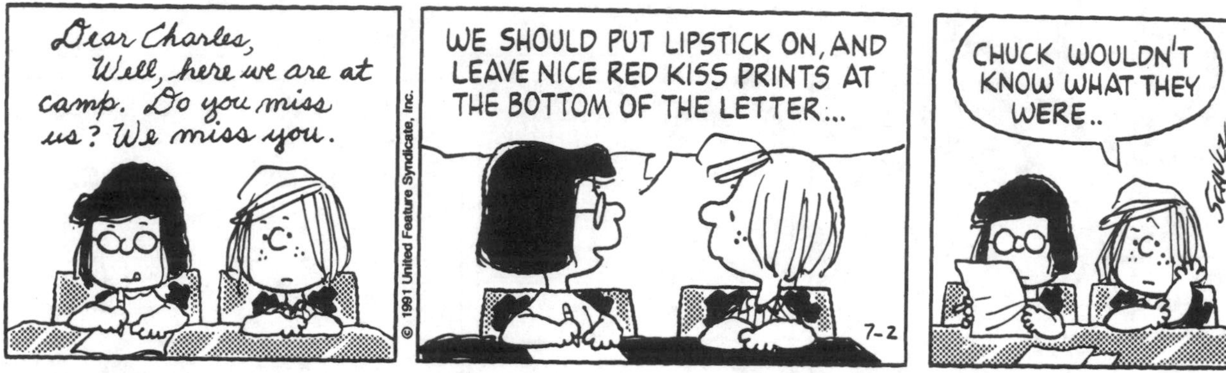
Dear Charles,
Well, here we are at camp. Do you miss us? We miss you.
© 1991 United Feature Syndicate, Inc.
WE SHOULD PUT LIPSTICK ON, AND LEAVE NICE RED KISS PRINTS AT THE BOTTOM OF THE LETTER...
7-2
CHUCK WOULDN'T KNOW WHAT THEY WERE..
SCHULZ

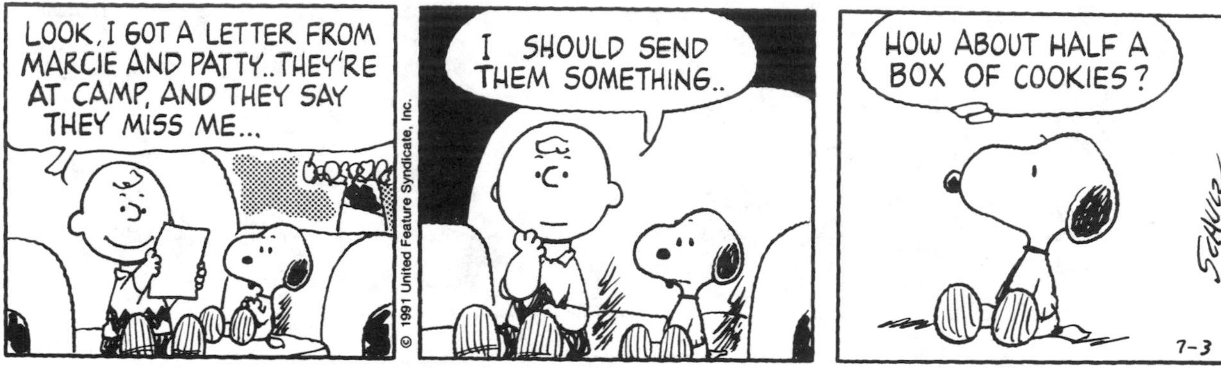
LOOK, I GOT A LETTER FROM MARCIE AND PATTY..THEY'RE AT CAMP, AND THEY SAY THEY MISS ME...
© 1991 United Feature Syndicate, Inc.
I SHOULD SEND THEM SOMETHING..
HOW ABOUT HALF A BOX OF COOKIES?
SCHULZ
7-3

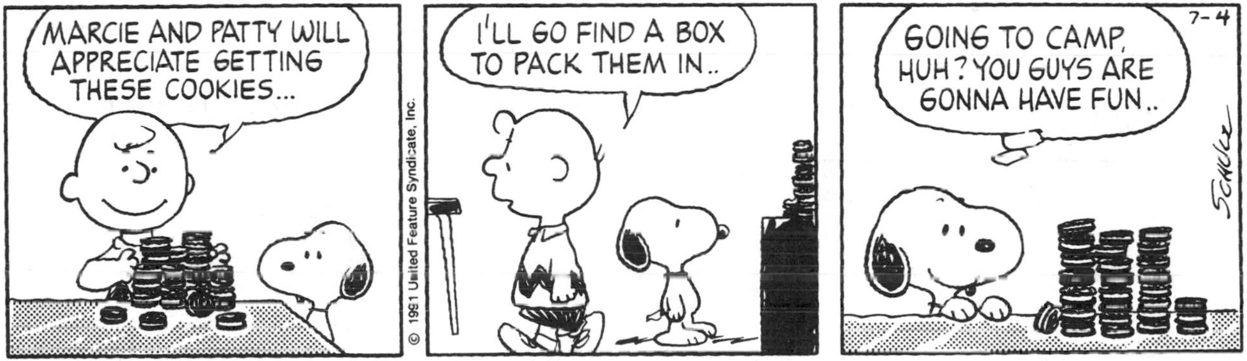
MARCIE AND PATTY WILL APPRECIATE GETTING THESE COOKIES...
© 1991 United Feature Syndicate, Inc.
I'LL GO FIND A BOX TO PACK THEM IN..
7-4
GOING TO CAMP, HUH? YOU GUYS ARE GONNA HAVE FUN..
SCHULZ

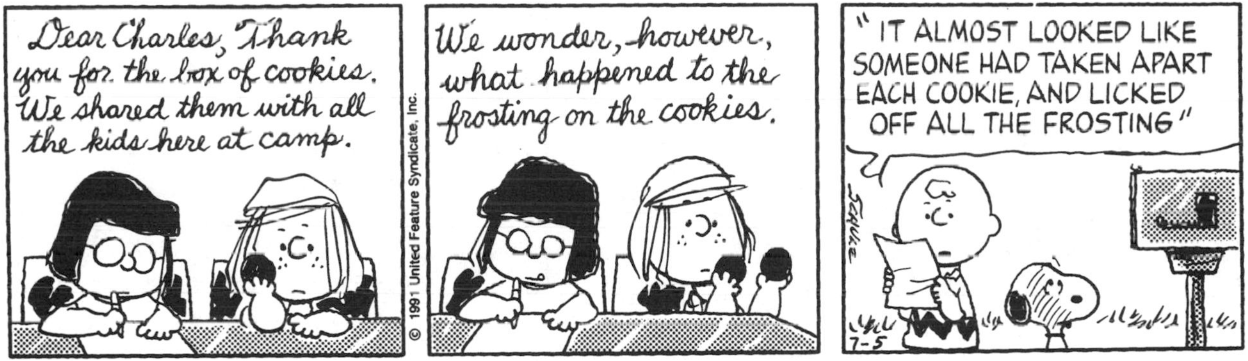
Dear Charles, Thank you for the box of cookies. We shared them with all the kids here at camp.
© 1991 United Feature Syndicate, Inc.
We wonder, however, what happened to the frosting on the cookies.
"IT ALMOST LOOKED LIKE SOMEONE HAD TAKEN APART EACH COOKIE, AND LICKED OFF ALL THE FROSTING"
SCHULZ
7-5

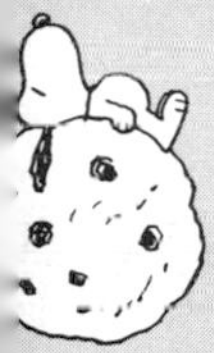

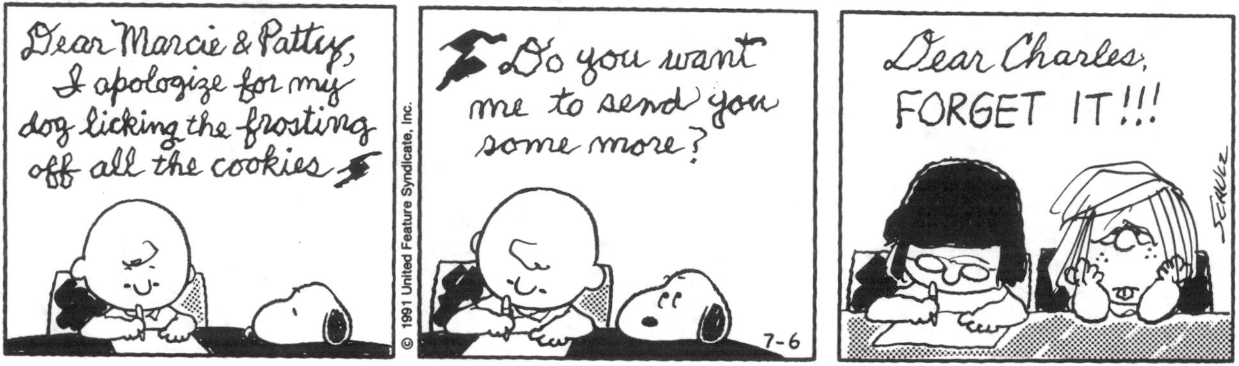
Dear Marcie & Patty,
I apologize for my dog licking the frosting off all the cookies
© 1991 United Feature Syndicate, Inc.
Do you want me to send you some more?
7-6
Dear Charles,
FORGET IT!!!
SCHULZ

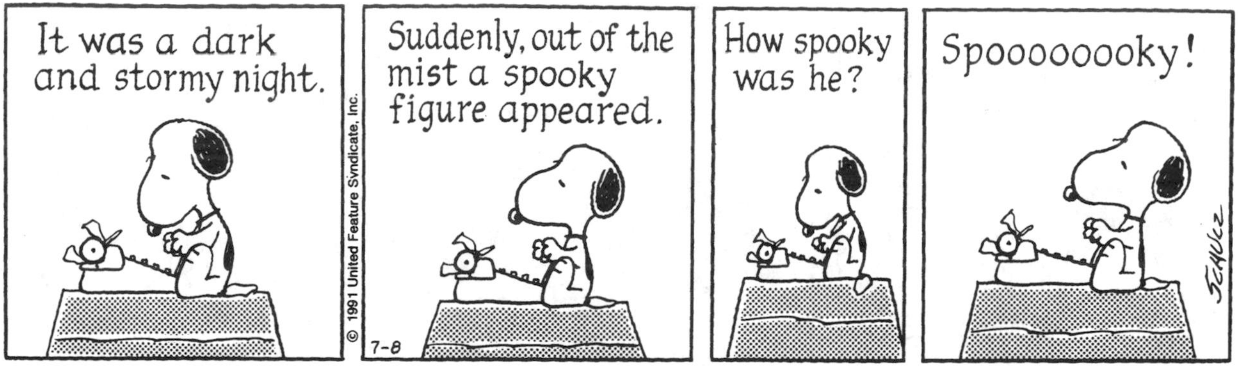
It was a dark and stormy night.
© 1991 United Feature Syndicate, Inc.
Suddenly, out of the mist a spooky figure appeared.
7-8
How spooky was he?
Spooooooooky!
SCHULZ

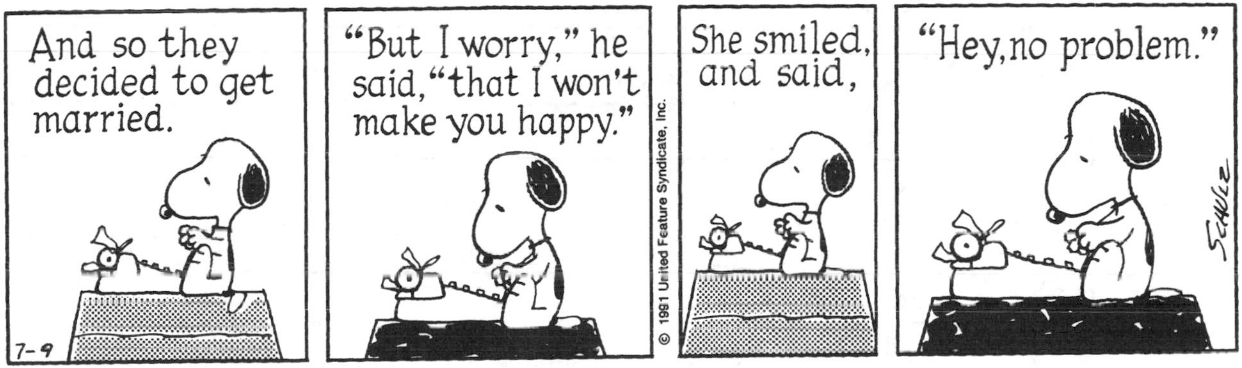
And so they decided to get married.
7-9
"But I worry," he said, "that I won't make you happy."
© 1991 United Feature Syndicate, Inc.
She smiled, and said,
"Hey, no problem."
SCHULZ

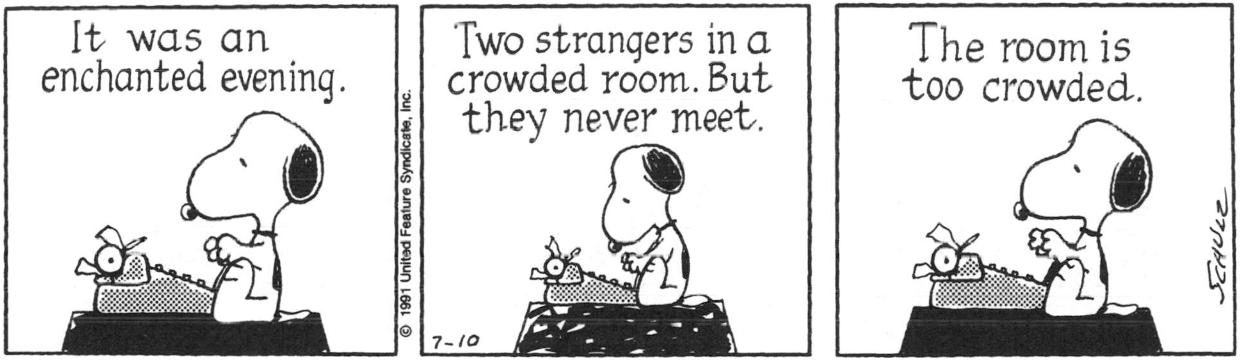
It was an enchanted evening.
© 1991 United Feature Syndicate, Inc.
Two strangers in a crowded room. But they never meet.
7-10
The room is too crowded.
SCHULZ

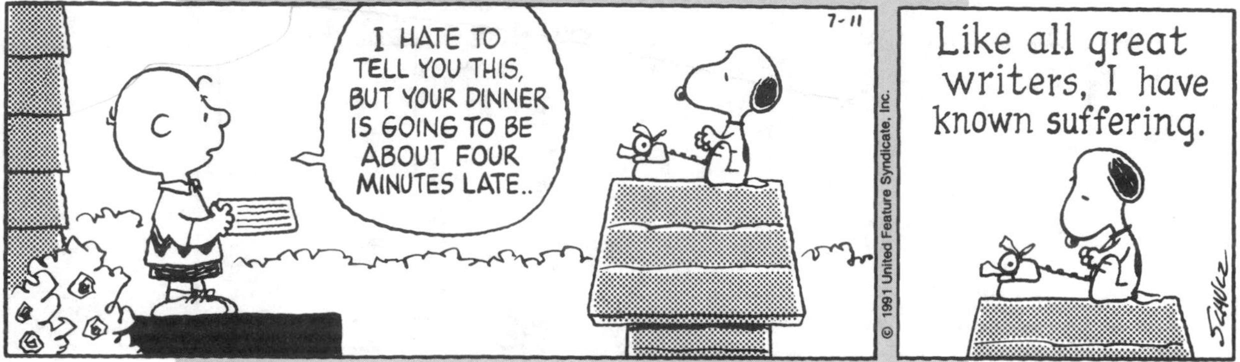
7-11
I HATE TO TELL YOU THIS, BUT YOUR DINNER IS GOING TO BE ABOUT FOUR MINUTES LATE..
© 1991 United Feature Syndicate, Inc.
Like all great writers, I have known suffering.
SCHULZ

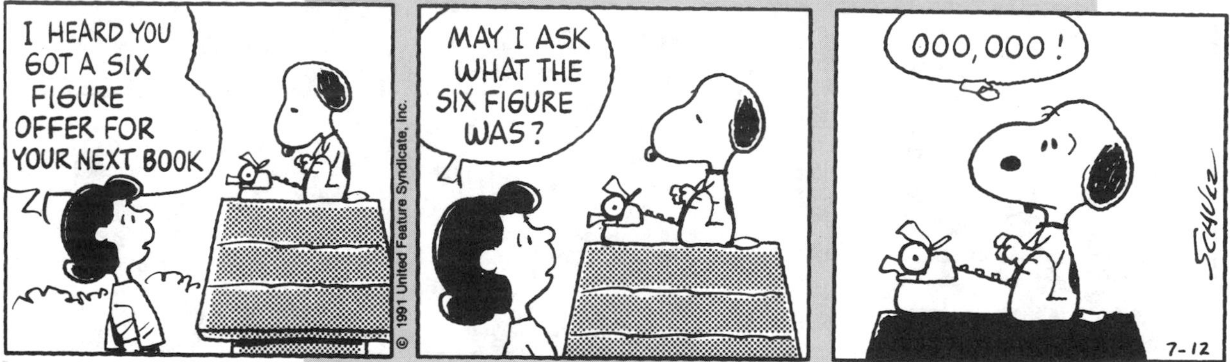
I HEARD YOU GOT A SIX FIGURE OFFER FOR YOUR NEXT BOOK
© 1991 United Feature Syndicate, Inc.
MAY I ASK WHAT THE SIX FIGURE WAS?
000,000!
SCHULZ
7-12

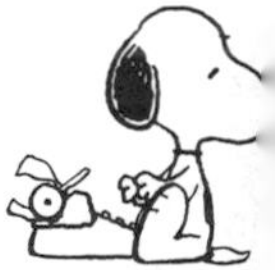

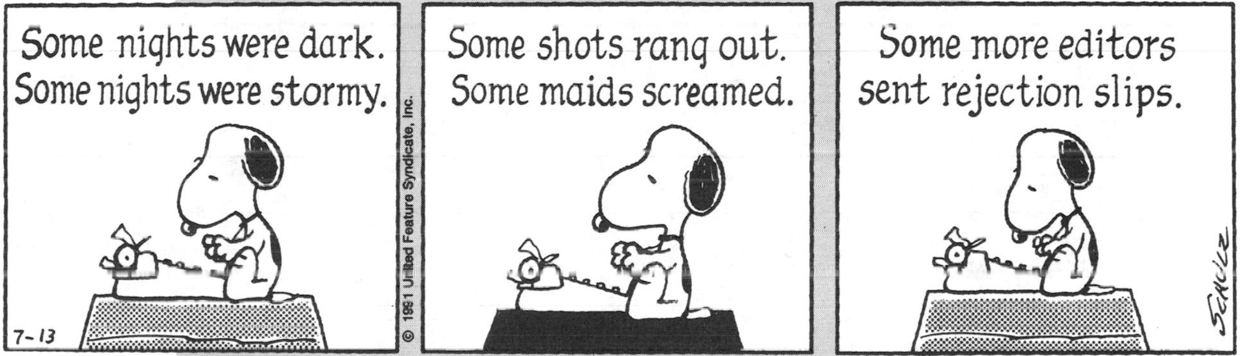
Some nights were dark.
Some nights were stormy.
7-13
© 1991 United Feature Syndicate, Inc.
Some shots rang out.
Some maids screamed.
Some more editors
sent rejection slips.
SCHULZ

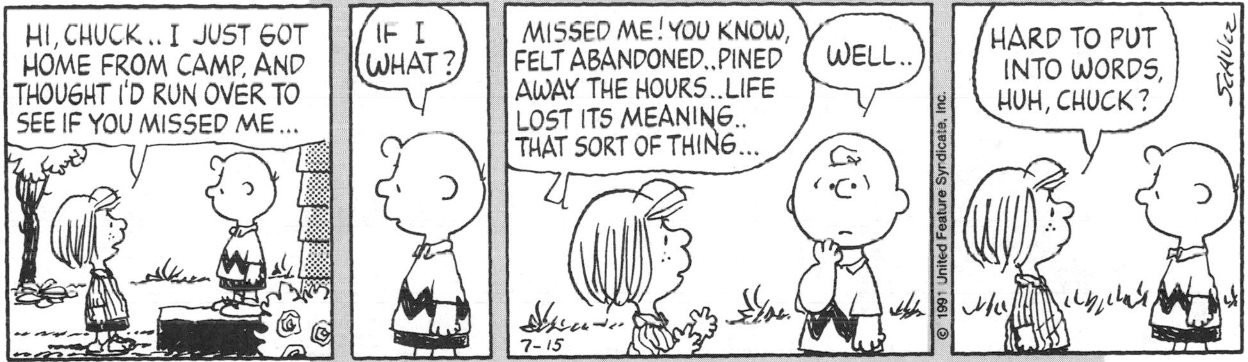
HI, CHUCK.. I JUST GOT HOME FROM CAMP, AND THOUGHT I'D RUN OVER TO SEE IF YOU MISSED ME...
IF I WHAT?
MISSED ME! YOU KNOW, FELT ABANDONED..PINED AWAY THE HOURS..LIFE LOST ITS MEANING.. THAT SORT OF THING...
WELL..
7-15
© 1991 United Feature Syndicate, Inc.
HARD TO PUT INTO WORDS, HUH, CHUCK?
SCHULZ

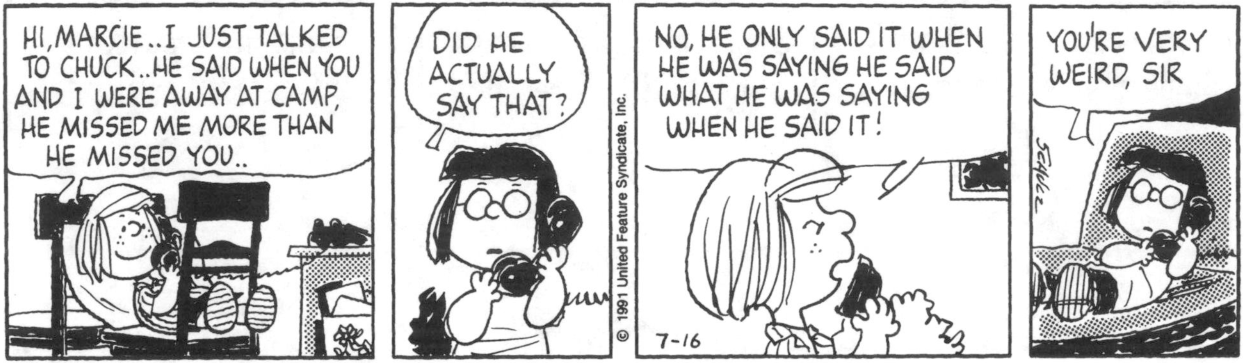
HI, MARCIE..I JUST TALKED TO CHUCK..HE SAID WHEN YOU AND I WERE AWAY AT CAMP, HE MISSED ME MORE THAN HE MISSED YOU..
DID HE ACTUALLY SAY THAT?
© 1991 United Feature Syndicate, Inc.
NO, HE ONLY SAID IT WHEN HE WAS SAYING HE SAID WHAT HE WAS SAYING WHEN HE SAID IT!
7-16
YOU'RE VERY WEIRD, SIR
SCHULZ

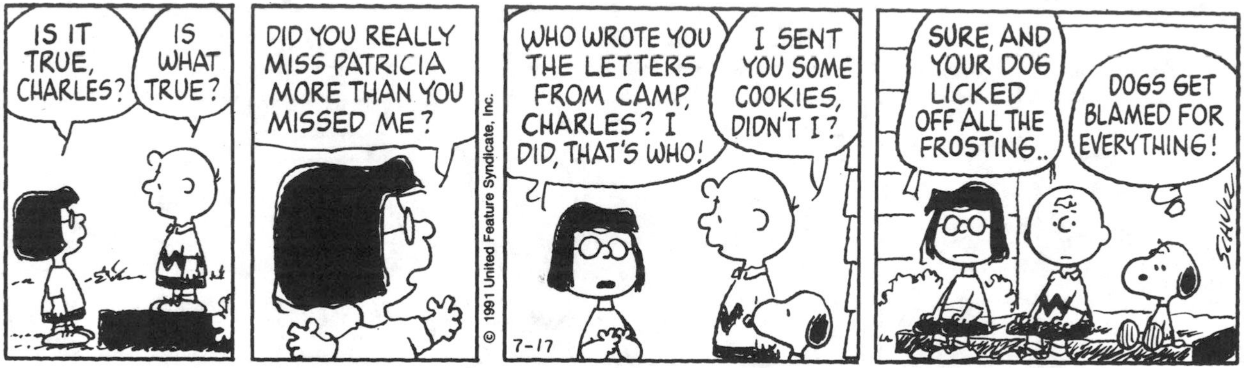
IS IT TRUE, CHARLES?
IS WHAT TRUE?
DID YOU REALLY MISS PATRICIA MORE THAN YOU MISSED ME?
© 1991 United Feature Syndicate, Inc.
WHO WROTE YOU THE LETTERS FROM CAMP, CHARLES? I DID, THAT'S WHO!
I SENT YOU SOME COOKIES, DIDN'T I?
7-17
SURE, AND YOUR DOG LICKED OFF ALL THE FROSTING..
DOGS GET BLAMED FOR EVERYTHING!
SCHULZ

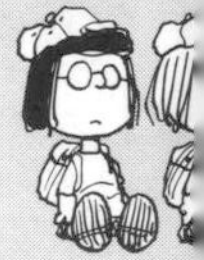

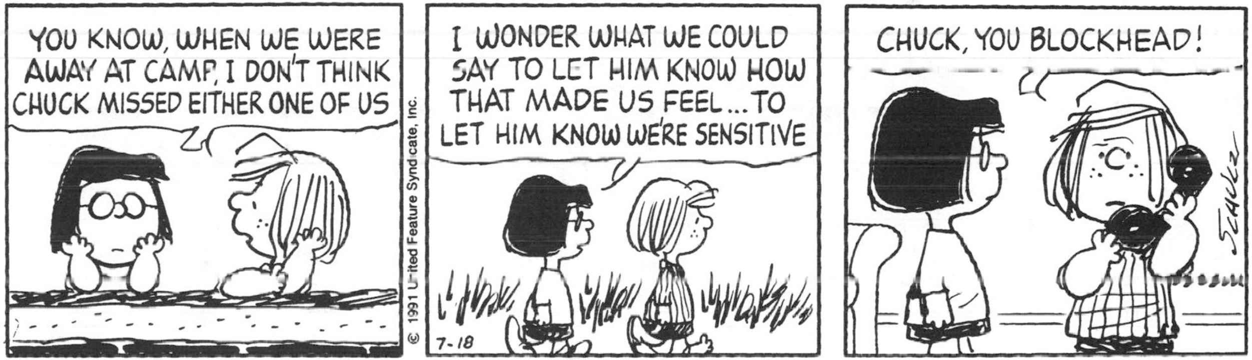
YOU KNOW, WHEN WE WERE AWAY AT CAMP, I DON'T THINK CHUCK MISSED EITHER ONE OF US
© 1991 United Feature Syndicate, Inc.
I WONDER WHAT WE COULD SAY TO LET HIM KNOW HOW THAT MADE US FEEL... TO LET HIM KNOW WE'RE SENSITIVE
7-18
CHUCK, YOU BLOCKHEAD!
SCHULZ

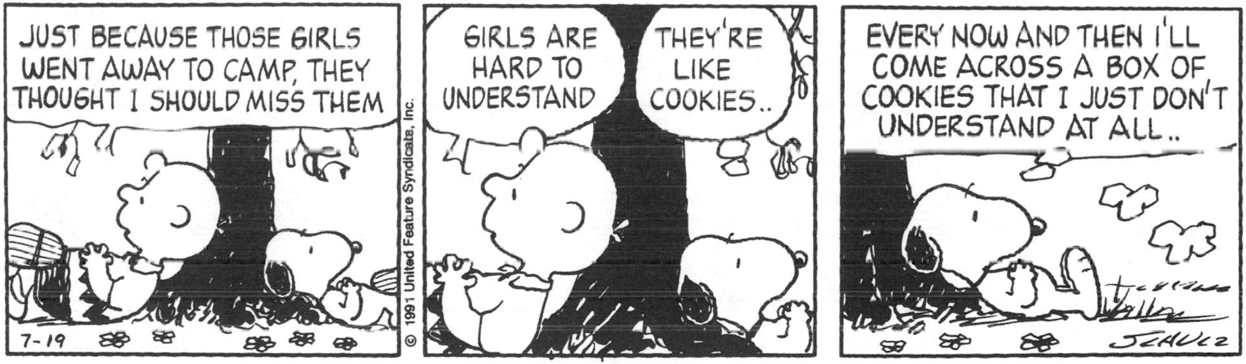
JUST BECAUSE THOSE GIRLS WENT AWAY TO CAMP, THEY THOUGHT I SHOULD MISS THEM
7-19
© 1991 United Feature Syndicate, Inc.
GIRLS ARE HARD TO UNDERSTAND
THEY'RE LIKE COOKIES..
EVERY NOW AND THEN I'LL COME ACROSS A BOX OF COOKIES THAT I JUST DON'T UNDERSTAND AT ALL..
SCHULZ

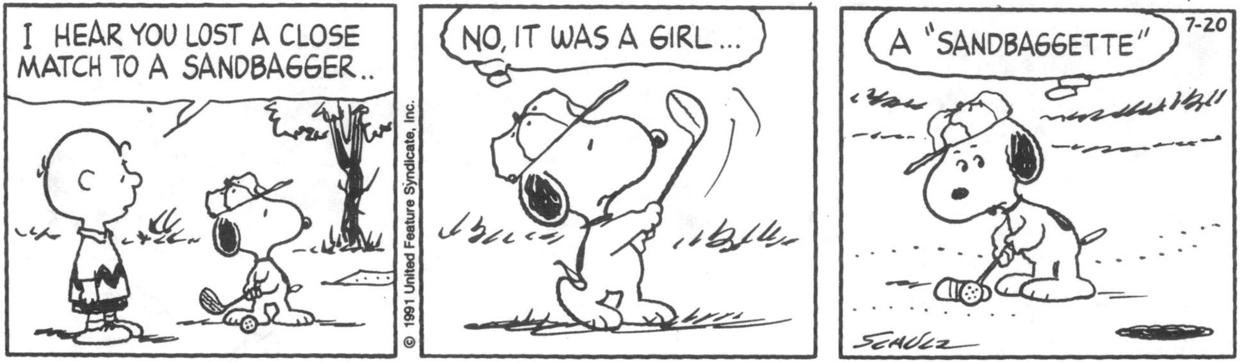
I HEAR YOU LOST A CLOSE MATCH TO A SANDBAGGER..
© 1991 United Feature Syndicate, Inc.
NO, IT WAS A GIRL...
7-20
A "SANDBAGGETTE"
SCHULZ

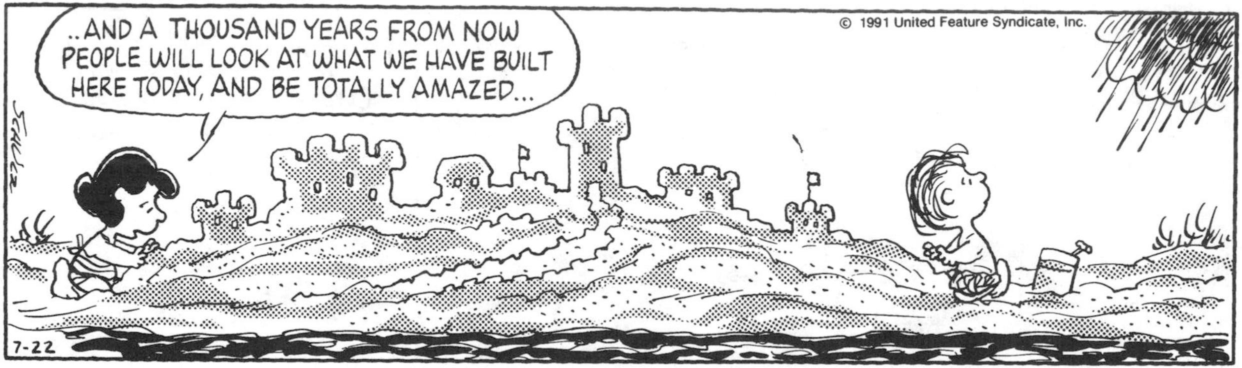
..AND A THOUSAND YEARS FROM NOW PEOPLE WILL LOOK AT WHAT WE HAVE BUILT HERE TODAY, AND BE TOTALLY AMAZED...
© 1991 United Feature Syndicate, Inc.
SCHULZ
7-22

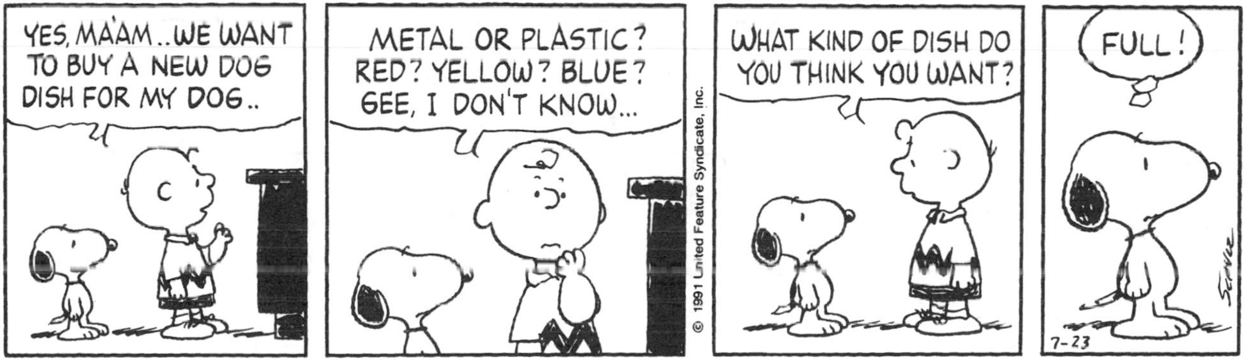
YES, MA'AM..WE WANT TO BUY A NEW DOG DISH FOR MY DOG..
METAL OR PLASTIC? RED? YELLOW? BLUE? GEE, I DON'T KNOW...
© 1991 United Feature Syndicate, Inc.
WHAT KIND OF DISH DO YOU THINK YOU WANT?
FULL!
7-23
SCHULZ

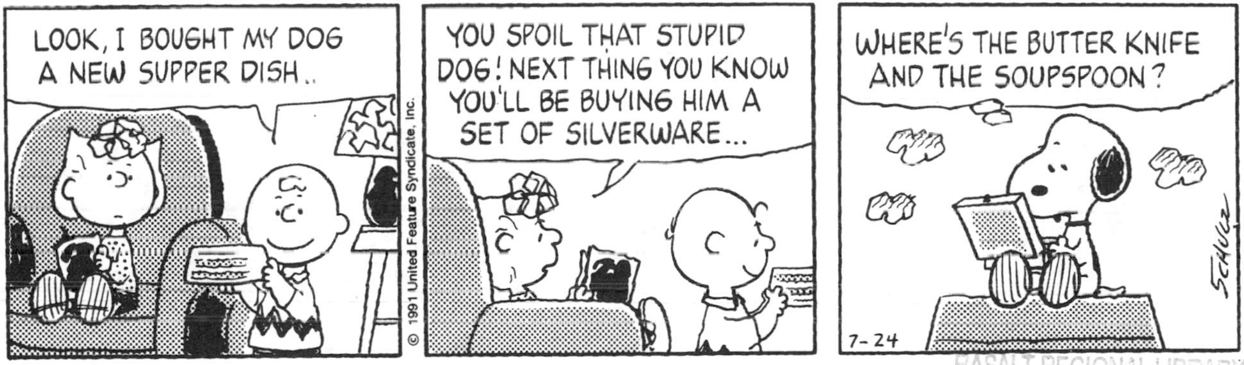
LOOK, I BOUGHT MY DOG A NEW SUPPER DISH..
© 1991 United Feature Syndicate, Inc.
YOU SPOIL THAT STUPID DOG! NEXT THING YOU KNOW YOU'LL BE BUYING HIM A SET OF SILVERWARE...
WHERE'S THE BUTTER KNIFE AND THE SOUPSPOON?
7-24
SCHULZ

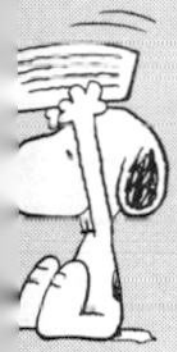

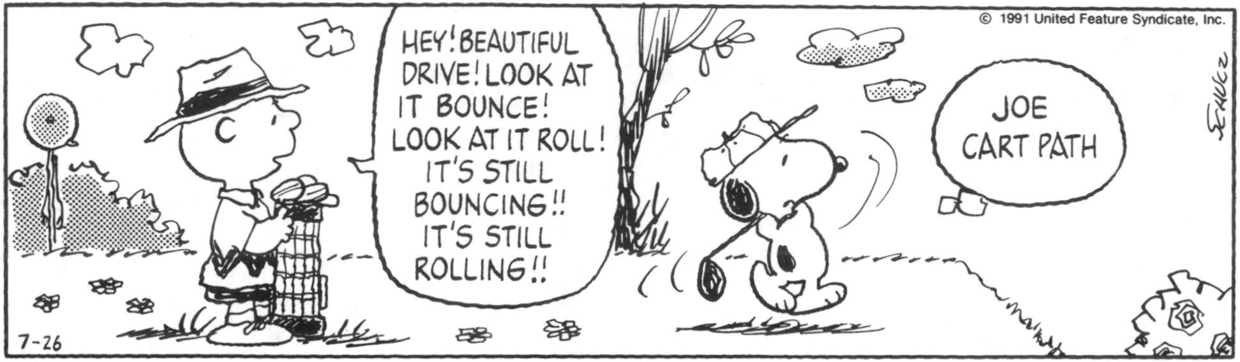
© 1991 United Feature Syndicate, Inc.
HEY! BEAUTIFUL DRIVE! LOOK AT IT BOUNCE! LOOK AT IT ROLL! IT'S STILL BOUNCING!! IT'S STILL ROLLING!!
JOE CART PATH
SCHULZ
7-26

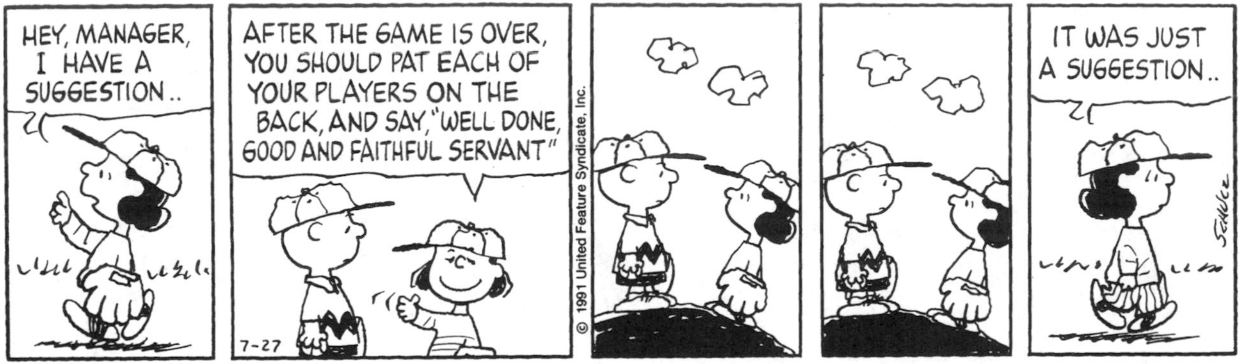
HEY, MANAGER, I HAVE A SUGGESTION..
AFTER THE GAME IS OVER, YOU SHOULD PAT EACH OF YOUR PLAYERS ON THE BACK, AND SAY, "WELL DONE, GOOD AND FAITHFUL SERVANT"
7-27
© 1991 United Feature Syndicate, Inc.
IT WAS JUST A SUGGESTION..
SCHULZ

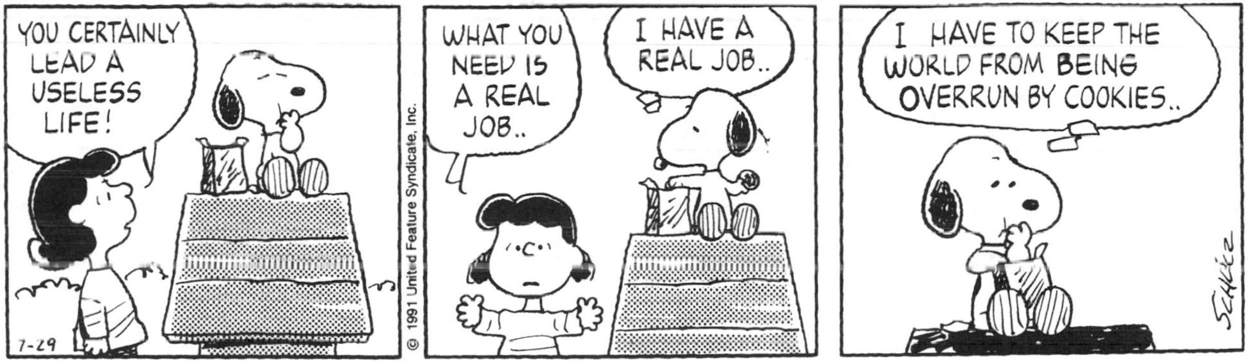
YOU CERTAINLY LEAD A USELESS LIFE!
7-29
© 1991 United Feature Syndicate, Inc.
WHAT YOU NEED IS A REAL JOB..
I HAVE A REAL JOB..
I HAVE TO KEEP THE WORLD FROM BEING OVERRUN BY COOKIES..
SCHULZ

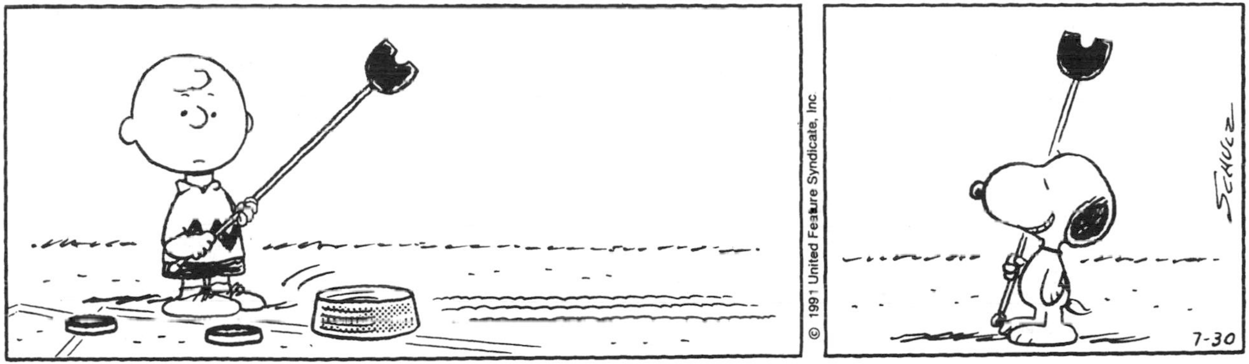
© 1991 United Feature Syndicate, Inc.
SCHULZ
7-30

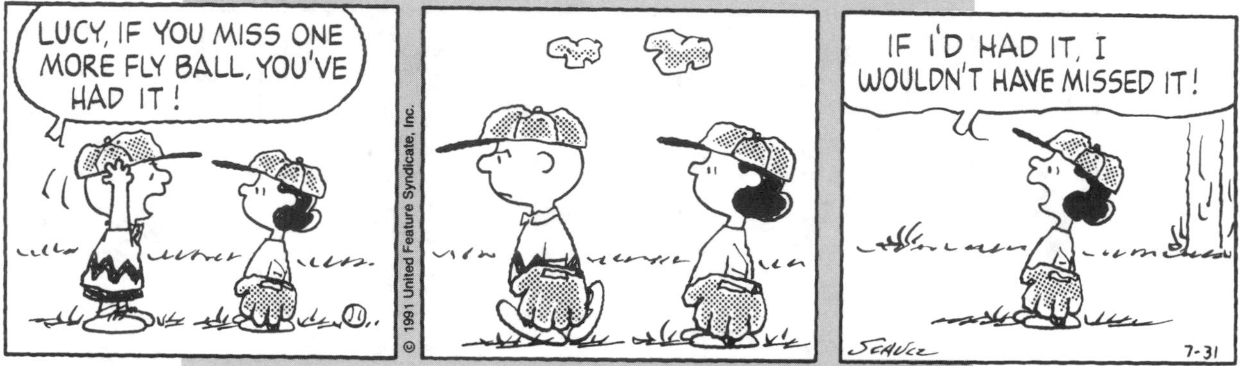
LUCY, IF YOU MISS ONE MORE FLY BALL, YOU'VE HAD IT!
IF I'D HAD IT, I WOULDN'T HAVE MISSED IT!
SCHULZ
7-31
© 1991 United Feature Syndicate, Inc.

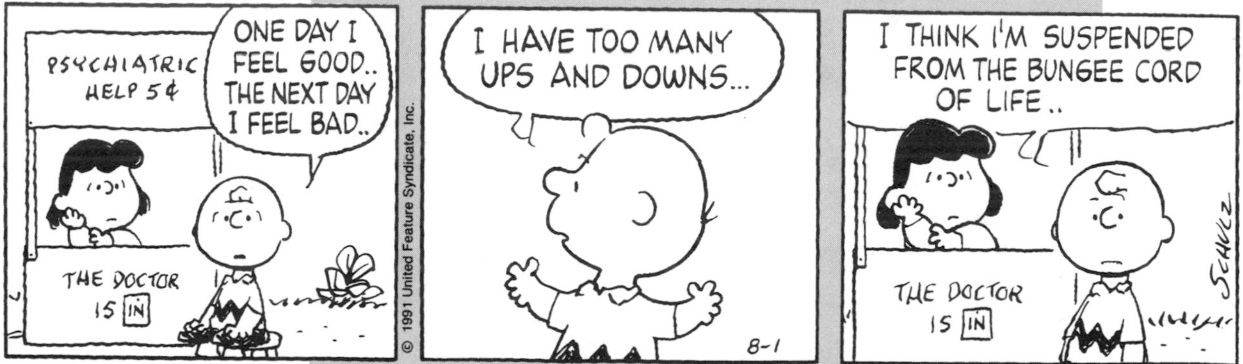
PSYCHIATRIC HELP 5¢
THE DOCTOR IS IN
ONE DAY I FEEL GOOD.. THE NEXT DAY I FEEL BAD..
I HAVE TOO MANY UPS AND DOWNS...
8-1
I THINK I'M SUSPENDED FROM THE BUNGEE CORD OF LIFE..
THE DOCTOR IS IN
SCHULZ
© 1991 United Feature Syndicate, Inc.

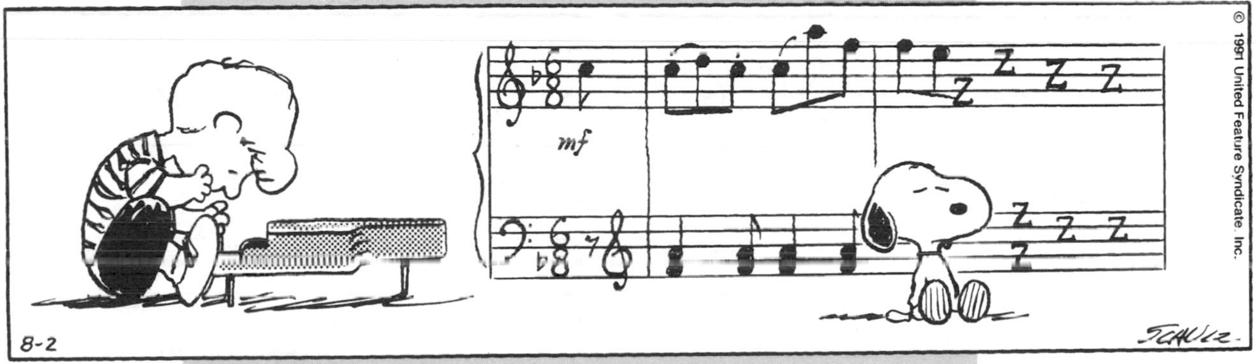
mf
Z Z Z
Z Z Z
Z Z Z
8-2
SCHULZ
© 1991 United Feature Syndicate, Inc.

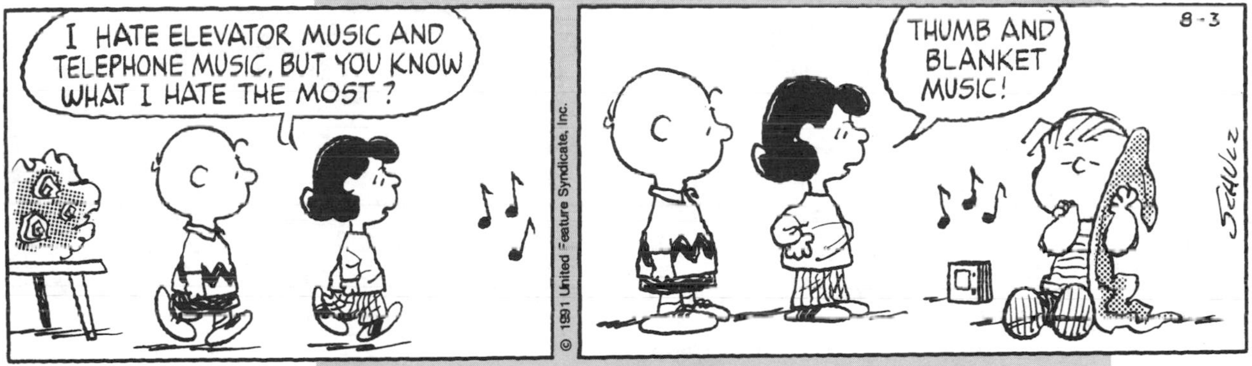
I HATE ELEVATOR MUSIC AND TELEPHONE MUSIC, BUT YOU KNOW WHAT I HATE THE MOST ?
© 1991 United Feature Syndicate, Inc.
8-3
THUMB AND BLANKET MUSIC!
SCHULZ

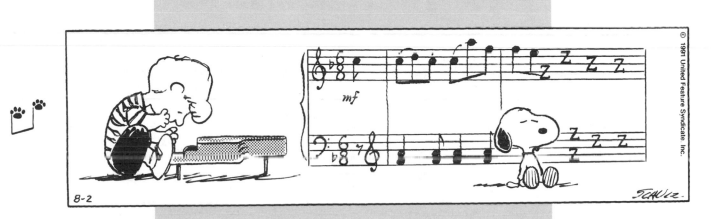

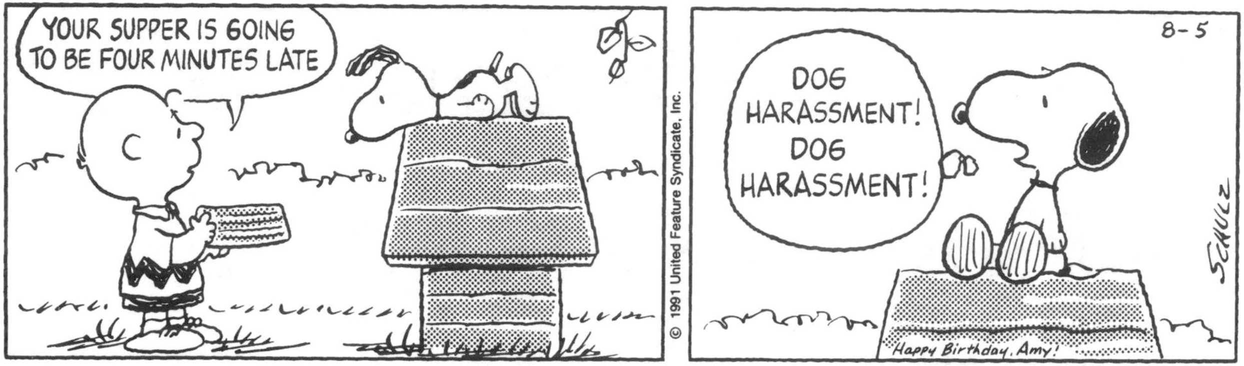
YOUR SUPPER IS GOING TO BE FOUR MINUTES LATE
© 1991 United Feature Syndicate, Inc.
8-5
DOG HARASSMENT! DOG HARASSMENT!
SCHULZ
Happy Birthday, Amy!

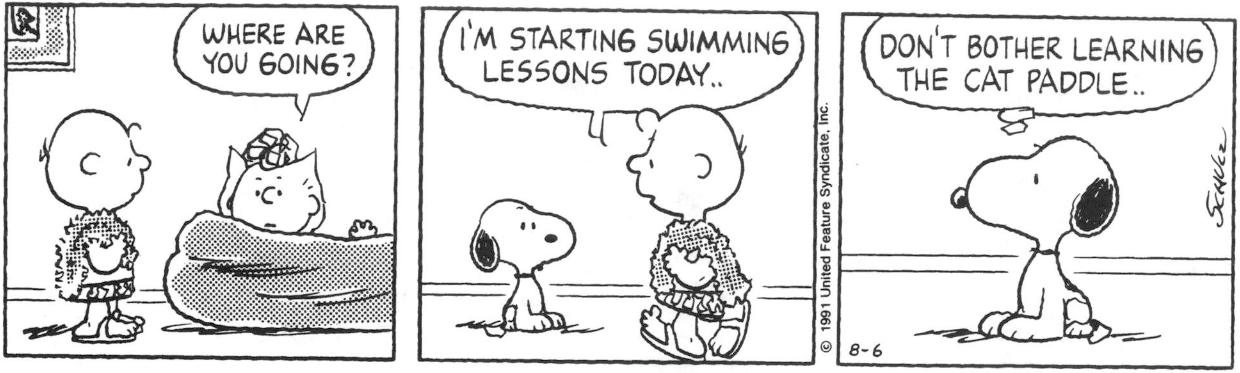
WHERE ARE YOU GOING?
I'M STARTING SWIMMING LESSONS TODAY..
© 1991 United Feature Syndicate, Inc.
DON'T BOTHER LEARNING THE CAT PADDLE..
SCHULZ
8-6

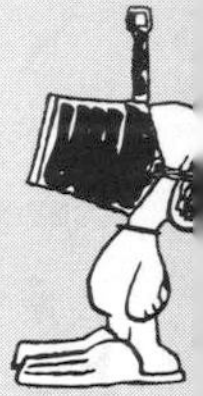

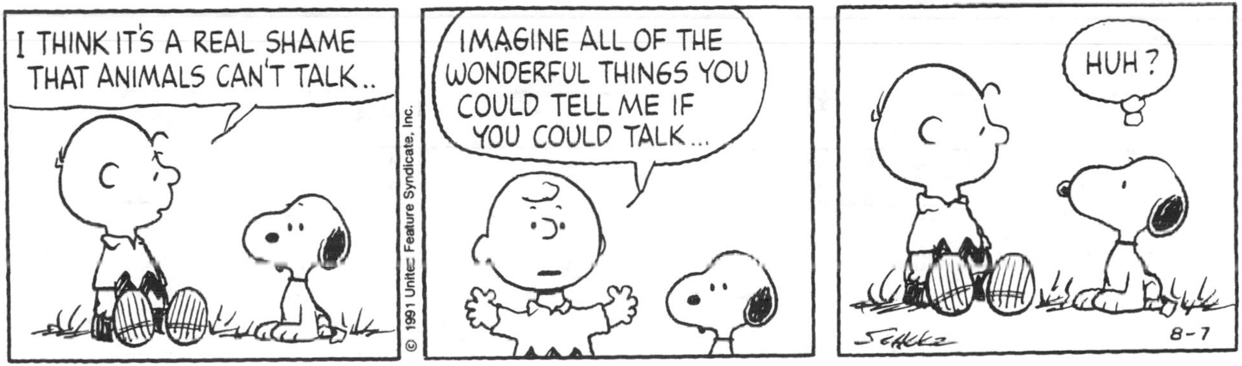
I THINK IT'S A REAL SHAME THAT ANIMALS CAN'T TALK..
IMAGINE ALL OF THE WONDERFUL THINGS YOU COULD TELL ME IF YOU COULD TALK...
HUH?
© 1991 United Feature Syndicate, Inc.
SCHULZ
8-7

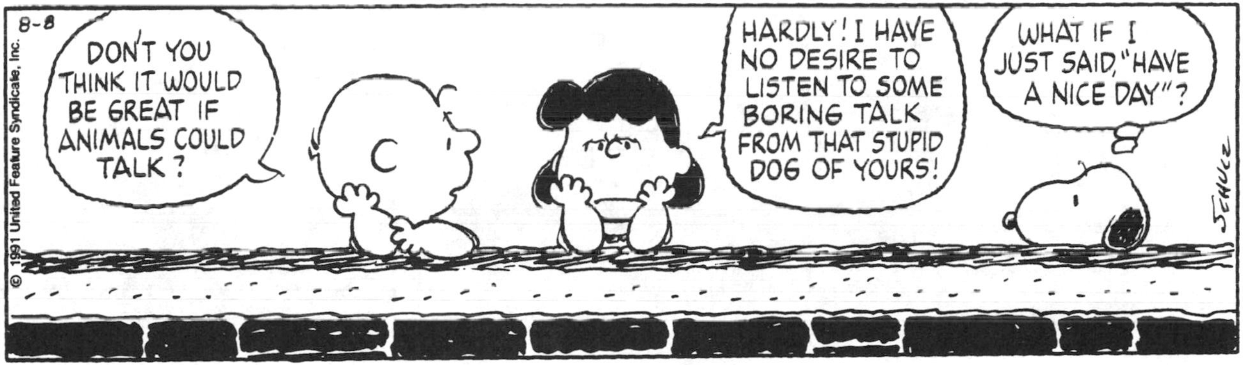
8-8
DON'T YOU THINK IT WOULD BE GREAT IF ANIMALS COULD TALK?
HARDLY! I HAVE NO DESIRE TO LISTEN TO SOME BORING TALK FROM THAT STUPID DOG OF YOURS!
WHAT IF I JUST SAID, "HAVE A NICE DAY"?
© 1991 United Feature Syndicate, Inc.
SCHULZ

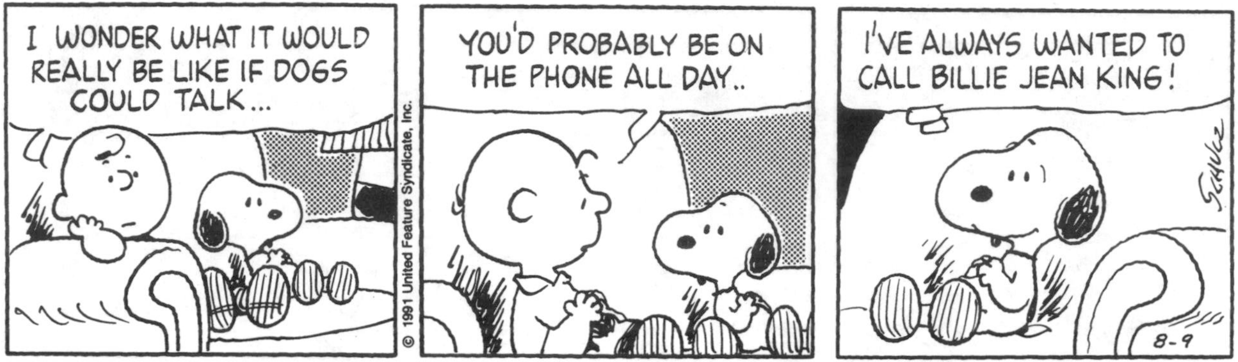
I WONDER WHAT IT WOULD REALLY BE LIKE IF DOGS COULD TALK...
© 1991 United Feature Syndicate, Inc.
YOU'D PROBABLY BE ON THE PHONE ALL DAY..
I'VE ALWAYS WANTED TO CALL BILLIE JEAN KING!
SCHULZ
8-9

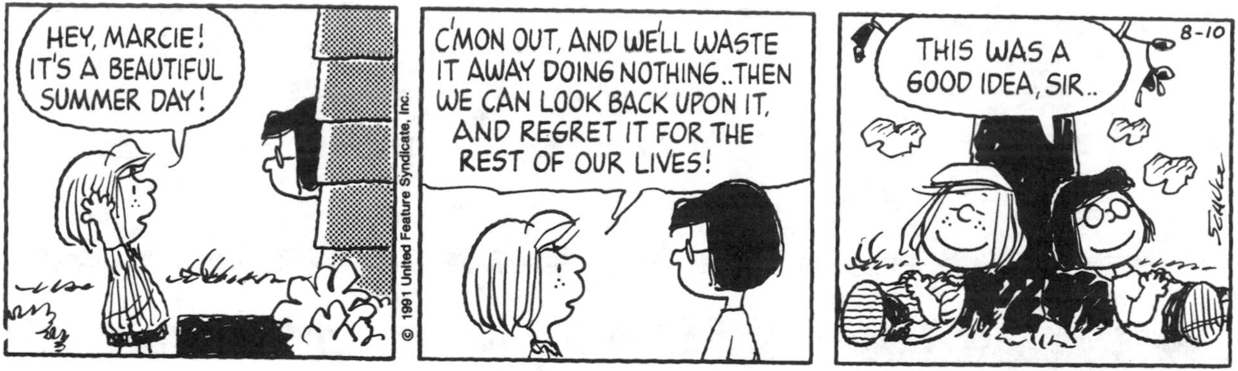
HEY, MARCIE! IT'S A BEAUTIFUL SUMMER DAY!
© 1991 United Feature Syndicate, Inc.
C'MON OUT, AND WE'LL WASTE IT AWAY DOING NOTHING..THEN WE CAN LOOK BACK UPON IT, AND REGRET IT FOR THE REST OF OUR LIVES!
8-10
THIS WAS A GOOD IDEA, SIR..
SCHULZ

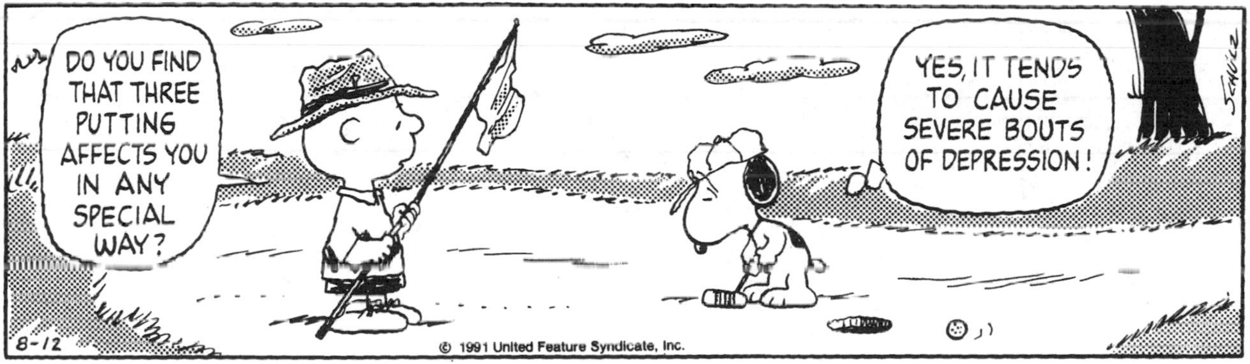
DO YOU FIND THAT THREE PUTTING AFFECTS YOU IN ANY SPECIAL WAY?
YES, IT TENDS TO CAUSE SEVERE BOUTS OF DEPRESSION!
SCHULZ
8-12
© 1991 United Feature Syndicate, Inc.

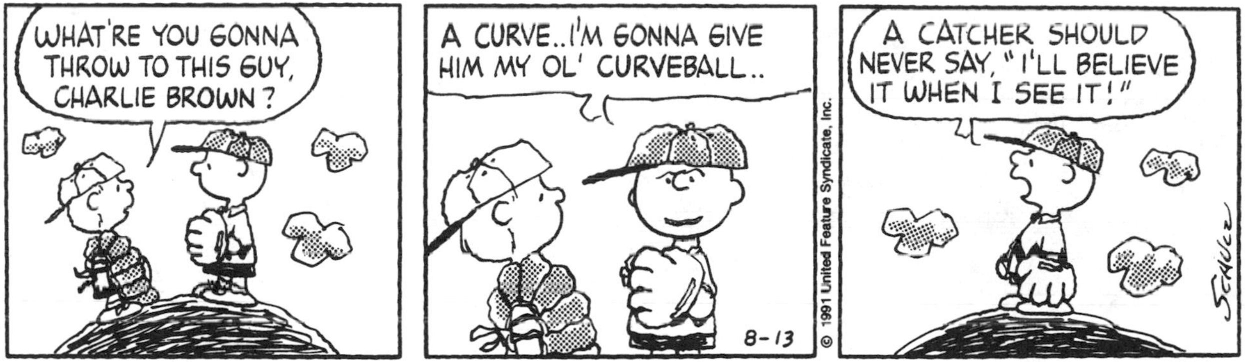
WHAT'RE YOU GONNA THROW TO THIS GUY, CHARLIE BROWN?
A CURVE.. I'M GONNA GIVE HIM MY OL' CURVEBALL..
8-13
© 1991 United Feature Syndicate, Inc.
A CATCHER SHOULD NEVER SAY, "I'LL BELIEVE IT WHEN I SEE IT!"
SCHULZ

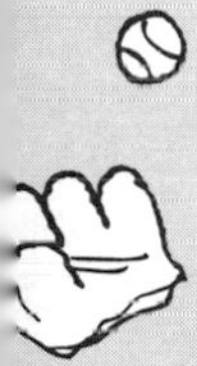

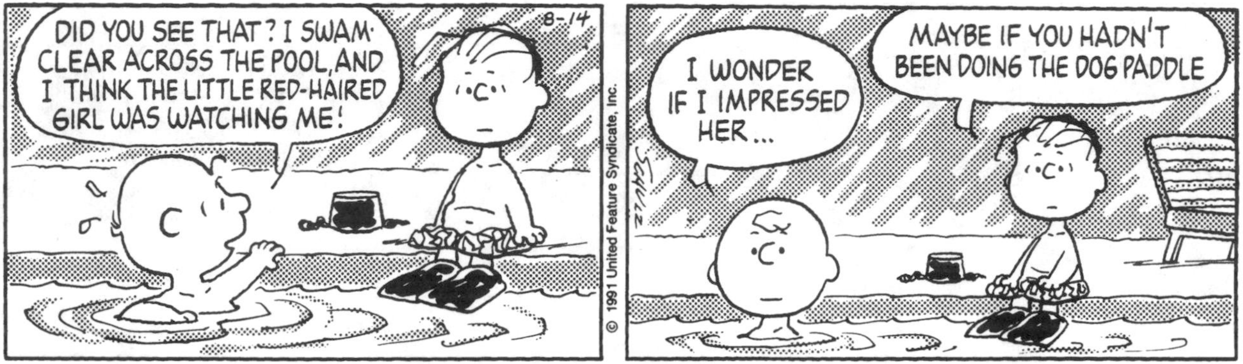
8-14
DID YOU SEE THAT? I SWAM CLEAR ACROSS THE POOL, AND I THINK THE LITTLE RED-HAIRED GIRL WAS WATCHING ME!
© 1991 United Feature Syndicate, Inc.
SCHULZ
I WONDER IF I IMPRESSED HER...
MAYBE IF YOU HADN'T BEEN DOING THE DOG PADDLE

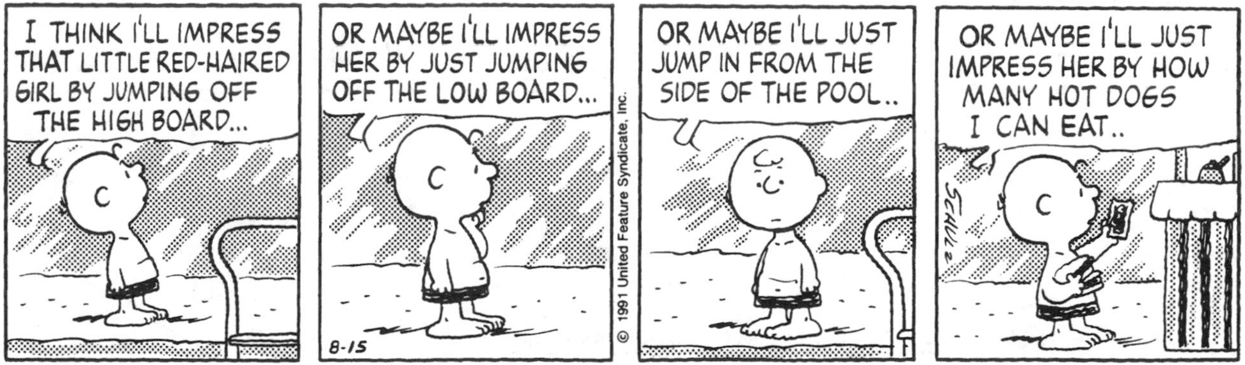
I THINK I'LL IMPRESS THAT LITTLE RED-HAIRED GIRL BY JUMPING OFF THE HIGH BOARD...
OR MAYBE I'LL IMPRESS HER BY JUST JUMPING OFF THE LOW BOARD...
8-15
© 1991 United Feature Syndicate, Inc.
OR MAYBE I'LL JUST JUMP IN FROM THE SIDE OF THE POOL..
OR MAYBE I'LL JUST IMPRESS HER BY HOW MANY HOT DOGS I CAN EAT..
SCHULZ

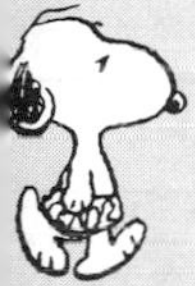

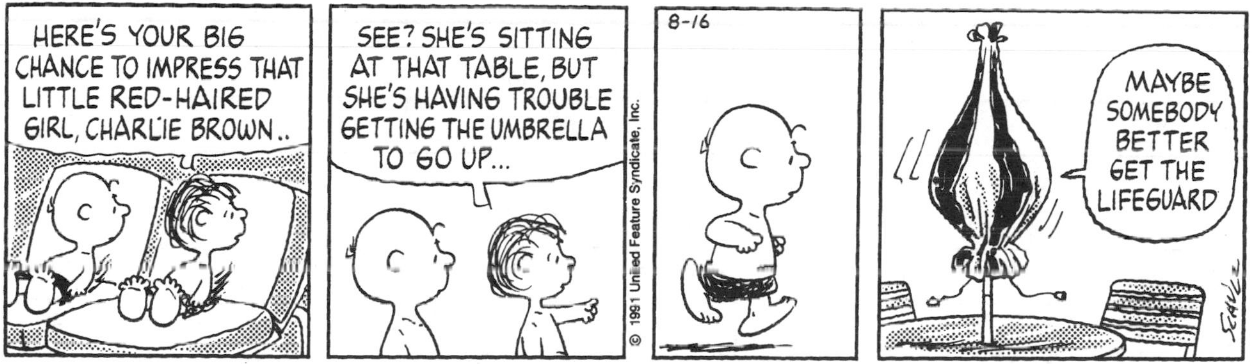
HERE'S YOUR BIG CHANCE TO IMPRESS THAT LITTLE RED-HAIRED GIRL, CHARLIE BROWN..
SEE? SHE'S SITTING AT THAT TABLE, BUT SHE'S HAVING TROUBLE GETTING THE UMBRELLA TO GO UP...
© 1991 United Feature Syndicate, Inc.
8-16
MAYBE SOMEBODY BETTER GET THE LIFEGUARD

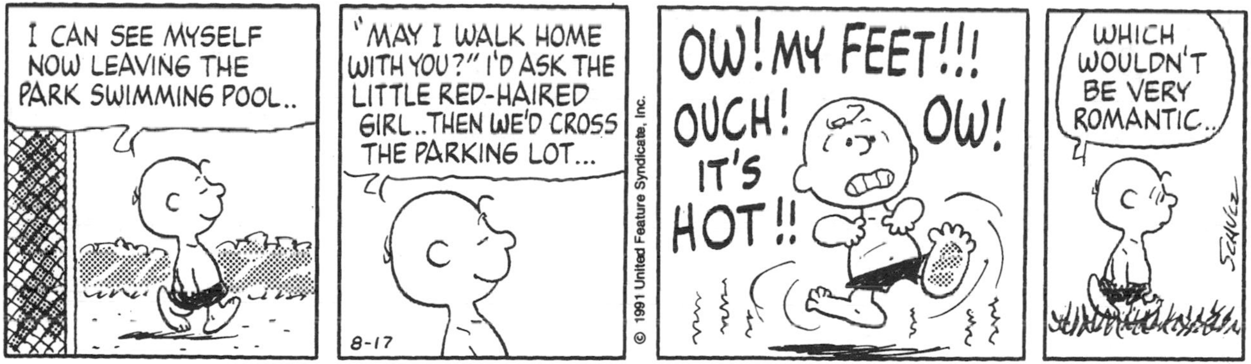
I CAN SEE MYSELF NOW LEAVING THE PARK SWIMMING POOL..
"MAY I WALK HOME WITH YOU?" I'D ASK THE LITTLE RED-HAIRED GIRL..THEN WE'D CROSS THE PARKING LOT...
8-17
© 1991 United Feature Syndicate, Inc.
OW! MY FEET!!!
OUCH!
OW!
IT'S HOT!!
WHICH WOULDN'T BE VERY ROMANTIC..

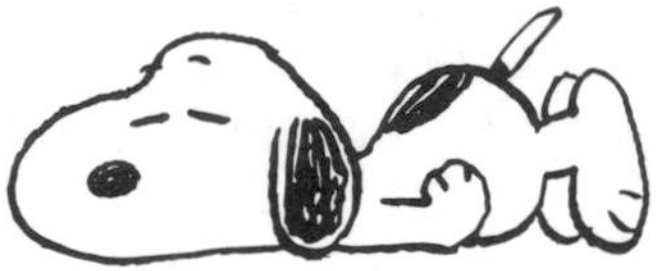

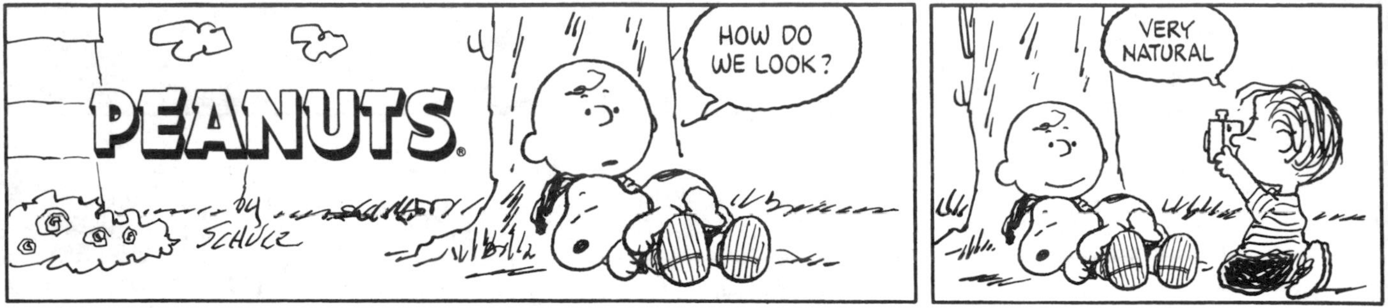
PEANUTS®
by SCHULZ
HOW DO WE LOOK?
VERY NATURAL

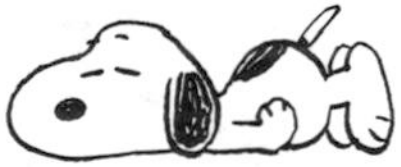

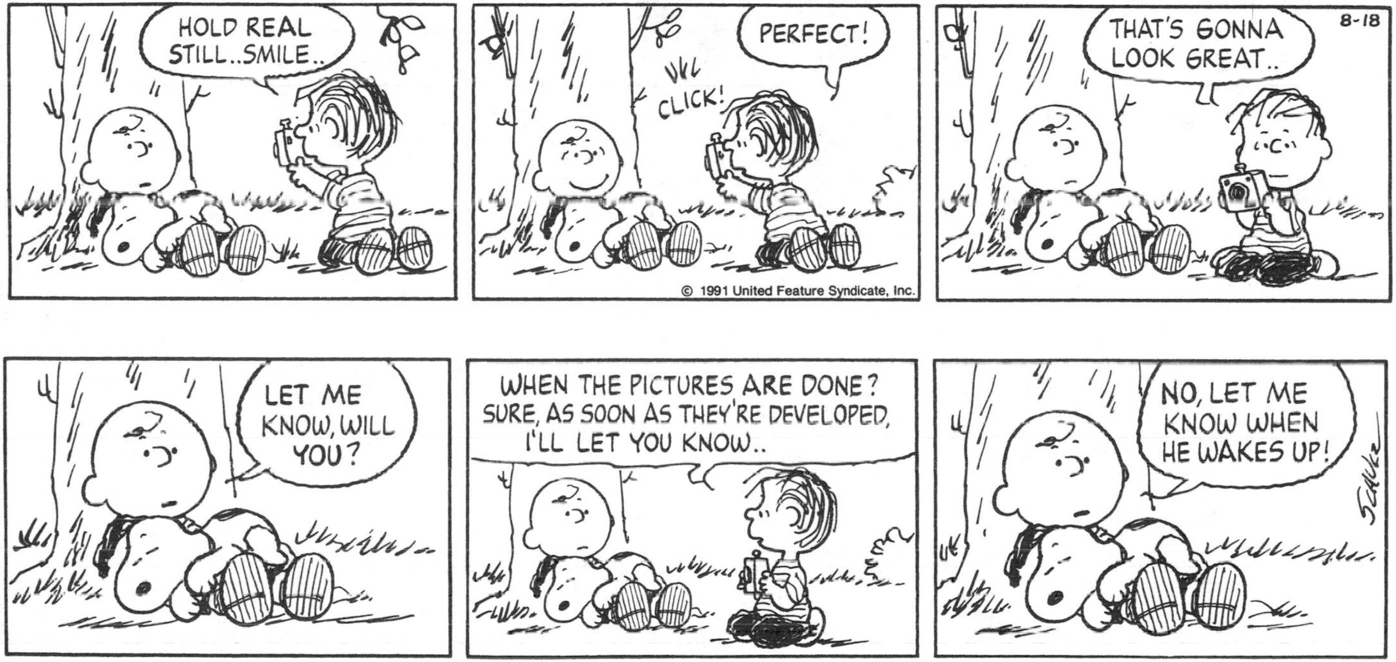
HOLD REAL STILL..SMILE..
CLICK!
PERFECT!
© 1991 United Feature Syndicate, Inc.
8-18
THAT'S GONNA LOOK GREAT..
LET ME KNOW, WILL YOU?
WHEN THE PICTURES ARE DONE? SURE, AS SOON AS THEY'RE DEVELOPED, I'LL LET YOU KNOW..
NO, LET ME KNOW WHEN HE WAKES UP!

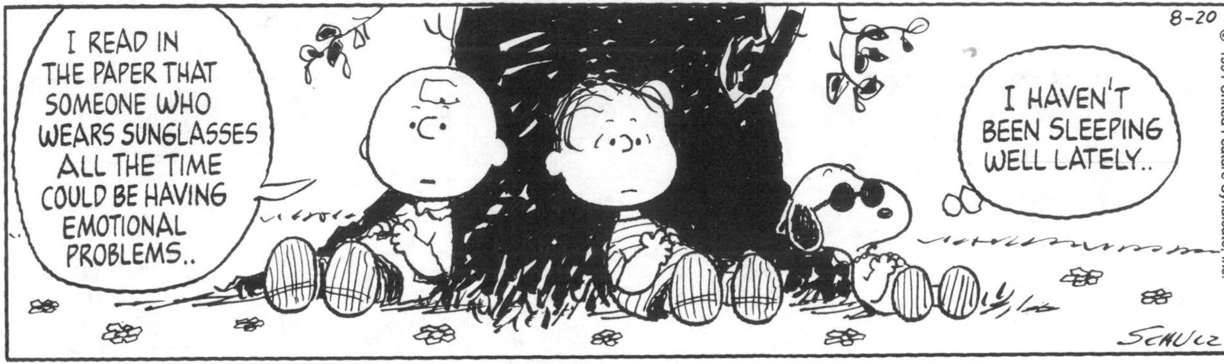
I READ IN THE PAPER THAT SOMEONE WHO WEARS SUNGLASSES ALL THE TIME COULD BE HAVING EMOTIONAL PROBLEMS..
I HAVEN'T BEEN SLEEPING WELL LATELY..
8-20
© 1991 United Feature Syndicate, Inc.
SCHULZ

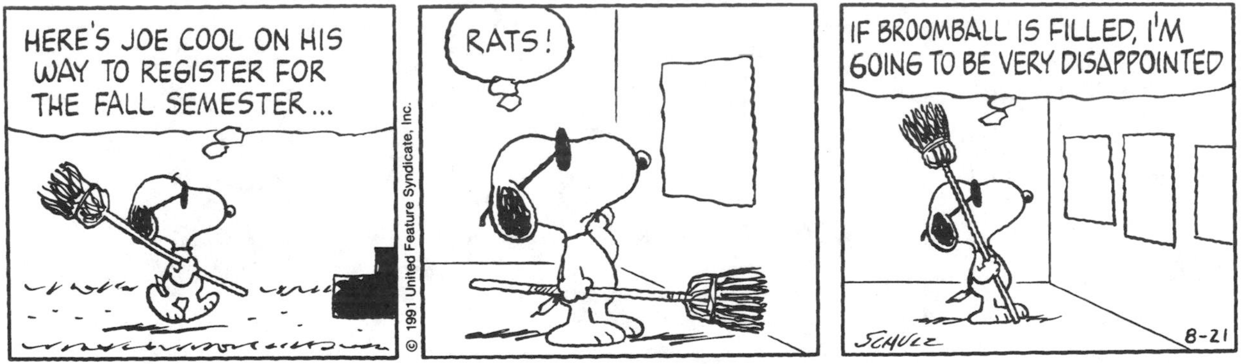
HERE'S JOE COOL ON HIS WAY TO REGISTER FOR THE FALL SEMESTER...
© 1991 United Feature Syndicate, Inc.
RATS!
IF BROOMBALL IS FILLED, I'M GOING TO BE VERY DISAPPOINTED
SCHULZ
8-21

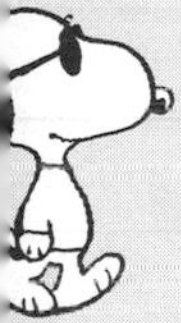

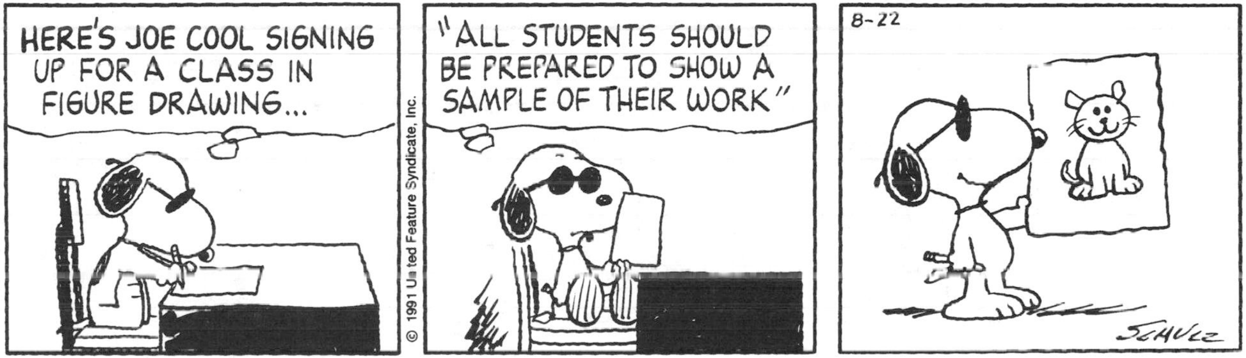
HERE'S JOE COOL SIGNING UP FOR A CLASS IN FIGURE DRAWING...
© 1991 United Feature Syndicate, Inc.
"ALL STUDENTS SHOULD BE PREPARED TO SHOW A SAMPLE OF THEIR WORK"
8-22
SCHULZ

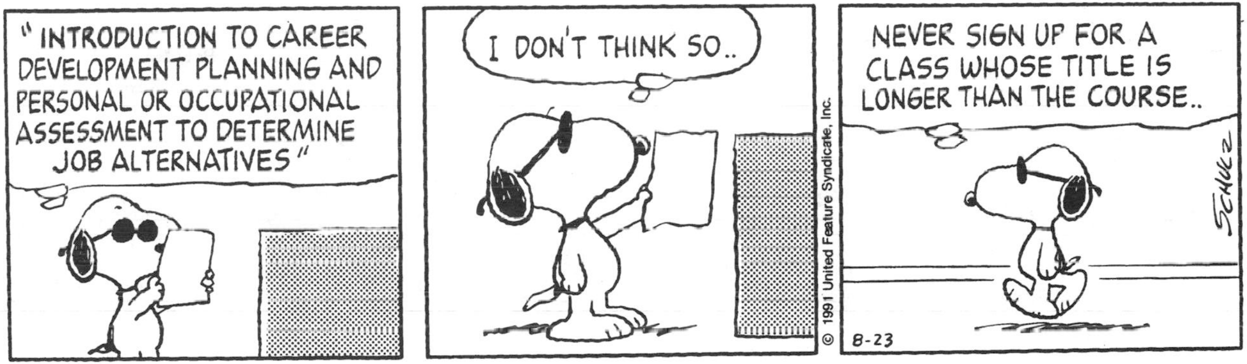
"INTRODUCTION TO CAREER DEVELOPMENT PLANNING AND PERSONAL OR OCCUPATIONAL ASSESSMENT TO DETERMINE JOB ALTERNATIVES"
I DON'T THINK SO..
© 1991 United Feature Syndicate, Inc.
NEVER SIGN UP FOR A CLASS WHOSE TITLE IS LONGER THAN THE COURSE..
SCHULZ
8-23

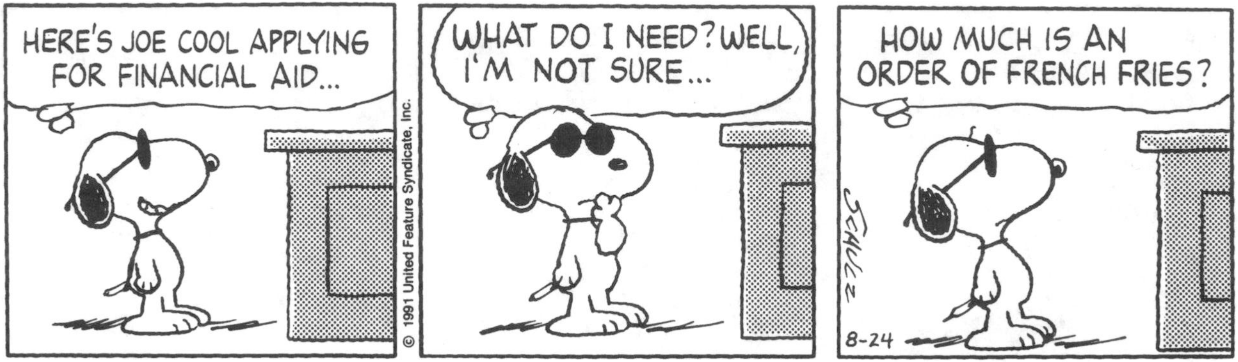
HERE'S JOE COOL APPLYING FOR FINANCIAL AID...
© 1991 United Feature Syndicate, Inc.
WHAT DO I NEED? WELL, I'M NOT SURE...
HOW MUCH IS AN ORDER OF FRENCH FRIES?
SCHULZ
8-24

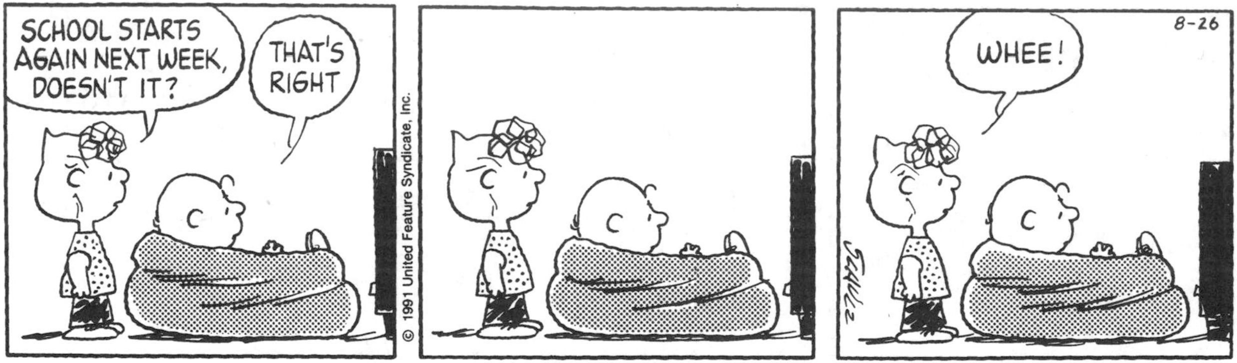
SCHOOL STARTS AGAIN NEXT WEEK, DOESN'T IT?
THAT'S RIGHT
© 1991 United Feature Syndicate, Inc.
8-26
WHEE!
SCHULZ

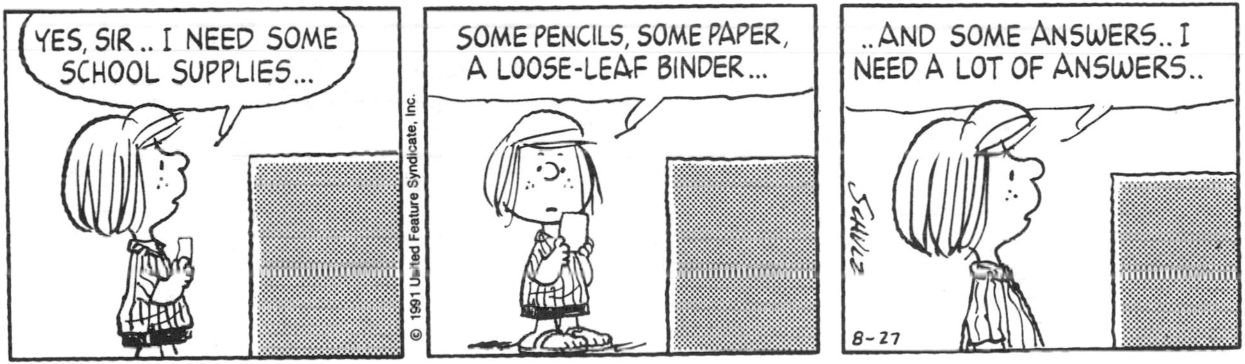
YES, SIR .. I NEED SOME SCHOOL SUPPLIES...
SOME PENCILS, SOME PAPER, A LOOSE-LEAF BINDER...
..AND SOME ANSWERS.. I NEED A LOT OF ANSWERS..
SCHULZ
8-27

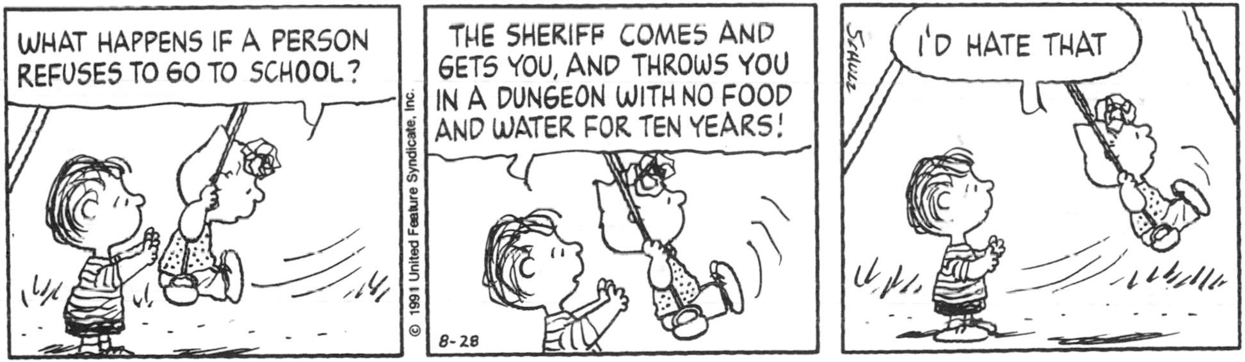
WHAT HAPPENS IF A PERSON REFUSES TO GO TO SCHOOL?
THE SHERIFF COMES AND GETS YOU, AND THROWS YOU IN A DUNGEON WITH NO FOOD AND WATER FOR TEN YEARS!
8-28
SCHULZ
I'D HATE THAT

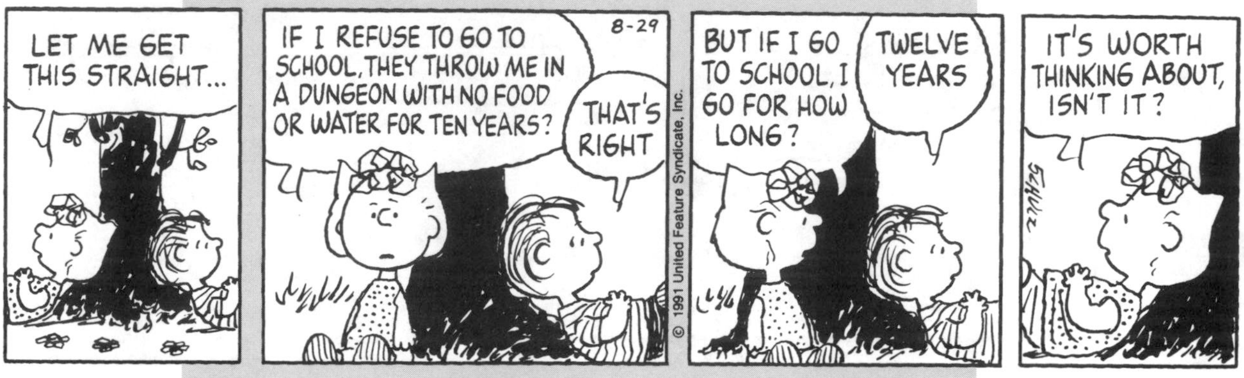
LET ME GET THIS STRAIGHT...
8-29
IF I REFUSE TO GO TO SCHOOL, THEY THROW ME IN A DUNGEON WITH NO FOOD OR WATER FOR TEN YEARS?
THAT'S RIGHT
© 1991 United Feature Syndicate, Inc.
BUT IF I GO TO SCHOOL, I GO FOR HOW LONG?
TWELVE YEARS
IT'S WORTH THINKING ABOUT, ISN'T IT?

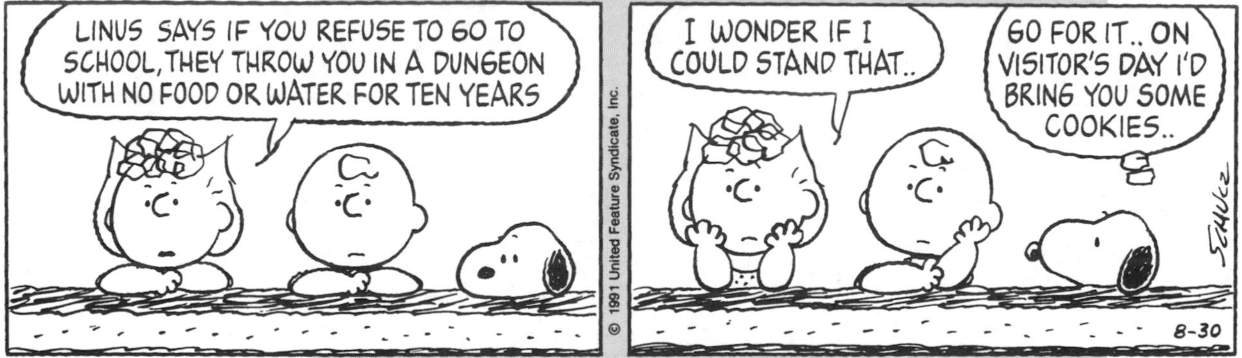
LINUS SAYS IF YOU REFUSE TO GO TO SCHOOL, THEY THROW YOU IN A DUNGEON WITH NO FOOD OR WATER FOR TEN YEARS
© 1991 United Feature Syndicate, Inc.
I WONDER IF I COULD STAND THAT..
GO FOR IT.. ON VISITOR'S DAY I'D BRING YOU SOME COOKIES..
8-30

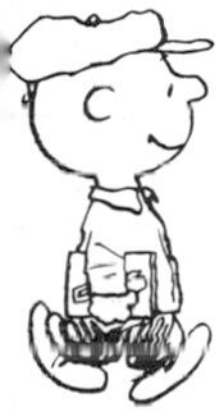

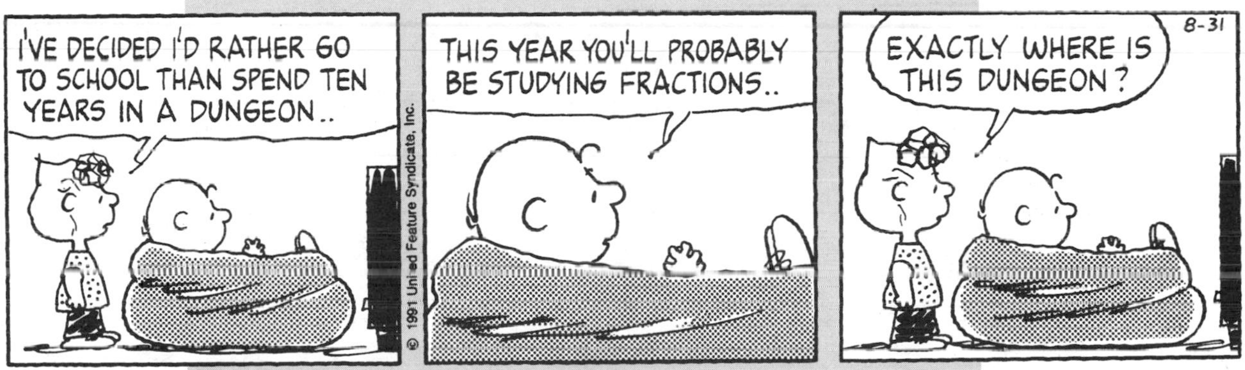

I'VE DECIDED I'D RATHER GO TO SCHOOL THAN SPEND TEN YEARS IN A DUNGEON..
© 1991 United Feature Syndicate, Inc.
THIS YEAR YOU'LL PROBABLY BE STUDYING FRACTIONS..
8-31
EXACTLY WHERE IS THIS DUNGEON?

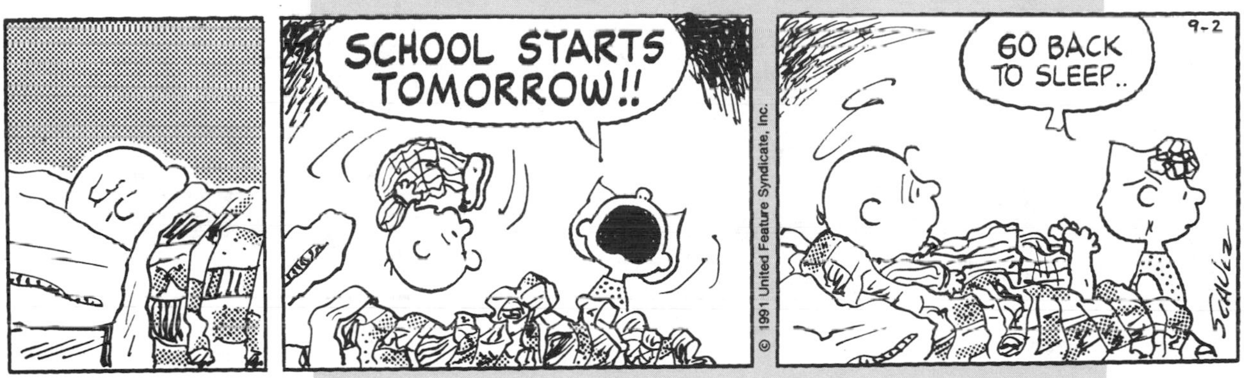

SCHOOL STARTS TOMORROW!!
© 1991 United Feature Syndicate, Inc.
9-2
GO BACK TO SLEEP..
SCHULZ

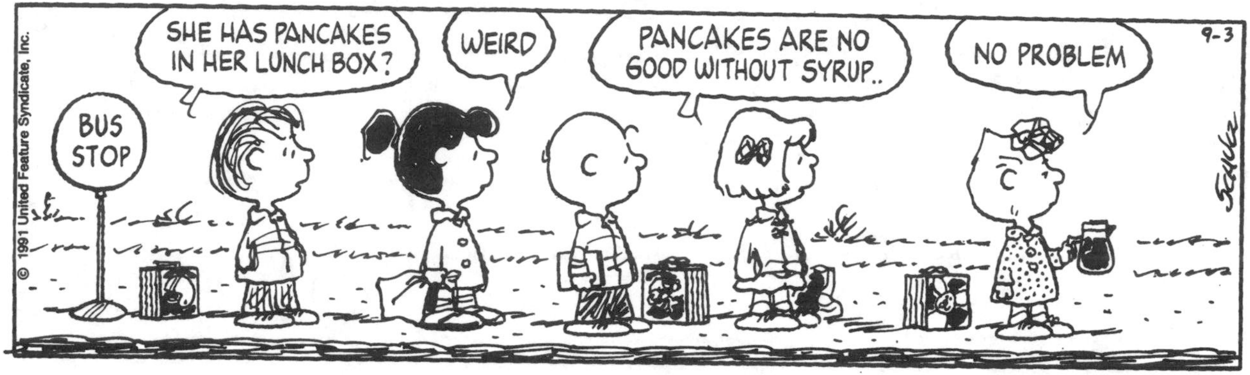
BUS STOP
SHE HAS PANCAKES IN HER LUNCH BOX?
WEIRD
PANCAKES ARE NO GOOD WITHOUT SYRUP..
NO PROBLEM
9-3
© 1991 United Feature Syndicate, Inc.
SCHULZ

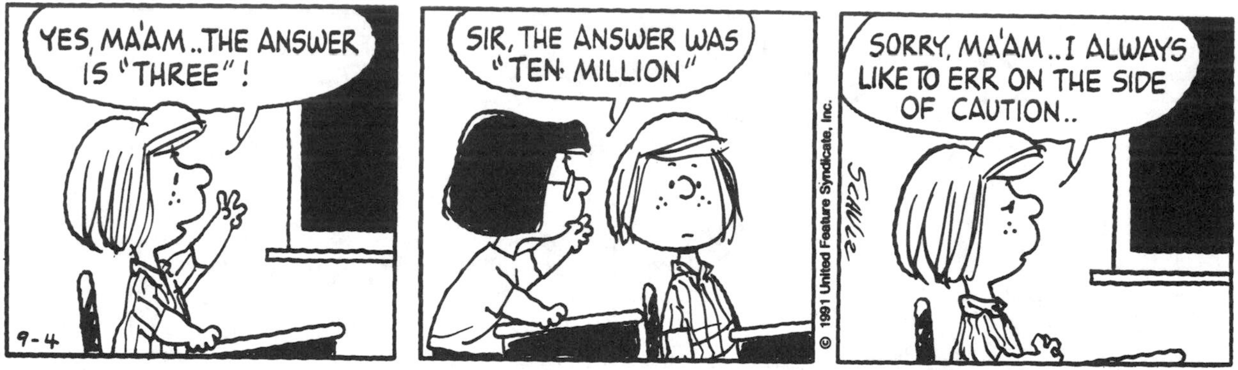
YES, MA'AM..THE ANSWER IS "THREE"!
9-4
SIR, THE ANSWER WAS "TEN MILLION"
© 1991 United Feature Syndicate, Inc.
SCHULZ
SORRY, MA'AM..I ALWAYS LIKE TO ERR ON THE SIDE OF CAUTION..

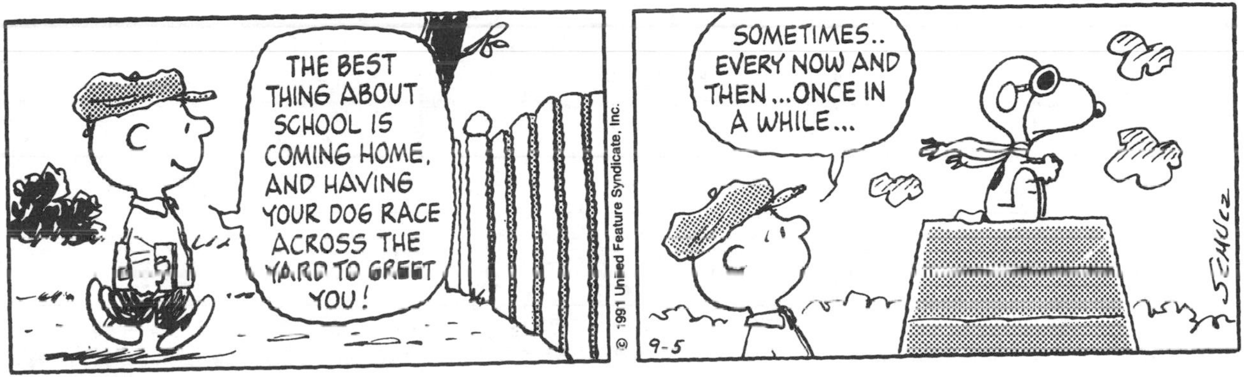
THE BEST THING ABOUT SCHOOL IS COMING HOME, AND HAVING YOUR DOG RACE ACROSS THE YARD TO GREET YOU!
© 1991 United Feature Syndicate, Inc.
SOMETIMES.. EVERY NOW AND THEN...ONCE IN A WHILE...
9-5
SCHULZ

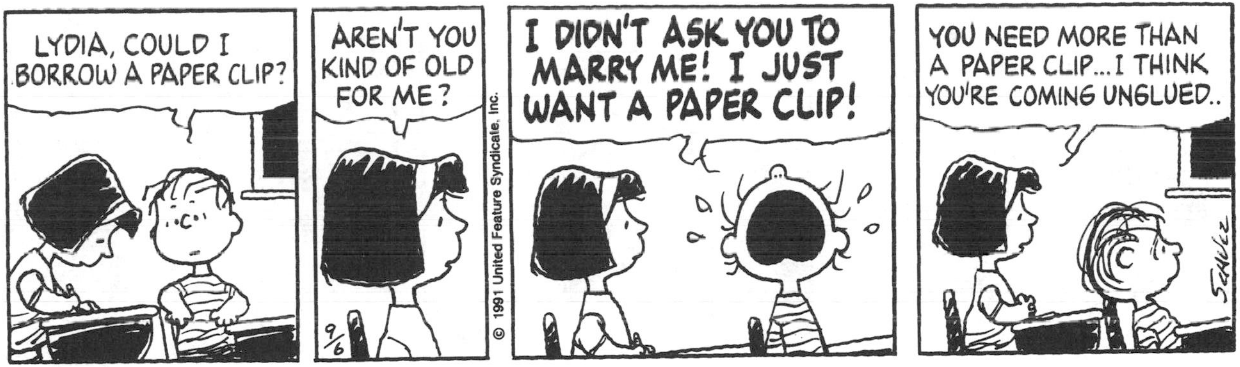
LYDIA, COULD I BORROW A PAPER CLIP?
AREN'T YOU KIND OF OLD FOR ME?
9/6
© 1991 United Feature Syndicate, Inc.
I DIDN'T ASK YOU TO MARRY ME! I JUST WANT A PAPER CLIP!
YOU NEED MORE THAN A PAPER CLIP...I THINK YOU'RE COMING UNGLUED..
SCHULZ

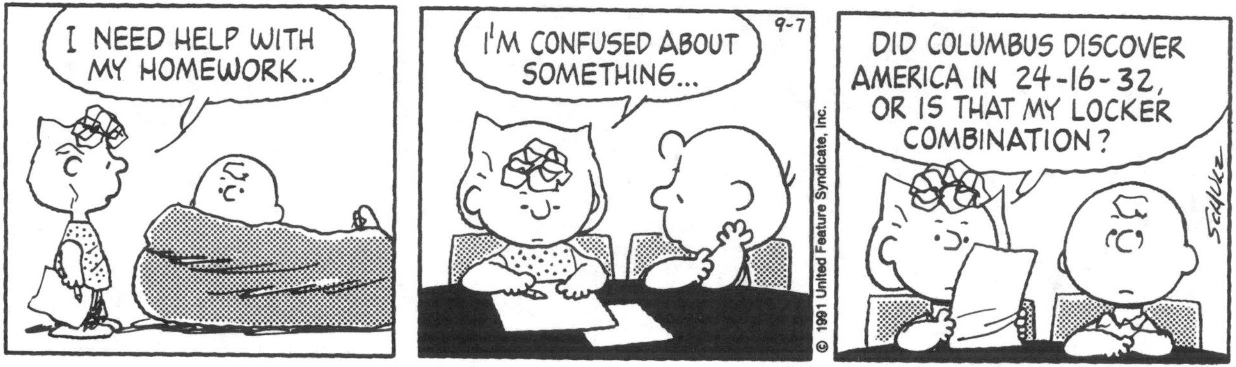
I NEED HELP WITH MY HOMEWORK..
9-7
I'M CONFUSED ABOUT SOMETHING...
© 1991 United Feature Syndicate, Inc.
DID COLUMBUS DISCOVER AMERICA IN 24-16-32, OR IS THAT MY LOCKER COMBINATION?
SCHULZ

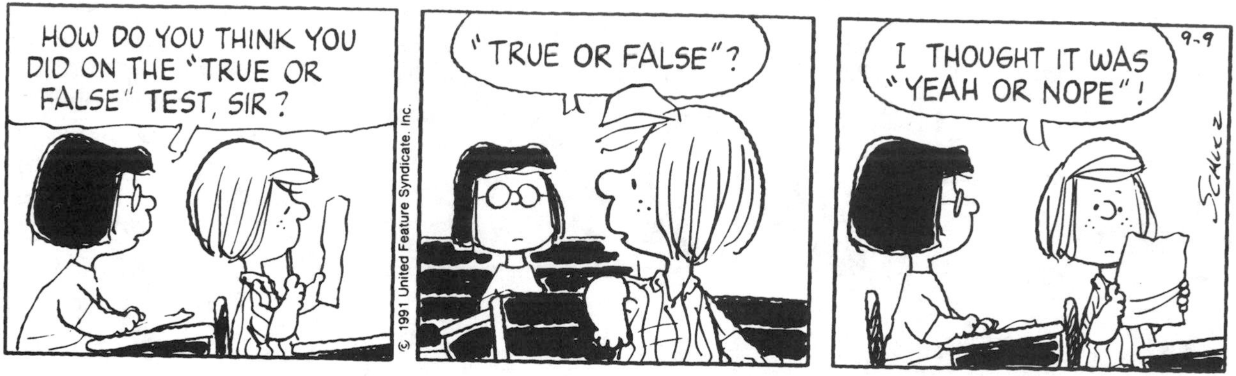
HOW DO YOU THINK YOU DID ON THE "TRUE OR FALSE" TEST, SIR?
© 1991 United Feature Syndicate, Inc.
"TRUE OR FALSE"?
9-9
I THOUGHT IT WAS "YEAH OR NOPE"!
SCHULZ

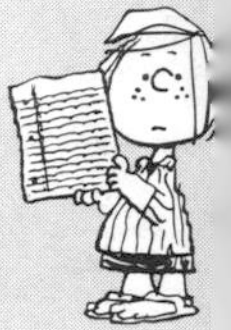

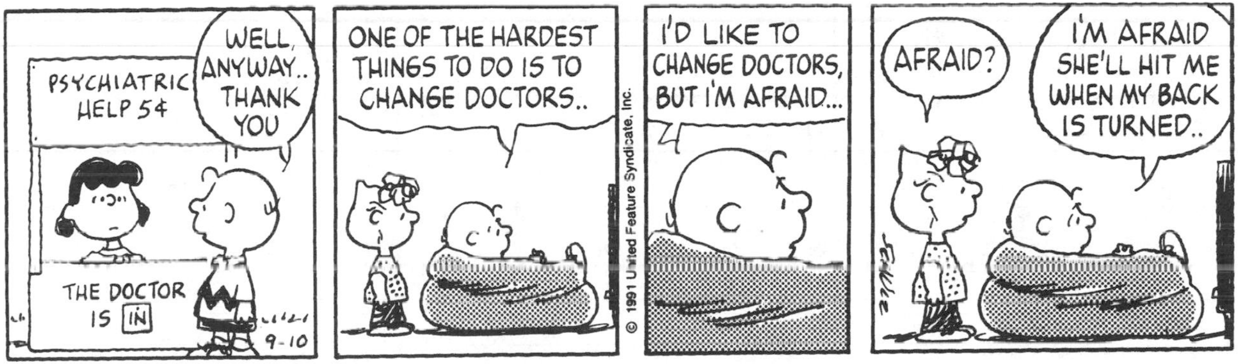
PSYCHIATRIC HELP 5¢
THE DOCTOR IS IN
WELL, ANYWAY.. THANK YOU
ONE OF THE HARDEST THINGS TO DO IS TO CHANGE DOCTORS..
© 1991 United Feature Syndicate, Inc.
I'D LIKE TO CHANGE DOCTORS, BUT I'M AFRAID...
AFRAID?
I'M AFRAID SHE'LL HIT ME WHEN MY BACK IS TURNED..
9-10

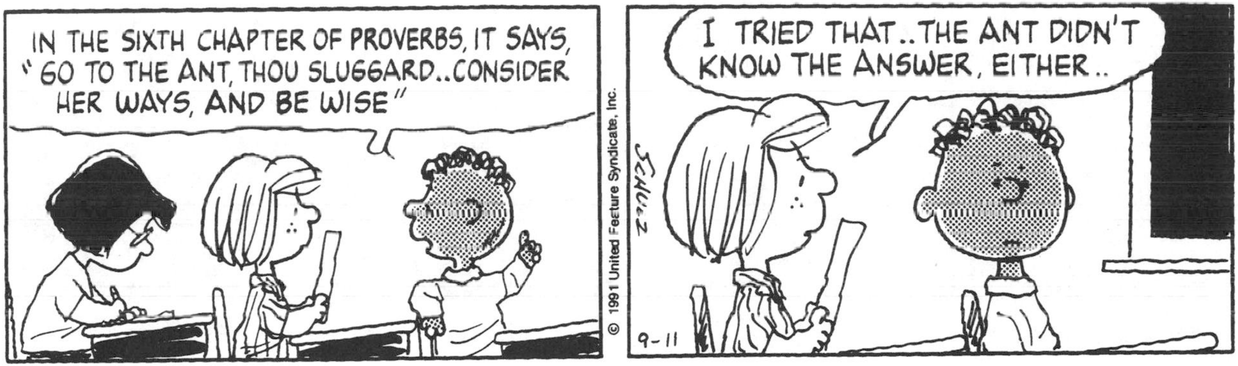
IN THE SIXTH CHAPTER OF PROVERBS, IT SAYS, "GO TO THE ANT, THOU SLUGGARD..CONSIDER HER WAYS, AND BE WISE"
© 1991 United Feature Syndicate, Inc.
I TRIED THAT..THE ANT DIDN'T KNOW THE ANSWER, EITHER..
9-11

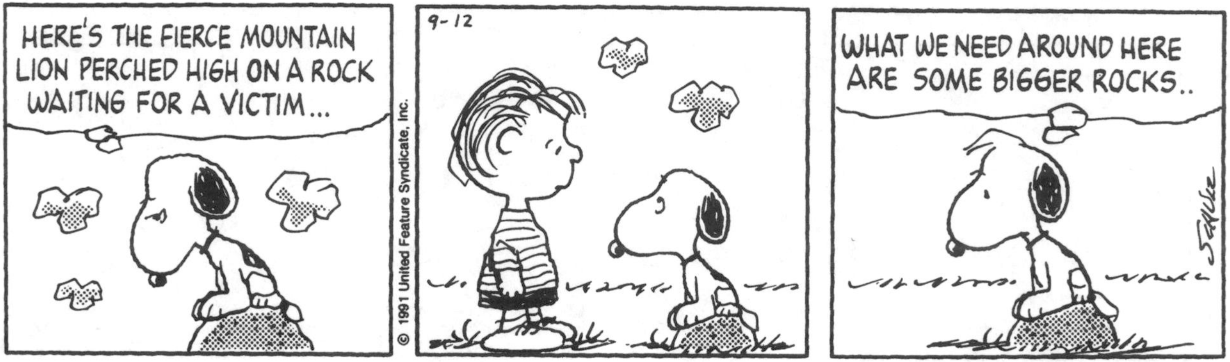
HERE'S THE FIERCE MOUNTAIN LION PERCHED HIGH ON A ROCK WAITING FOR A VICTIM...
© 1991 United Feature Syndicate, Inc.
9-12
WHAT WE NEED AROUND HERE ARE SOME BIGGER ROCKS..
SCHULZ

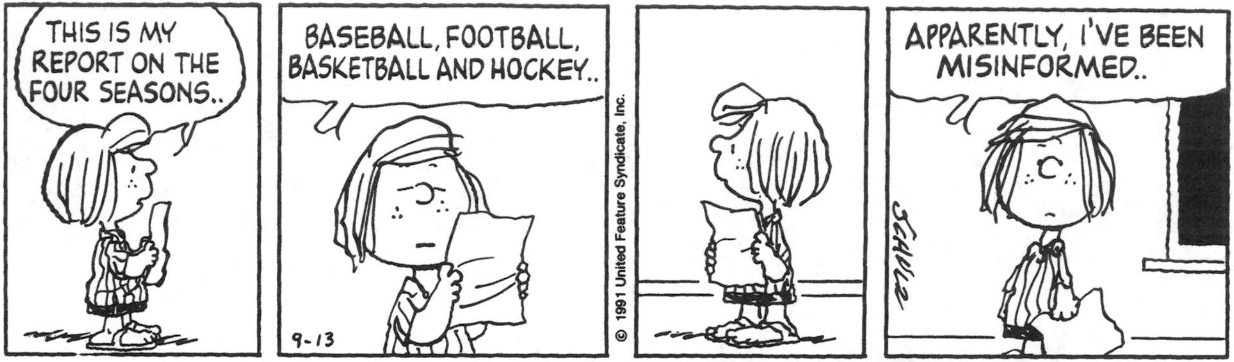
THIS IS MY REPORT ON THE FOUR SEASONS..
BASEBALL, FOOTBALL, BASKETBALL AND HOCKEY..
9-13
© 1991 United Feature Syndicate, Inc.
APPARENTLY, I'VE BEEN MISINFORMED..
SCHULZ

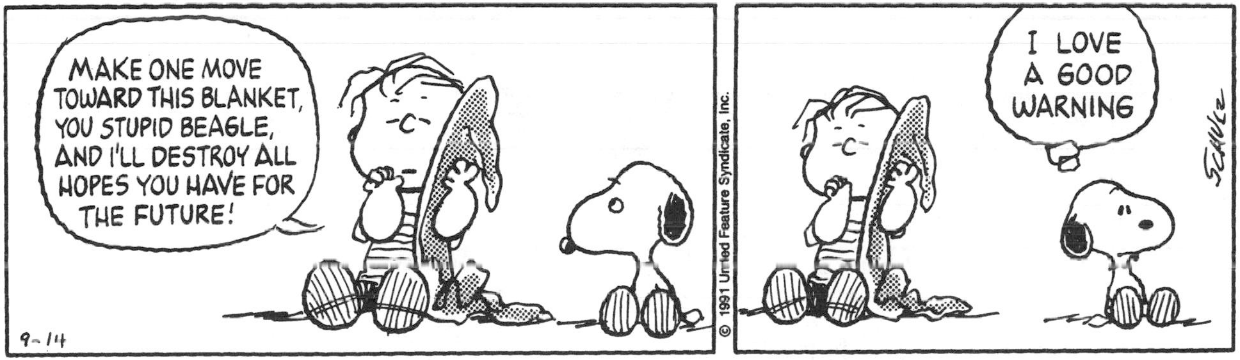
MAKE ONE MOVE TOWARD THIS BLANKET, YOU STUPID BEAGLE, AND I'LL DESTROY ALL HOPES YOU HAVE FOR THE FUTURE!
9-14
© 1991 United Feature Syndicate, Inc.
I LOVE A GOOD WARNING
SCHULZ

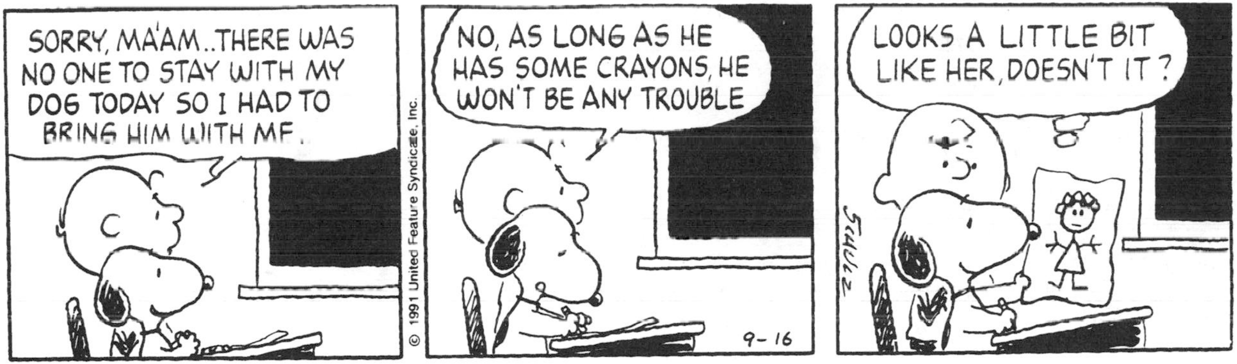
SORRY, MA'AM..THERE WAS NO ONE TO STAY WITH MY DOG TODAY SO I HAD TO BRING HIM WITH ME..
© 1991 United Feature Syndicate, Inc.
NO, AS LONG AS HE HAS SOME CRAYONS, HE WON'T BE ANY TROUBLE
9-16
LOOKS A LITTLE BIT LIKE HER, DOESN'T IT ?
SCHULZ

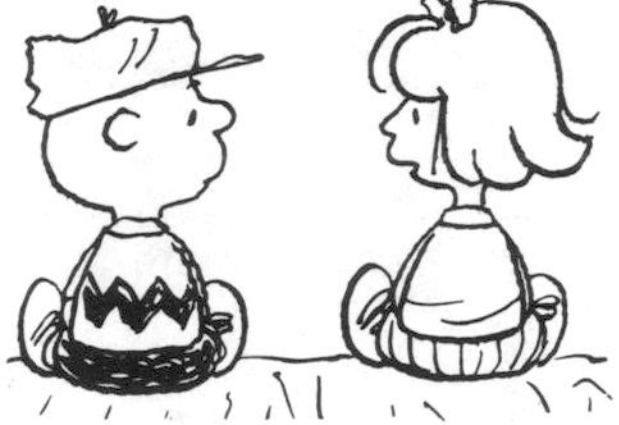

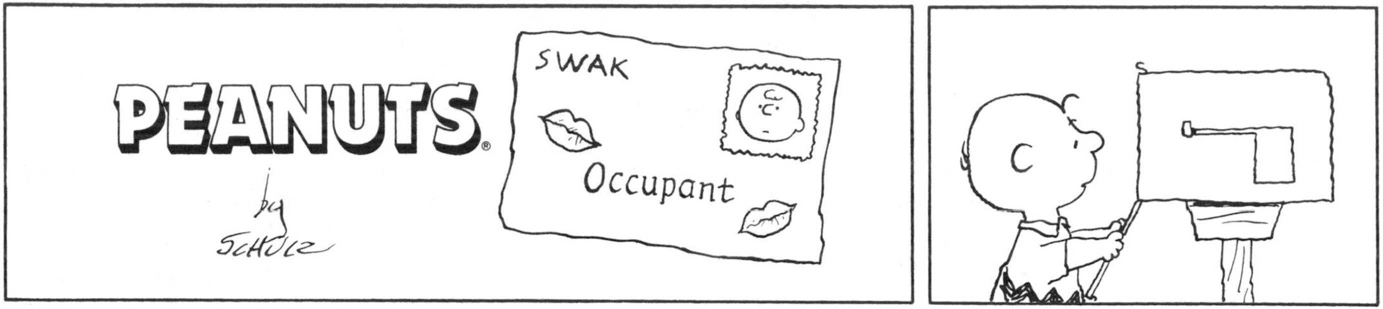
PEANUTS
by SCHULZ
SWAK
Occupant

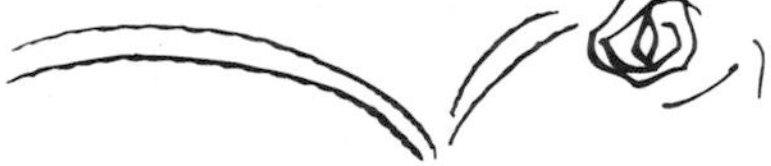

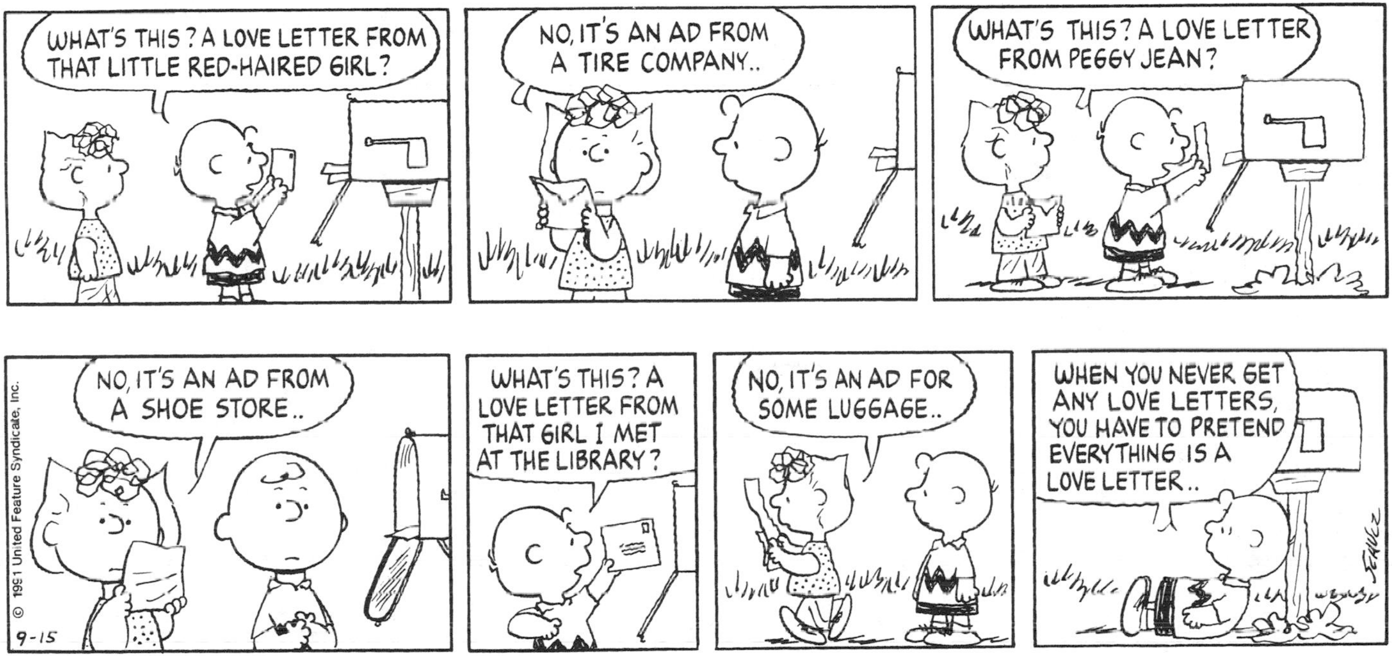
WHAT'S THIS? A LOVE LETTER FROM THAT LITTLE RED-HAIRED GIRL?
NO, IT'S AN AD FROM A TIRE COMPANY..
WHAT'S THIS? A LOVE LETTER FROM PEGGY JEAN?
NO, IT'S AN AD FROM A SHOE STORE..
WHAT'S THIS? A LOVE LETTER FROM THAT GIRL I MET AT THE LIBRARY?
NO, IT'S AN AD FOR SOME LUGGAGE..
WHEN YOU NEVER GET ANY LOVE LETTERS, YOU HAVE TO PRETEND EVERYTHING IS A LOVE LETTER..
© 1991 United Feature Syndicate, Inc.
9-15
SCHULZ

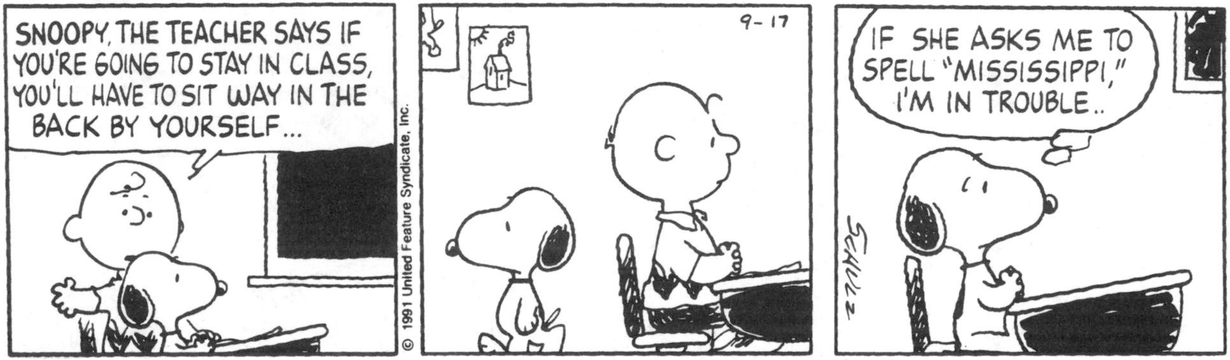
SNOOPY, THE TEACHER SAYS IF YOU'RE GOING TO STAY IN CLASS, YOU'LL HAVE TO SIT WAY IN THE BACK BY YOURSELF...
© 1991 United Feature Syndicate, Inc.
9-17
IF SHE ASKS ME TO SPELL "MISSISSIPPI," I'M IN TROUBLE..
SCHULZ

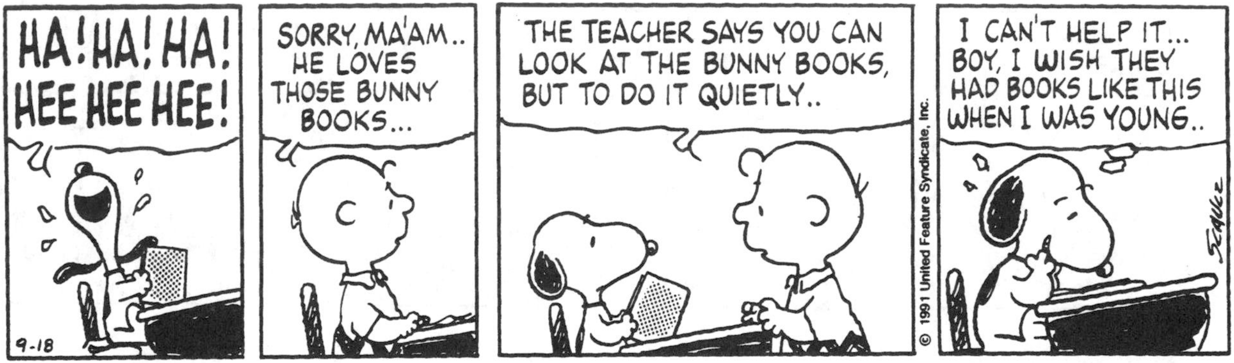
HA! HA! HA! HEE HEE HEE!
9-18
SORRY, MA'AM.. HE LOVES THOSE BUNNY BOOKS...
THE TEACHER SAYS YOU CAN LOOK AT THE BUNNY BOOKS, BUT TO DO IT QUIETLY..
© 1991 United Feature Syndicate, Inc.
I CAN'T HELP IT... BOY, I WISH THEY HAD BOOKS LIKE THIS WHEN I WAS YOUNG..
SCHULZ

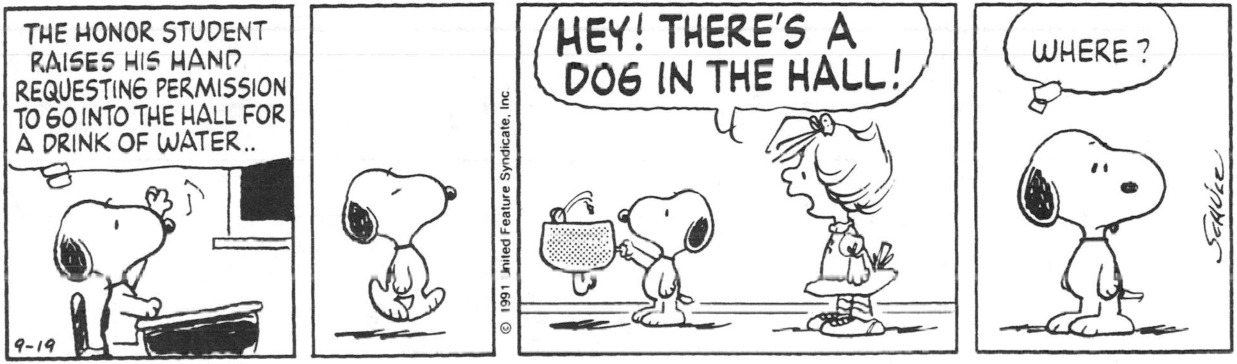
THE HONOR STUDENT RAISES HIS HAND REQUESTING PERMISSION TO GO INTO THE HALL FOR A DRINK OF WATER..
9-19
© 1991 United Feature Syndicate, Inc.
HEY! THERE'S A DOG IN THE HALL!
WHERE ?

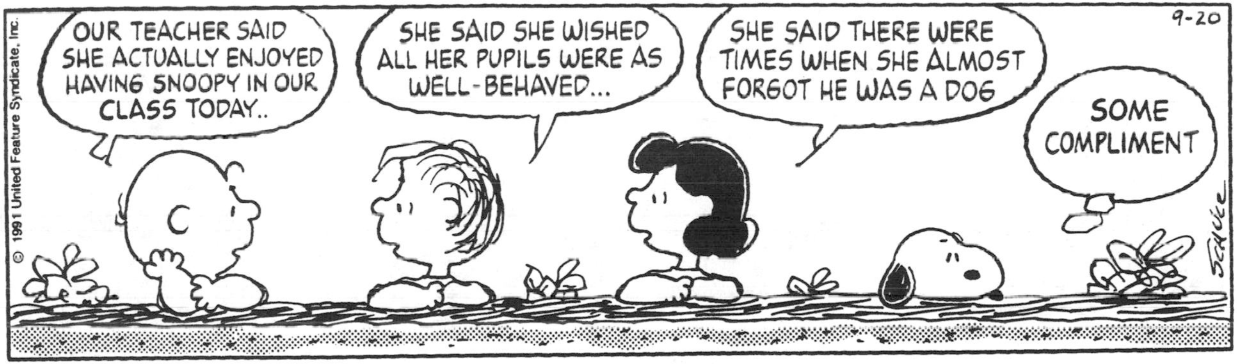
© 1991 United Feature Syndicate, Inc.
9-20
OUR TEACHER SAID SHE ACTUALLY ENJOYED HAVING SNOOPY IN OUR CLASS TODAY..
SHE SAID SHE WISHED ALL HER PUPILS WERE AS WELL-BEHAVED...
SHE SAID THERE WERE TIMES WHEN SHE ALMOST FORGOT HE WAS A DOG
SOME COMPLIMENT

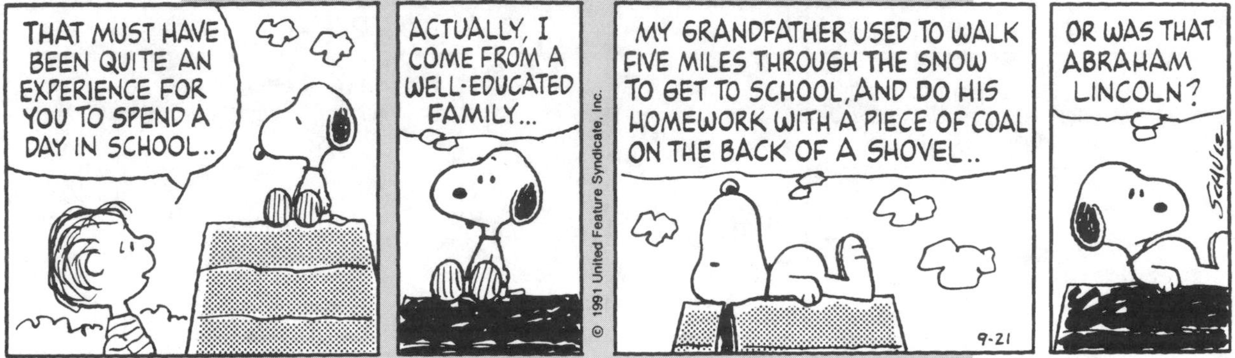
THAT MUST HAVE BEEN QUITE AN EXPERIENCE FOR YOU TO SPEND A DAY IN SCHOOL..
ACTUALLY, I COME FROM A WELL-EDUCATED FAMILY...
© 1991 United Feature Syndicate, Inc.
MY GRANDFATHER USED TO WALK FIVE MILES THROUGH THE SNOW TO GET TO SCHOOL, AND DO HIS HOMEWORK WITH A PIECE OF COAL ON THE BACK OF A SHOVEL..
9-21
OR WAS THAT ABRAHAM LINCOLN?
SCHULZ

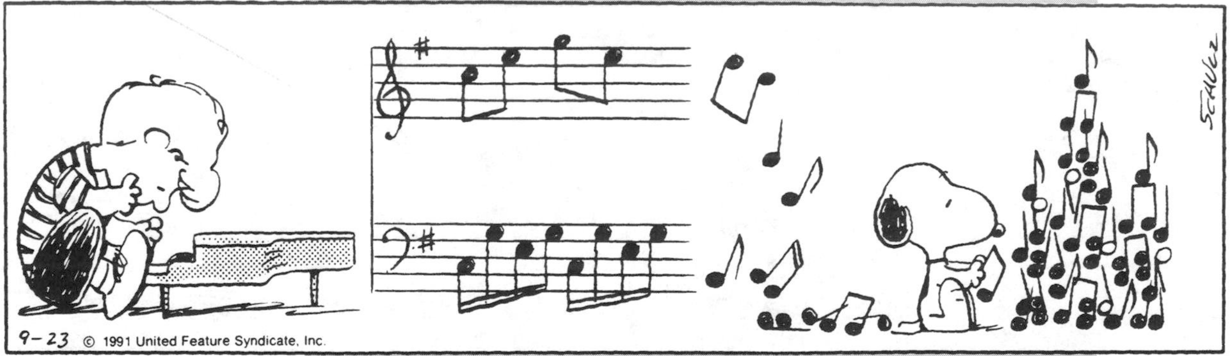
SCHULZ
9-23 © 1991 United Feature Syndicate, Inc.

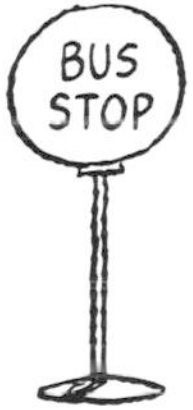
BUS STOP

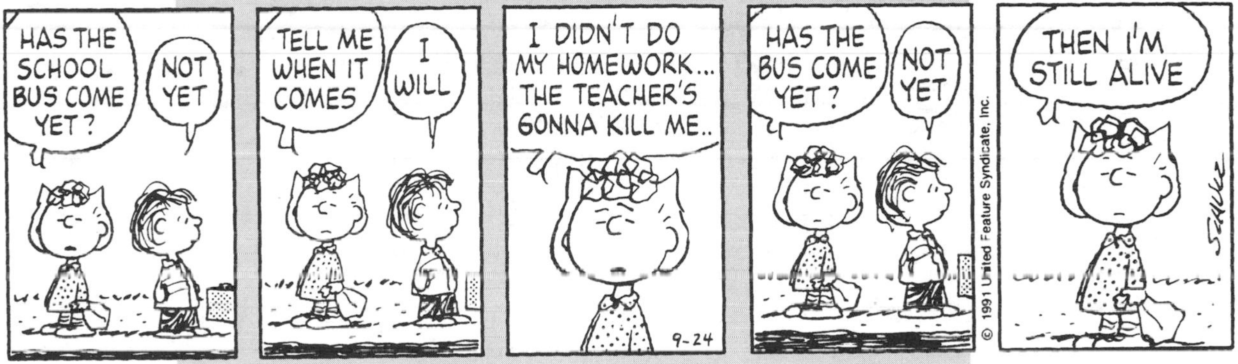
HAS THE SCHOOL BUS COME YET?
NOT YET
TELL ME WHEN IT COMES
I WILL
I DIDN'T DO MY HOMEWORK... THE TEACHER'S GONNA KILL ME..
9-24
HAS THE BUS COME YET?
NOT YET
© 1991 United Feature Syndicate, Inc.
THEN I'M STILL ALIVE

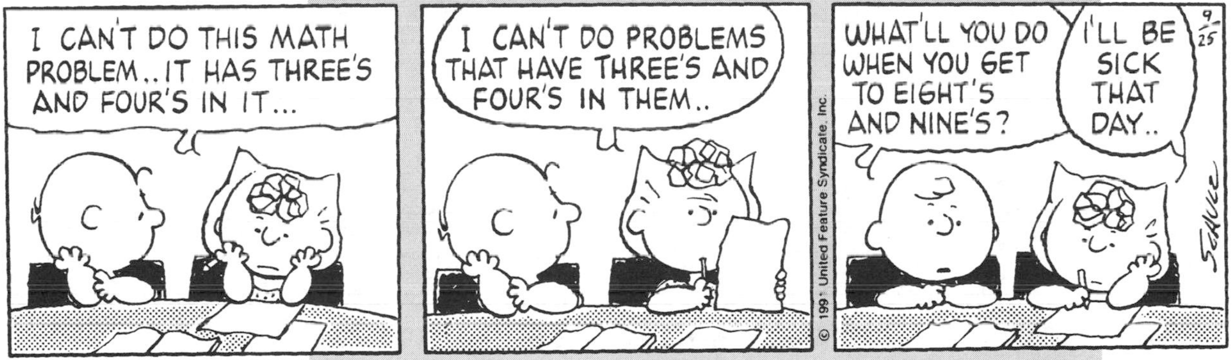
I CAN'T DO THIS MATH PROBLEM..IT HAS THREE'S AND FOUR'S IN IT...
I CAN'T DO PROBLEMS THAT HAVE THREE'S AND FOUR'S IN THEM..
© 1991 United Feature Syndicate, Inc.
WHAT'LL YOU DO WHEN YOU GET TO EIGHT'S AND NINE'S?
I'LL BE SICK THAT DAY..
9/25

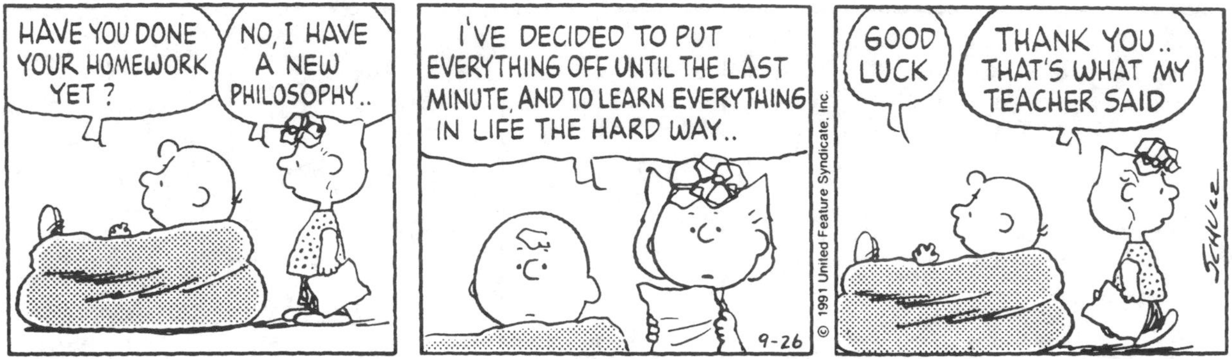
HAVE YOU DONE YOUR HOMEWORK YET ?
NO, I HAVE A NEW PHILOSOPHY..
I'VE DECIDED TO PUT EVERYTHING OFF UNTIL THE LAST MINUTE, AND TO LEARN EVERYTHING IN LIFE THE HARD WAY..
© 1991 United Feature Syndicate, Inc.
9-26
GOOD LUCK
THANK YOU.. THAT'S WHAT MY TEACHER SAID
SCHULZ

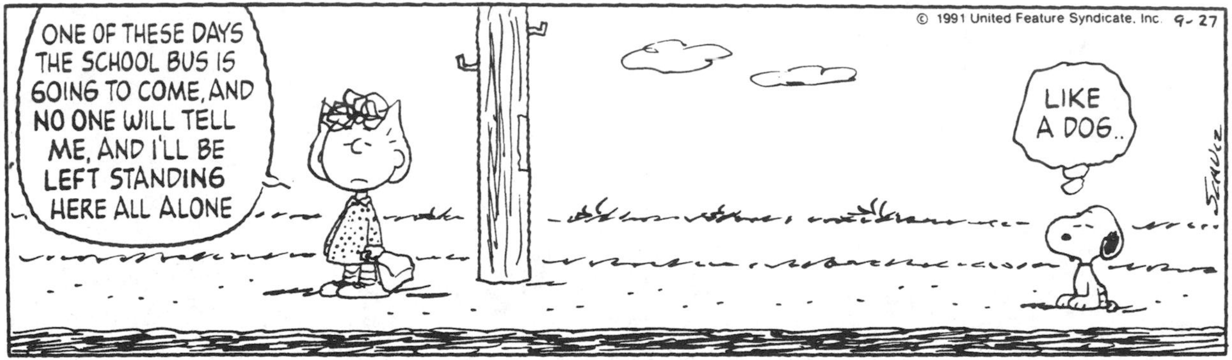
© 1991 United Feature Syndicate, Inc. 9-27
ONE OF THESE DAYS THE SCHOOL BUS IS GOING TO COME, AND NO ONE WILL TELL ME, AND I'LL BE LEFT STANDING HERE ALL ALONE
LIKE A DOG..
SCHULZ

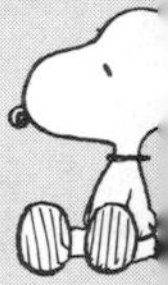

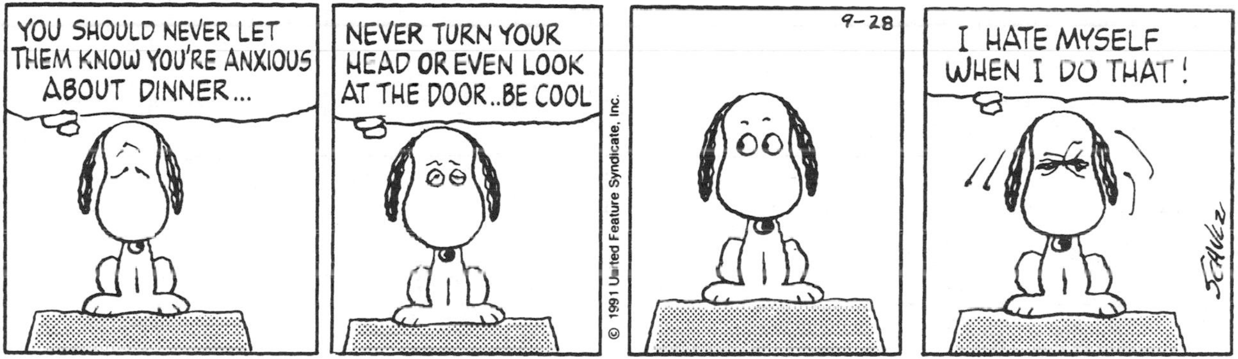
YOU SHOULD NEVER LET THEM KNOW YOU'RE ANXIOUS ABOUT DINNER...
NEVER TURN YOUR HEAD OR EVEN LOOK AT THE DOOR..BE COOL
© 1991 United Feature Syndicate, Inc.
9-28
I HATE MYSELF WHEN I DO THAT!
SCHULZ

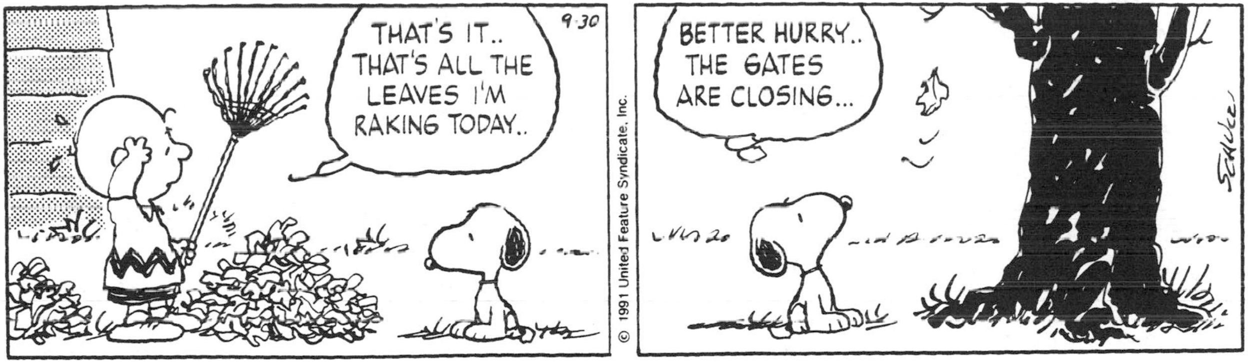
9-30
THAT'S IT.. THAT'S ALL THE LEAVES I'M RAKING TODAY..
© 1991 United Feature Syndicate, Inc.
BETTER HURRY.. THE GATES ARE CLOSING...
SCHULZ

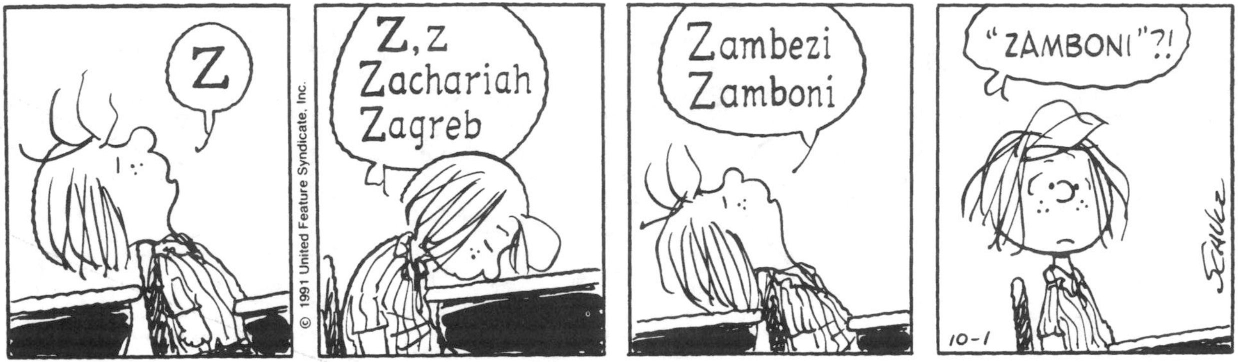
Z
Z, z
Zachariah
Zagreb
© 1991 United Feature Syndicate, Inc.
Zambezi
Zamboni
"ZAMBONI"?!
10-1
SCHULZ

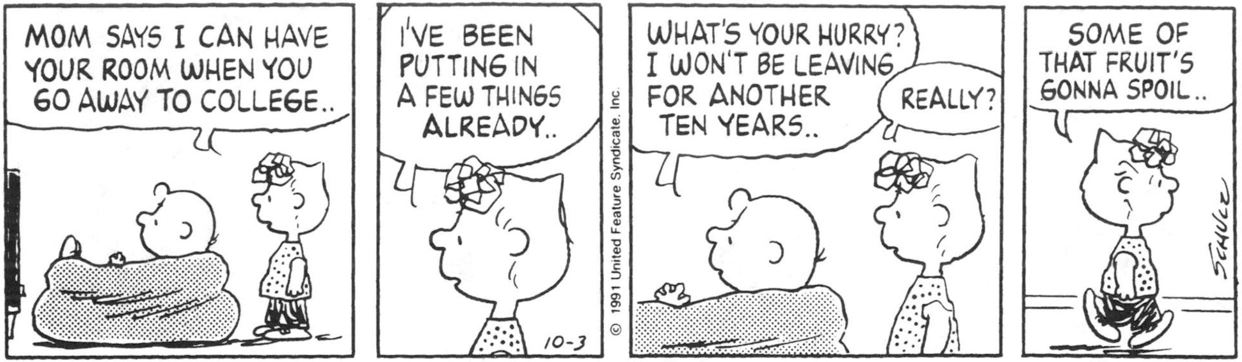
MOM SAYS I CAN HAVE YOUR ROOM WHEN YOU GO AWAY TO COLLEGE..
I'VE BEEN PUTTING IN A FEW THINGS ALREADY..
10-3
© 1991 United Feature Syndicate, Inc.
WHAT'S YOUR HURRY? I WON'T BE LEAVING FOR ANOTHER TEN YEARS..
REALLY?
SOME OF THAT FRUIT'S GONNA SPOIL..
SCHULZ

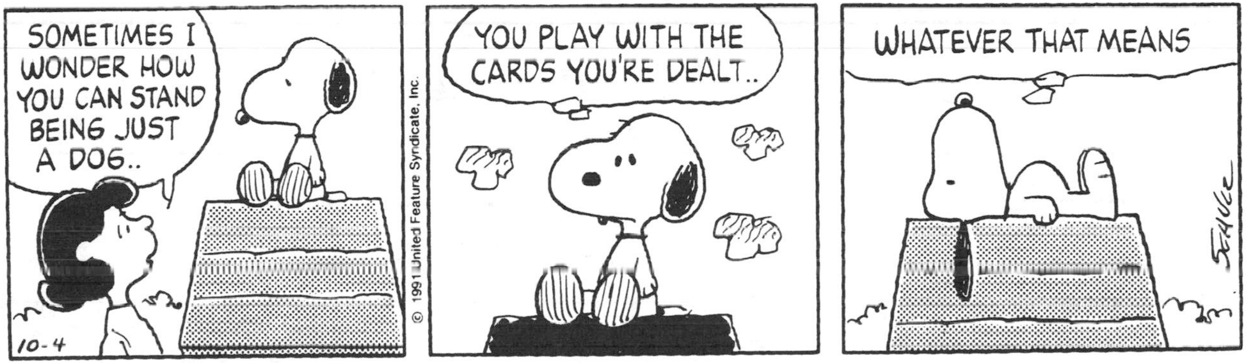
SOMETIMES I WONDER HOW YOU CAN STAND BEING JUST A DOG..
10-4
© 1991 United Feature Syndicate, Inc.
YOU PLAY WITH THE CARDS YOU'RE DEALT..
WHATEVER THAT MEANS

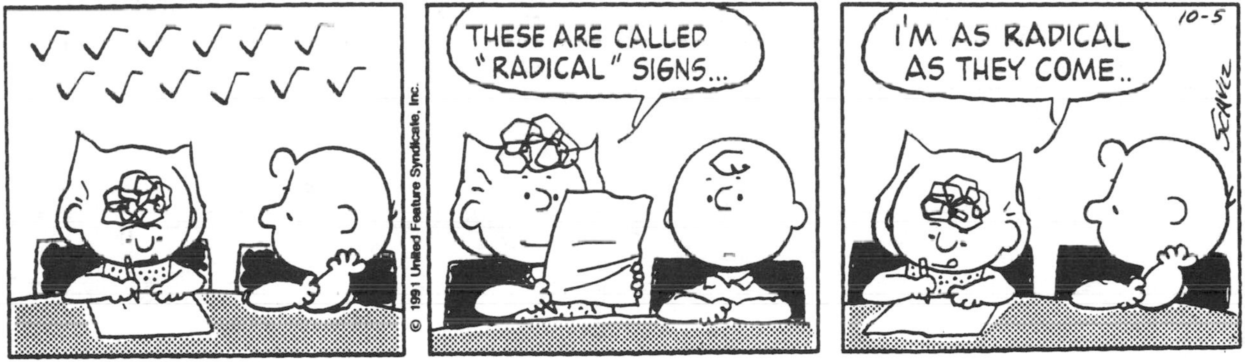
© 1991 United Feature Syndicate, Inc.
THESE ARE CALLED "RADICAL" SIGNS...
I'M AS RADICAL AS THEY COME..
10-5

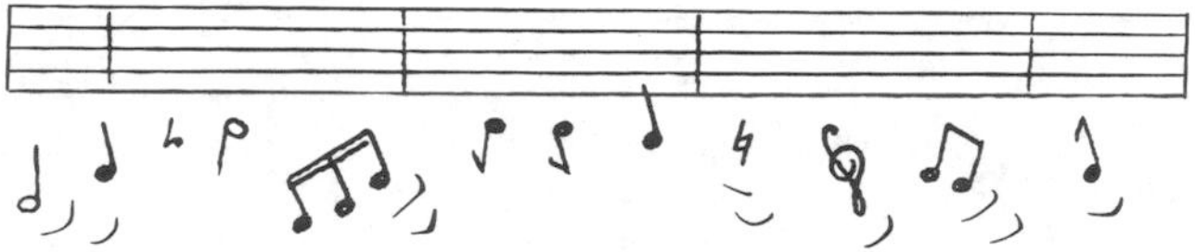

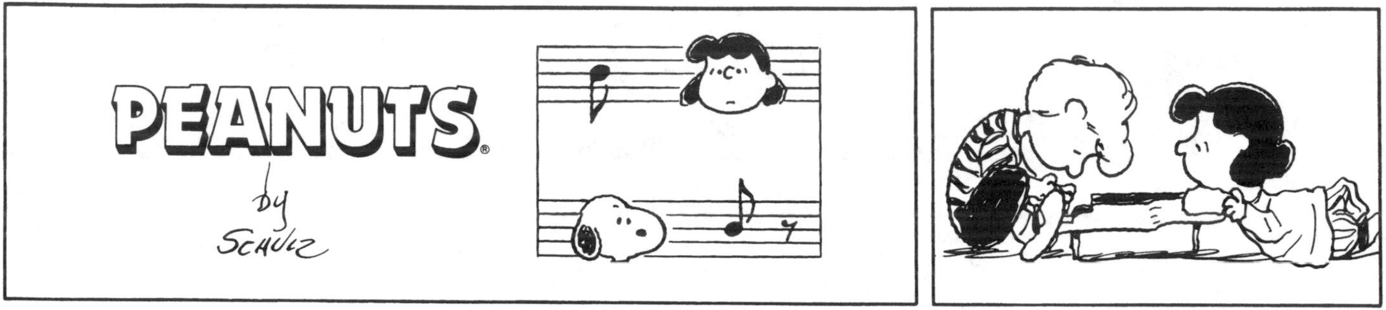
PEANUTS®
by
SCHULZ

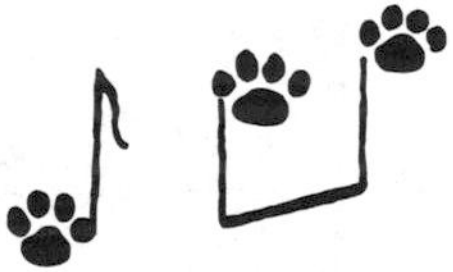

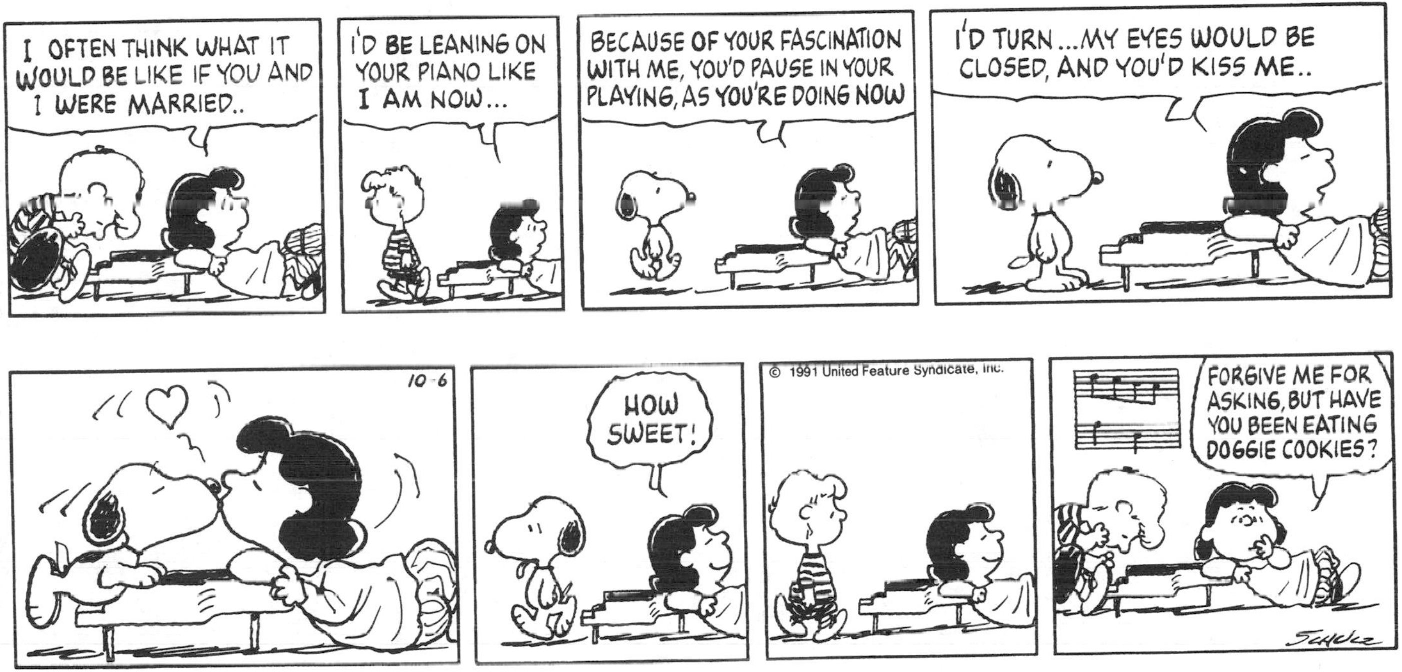
I OFTEN THINK WHAT IT WOULD BE LIKE IF YOU AND I WERE MARRIED..
I'D BE LEANING ON YOUR PIANO LIKE I AM NOW...
BECAUSE OF YOUR FASCINATION WITH ME, YOU'D PAUSE IN YOUR PLAYING, AS YOU'RE DOING NOW
I'D TURN ...MY EYES WOULD BE CLOSED, AND YOU'D KISS ME..
10-6
HOW SWEET!
© 1991 United Feature Syndicate, Inc.
FORGIVE ME FOR ASKING, BUT HAVE YOU BEEN EATING DOGGIE COOKIES?

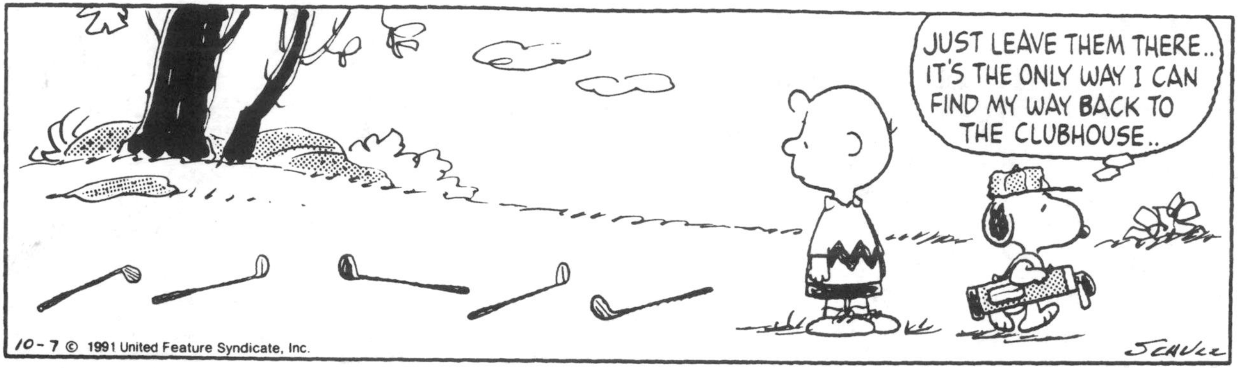
JUST LEAVE THEM THERE.. IT'S THE ONLY WAY I CAN FIND MY WAY BACK TO THE CLUBHOUSE..
10-7 © 1991 United Feature Syndicate, Inc.
SCHULZ

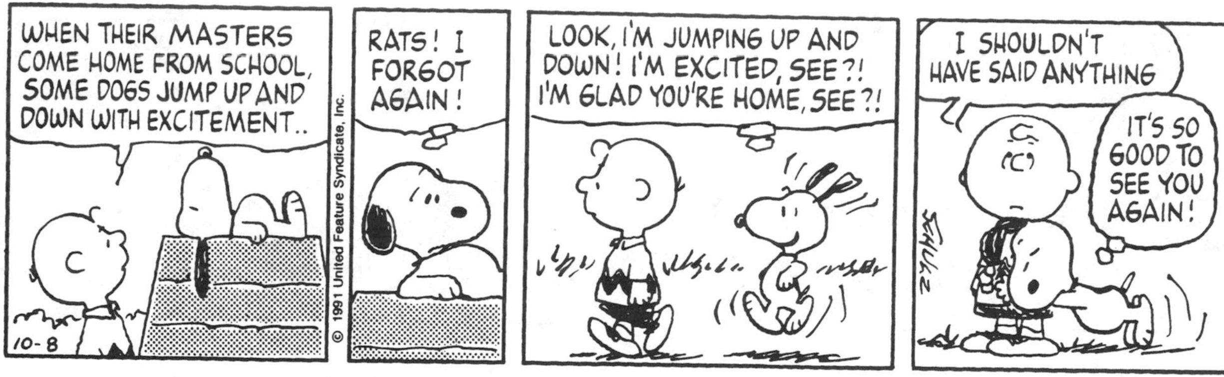
WHEN THEIR MASTERS COME HOME FROM SCHOOL, SOME DOGS JUMP UP AND DOWN WITH EXCITEMENT..
10-8
© 1991 United Feature Syndicate, Inc.
RATS! I FORGOT AGAIN!
LOOK, I'M JUMPING UP AND DOWN! I'M EXCITED, SEE?! I'M GLAD YOU'RE HOME, SEE?!
I SHOULDN'T HAVE SAID ANYTHING
IT'S SO GOOD TO SEE YOU AGAIN!
SCHULZ

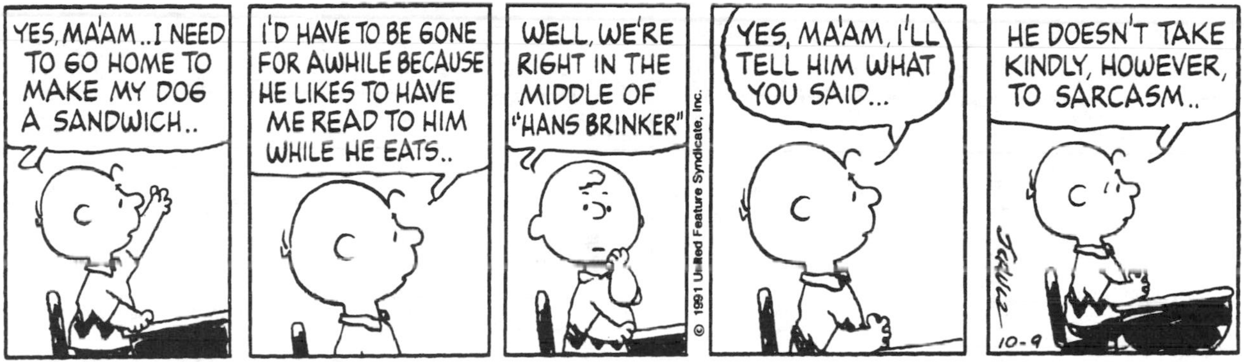
YES, MA'AM.. I NEED TO GO HOME TO MAKE MY DOG A SANDWICH..
I'D HAVE TO BE GONE FOR AWHILE BECAUSE HE LIKES TO HAVE ME READ TO HIM WHILE HE EATS..
WELL, WE'RE RIGHT IN THE MIDDLE OF "HANS BRINKER"
© 1991 United Feature Syndicate, Inc.
YES, MA'AM, I'LL TELL HIM WHAT YOU SAID...
HE DOESN'T TAKE KINDLY, HOWEVER, TO SARCASM..
10-9

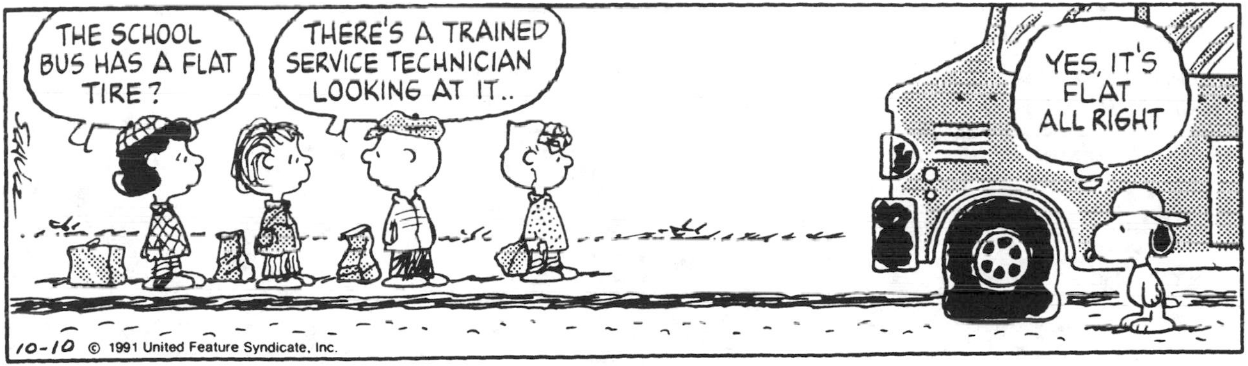
THE SCHOOL BUS HAS A FLAT TIRE?
THERE'S A TRAINED SERVICE TECHNICIAN LOOKING AT IT..
YES, IT'S FLAT ALL RIGHT
10-10 © 1991 United Feature Syndicate, Inc.

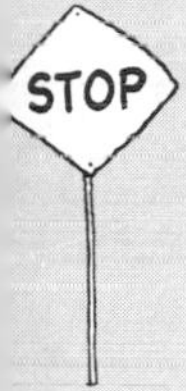
STOP

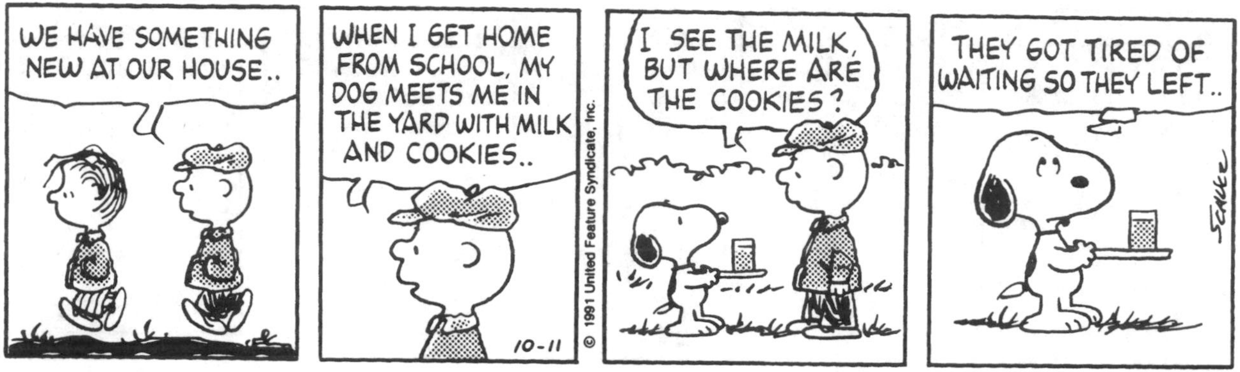
WE HAVE SOMETHING NEW AT OUR HOUSE..
WHEN I GET HOME FROM SCHOOL, MY DOG MEETS ME IN THE YARD WITH MILK AND COOKIES..
10-11
© 1991 United Feature Syndicate, Inc.
I SEE THE MILK, BUT WHERE ARE THE COOKIES?
THEY GOT TIRED OF WAITING SO THEY LEFT..
SCHULZ

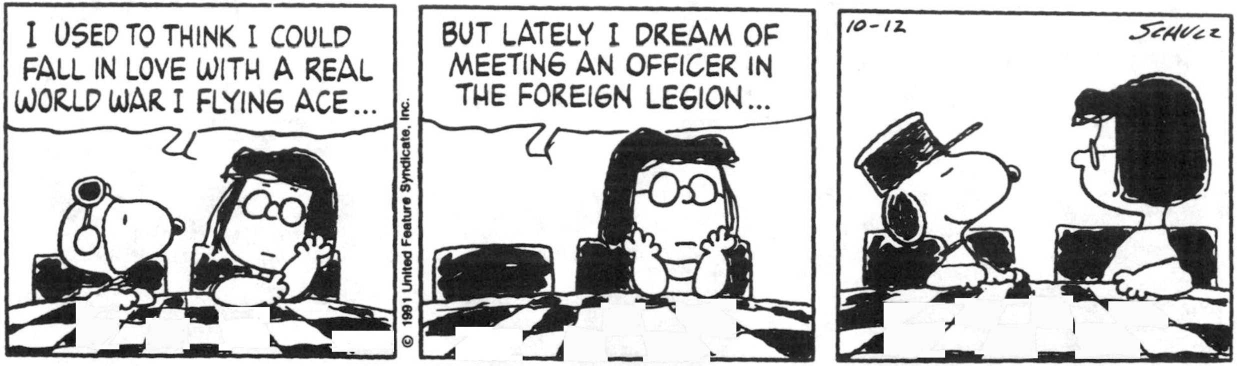
I USED TO THINK I COULD FALL IN LOVE WITH A REAL WORLD WAR I FLYING ACE...
© 1991 United Feature Syndicate, Inc.
BUT LATELY I DREAM OF MEETING AN OFFICER IN THE FOREIGN LEGION...
10-12
SCHULZ

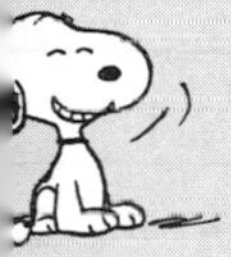

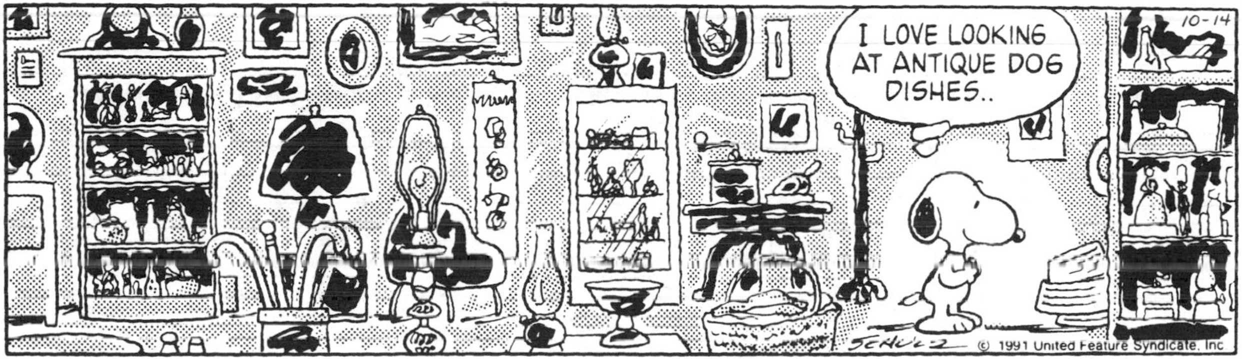
10-14
I LOVE LOOKING AT ANTIQUE DOG DISHES..
SCHULZ
© 1991 United Feature Syndicate, Inc

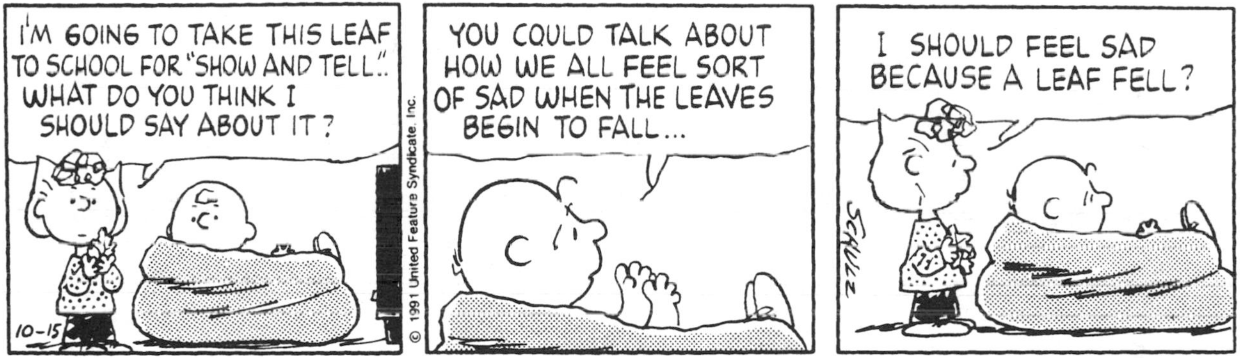
I'M GOING TO TAKE THIS LEAF TO SCHOOL FOR "SHOW AND TELL." WHAT DO YOU THINK I SHOULD SAY ABOUT IT?
10-15
© 1991 United Feature Syndicate, Inc.
YOU COULD TALK ABOUT HOW WE ALL FEEL SORT OF SAD WHEN THE LEAVES BEGIN TO FALL...
I SHOULD FEEL SAD BECAUSE A LEAF FELL?
SCHULZ

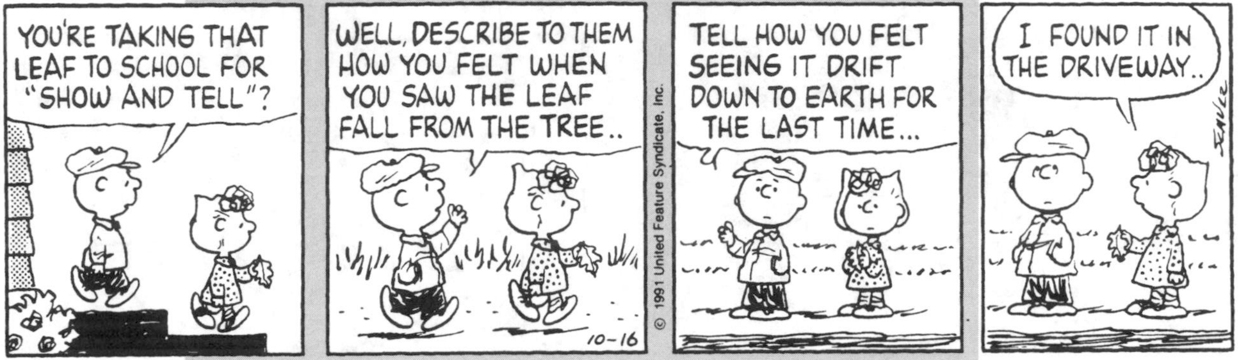
YOU'RE TAKING THAT LEAF TO SCHOOL FOR "SHOW AND TELL"?
WELL, DESCRIBE TO THEM HOW YOU FELT WHEN YOU SAW THE LEAF FALL FROM THE TREE..
10-16
© 1991 United Feature Syndicate, Inc.
TELL HOW YOU FELT SEEING IT DRIFT DOWN TO EARTH FOR THE LAST TIME...
I FOUND IT IN THE DRIVEWAY..

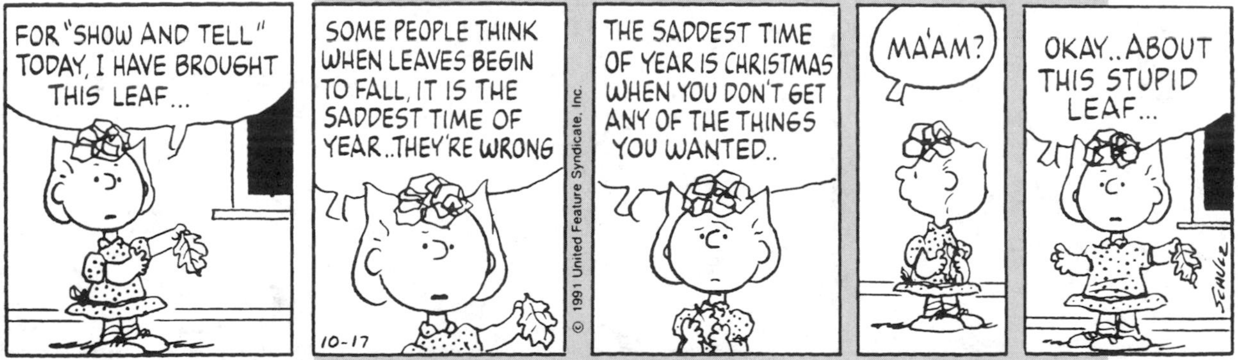
FOR "SHOW AND TELL" TODAY, I HAVE BROUGHT THIS LEAF...
SOME PEOPLE THINK WHEN LEAVES BEGIN TO FALL, IT IS THE SADDEST TIME OF YEAR..THEY'RE WRONG
10-17
© 1991 United Feature Syndicate, Inc.
THE SADDEST TIME OF YEAR IS CHRISTMAS WHEN YOU DON'T GET ANY OF THE THINGS YOU WANTED..
MA'AM?
OKAY..ABOUT THIS STUPID LEAF...

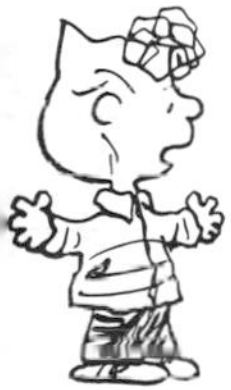

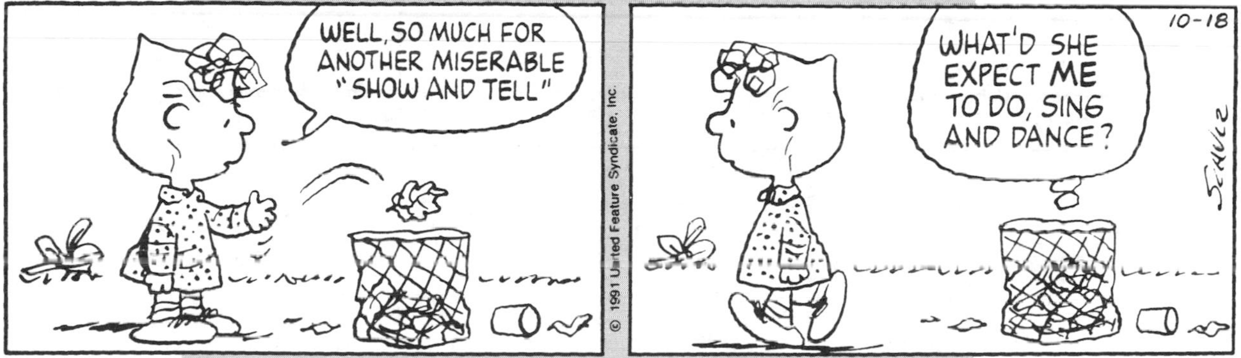
WELL, SO MUCH FOR ANOTHER MISERABLE "SHOW AND TELL"
© 1991 United Feature Syndicate, Inc.
10-18
WHAT'D SHE EXPECT ME TO DO, SING AND DANCE?

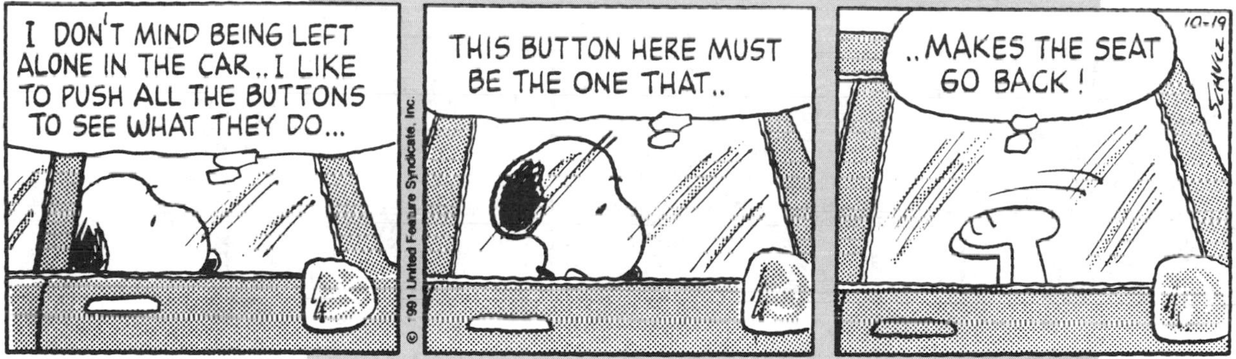
I DON'T MIND BEING LEFT ALONE IN THE CAR.. I LIKE TO PUSH ALL THE BUTTONS TO SEE WHAT THEY DO...
© 1991 United Feature Syndicate, Inc.
THIS BUTTON HERE MUST BE THE ONE THAT..
10-19
..MAKES THE SEAT GO BACK!

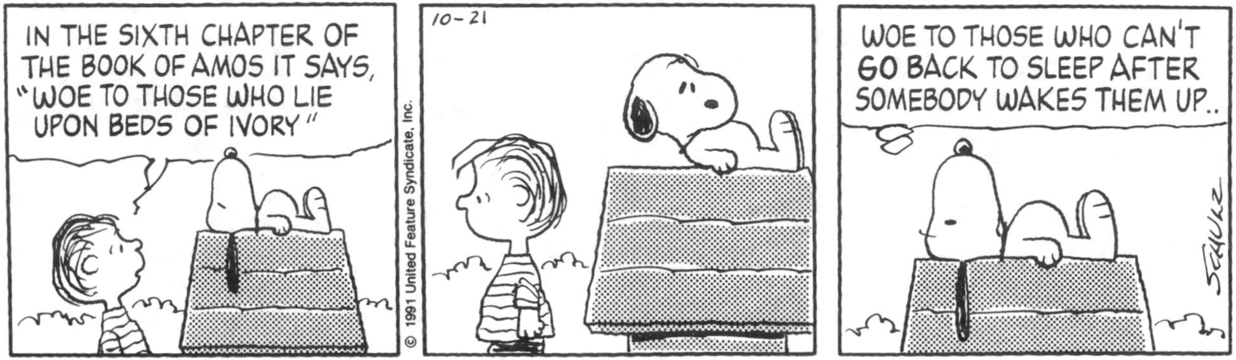
IN THE SIXTH CHAPTER OF THE BOOK OF AMOS IT SAYS, "WOE TO THOSE WHO LIE UPON BEDS OF IVORY"
© 1991 United Feature Syndicate, Inc.
10-21
WOE TO THOSE WHO CAN'T GO BACK TO SLEEP AFTER SOMEBODY WAKES THEM UP..
SCHULZ

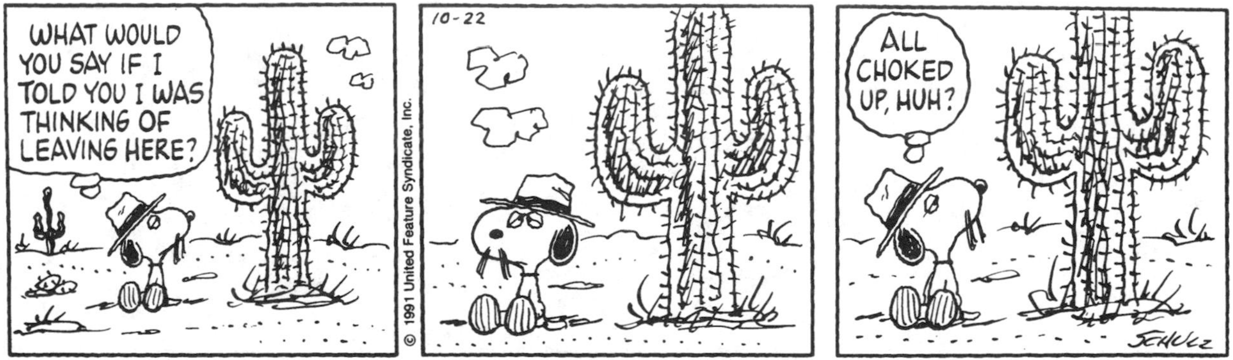
WHAT WOULD YOU SAY IF I TOLD YOU I WAS THINKING OF LEAVING HERE?
© 1991 United Feature Syndicate, Inc.
10-22
ALL CHOKED UP, HUH?
SCHULZ

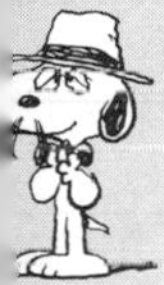

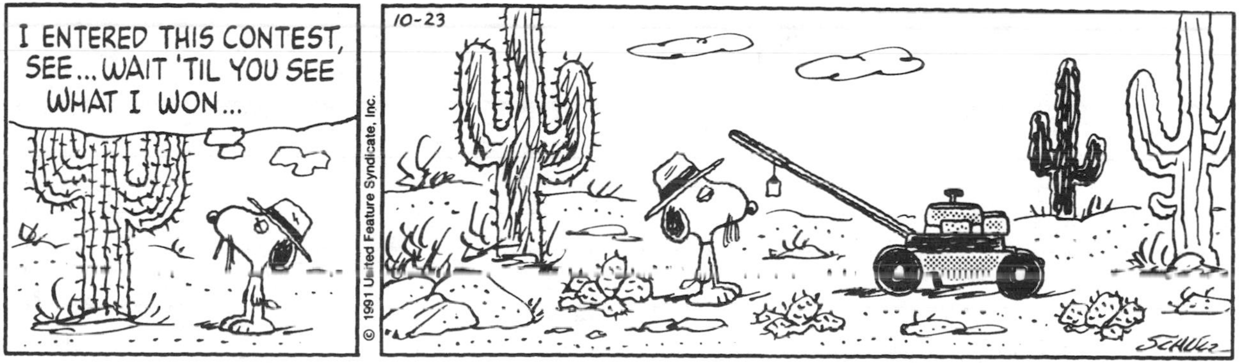

I ENTERED THIS CONTEST, SEE... WAIT 'TIL YOU SEE WHAT I WON...
© 1991 United Feature Syndicate, Inc.
10-23
SCHULZ

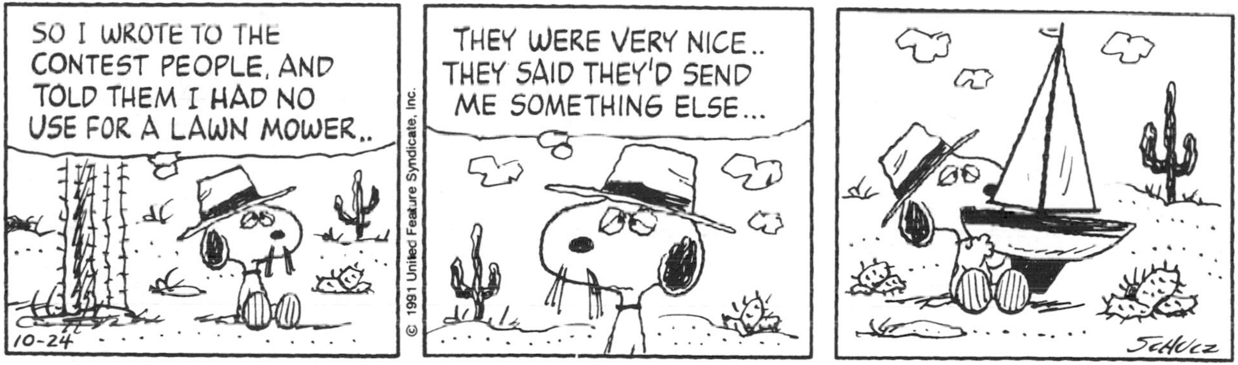

SO I WROTE TO THE CONTEST PEOPLE, AND TOLD THEM I HAD NO USE FOR A LAWN MOWER..
10-24
© 1991 United Feature Syndicate, Inc.
THEY WERE VERY NICE.. THEY SAID THEY'D SEND ME SOMETHING ELSE...
SCHULZ

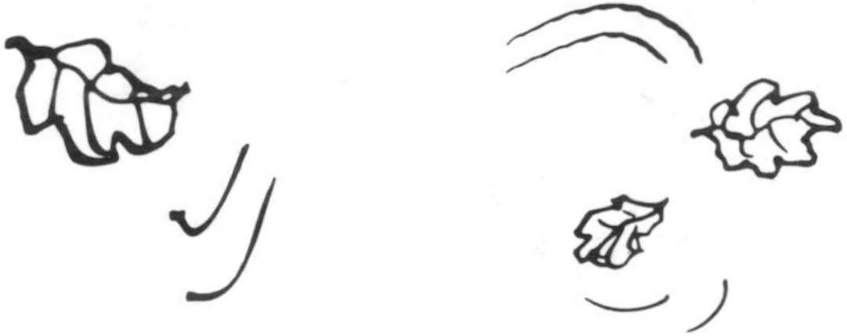

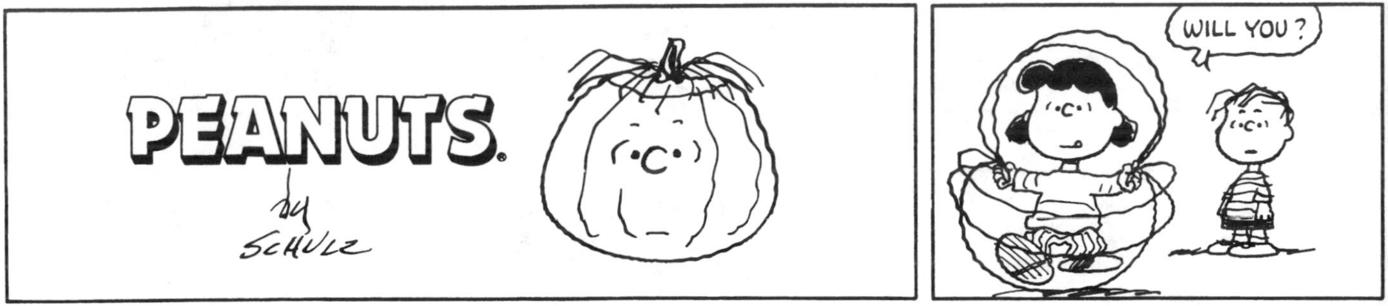
PEANUTS
by SCHULZ
WILL YOU?

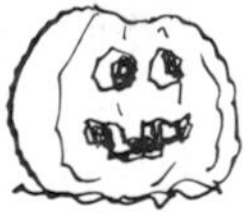

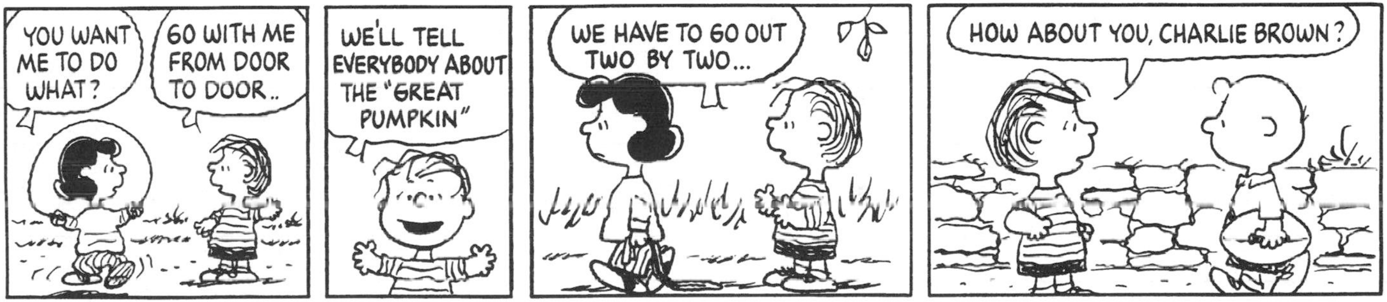
YOU WANT ME TO DO WHAT?
GO WITH ME FROM DOOR TO DOOR..
WE'LL TELL EVERYBODY ABOUT THE "GREAT PUMPKIN"
WE HAVE TO GO OUT TWO BY TWO...
HOW ABOUT YOU, CHARLIE BROWN?

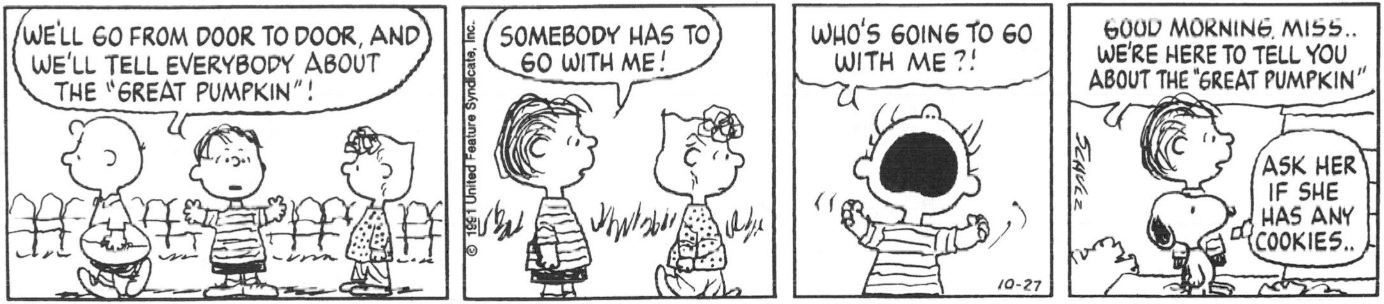
WE'LL GO FROM DOOR TO DOOR, AND WE'LL TELL EVERYBODY ABOUT THE "GREAT PUMPKIN"!
© 1991 United Feature Syndicate, Inc.
SOMEBODY HAS TO GO WITH ME!
WHO'S GOING TO GO WITH ME?!
10-27
GOOD MORNING, MISS.. WE'RE HERE TO TELL YOU ABOUT THE "GREAT PUMPKIN"
SCHULZ
ASK HER IF SHE HAS ANY COOKIES..

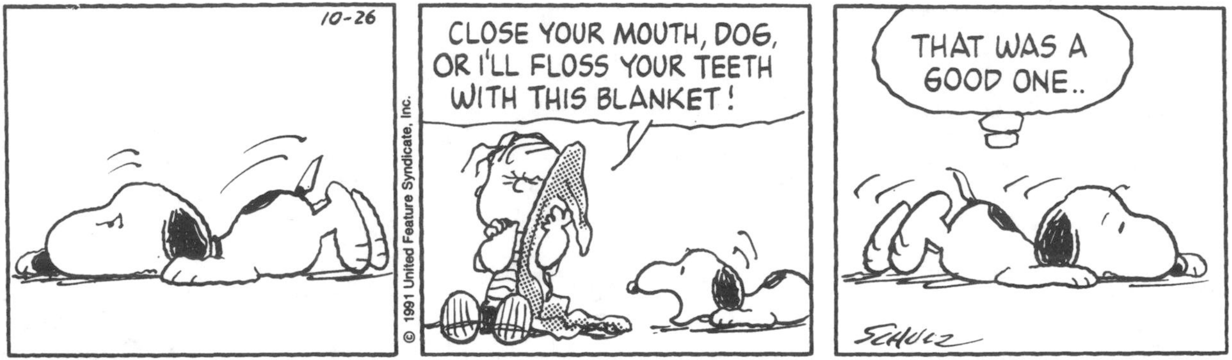
10-26
© 1991 United Feature Syndicate, Inc.
CLOSE YOUR MOUTH, DOG, OR I'LL FLOSS YOUR TEETH WITH THIS BLANKET!
THAT WAS A GOOD ONE..
SCHULZ

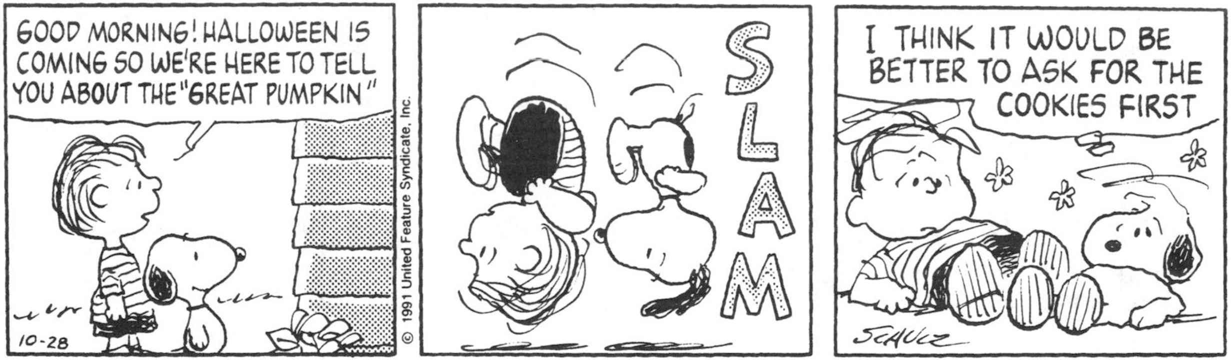
GOOD MORNING! HALLOWEEN IS COMING SO WE'RE HERE TO TELL YOU ABOUT THE "GREAT PUMPKIN"
10-28
© 1991 United Feature Syndicate, Inc.
SLAM
I THINK IT WOULD BE BETTER TO ASK FOR THE COOKIES FIRST
SCHULZ

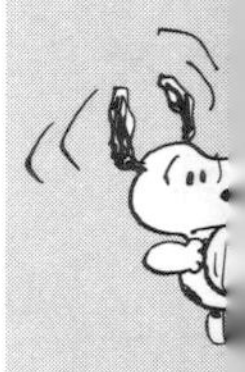

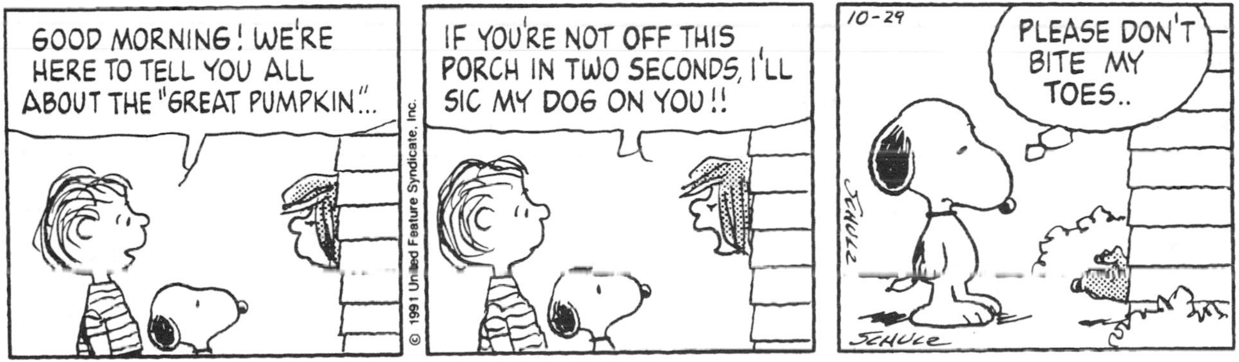
GOOD MORNING! WE'RE HERE TO TELL YOU ALL ABOUT THE "GREAT PUMPKIN"...
© 1991 United Feature Syndicate, Inc.
IF YOU'RE NOT OFF THIS PORCH IN TWO SECONDS, I'LL SIC MY DOG ON YOU!!
10-29
PLEASE DON'T BITE MY TOES..
SCHULZ

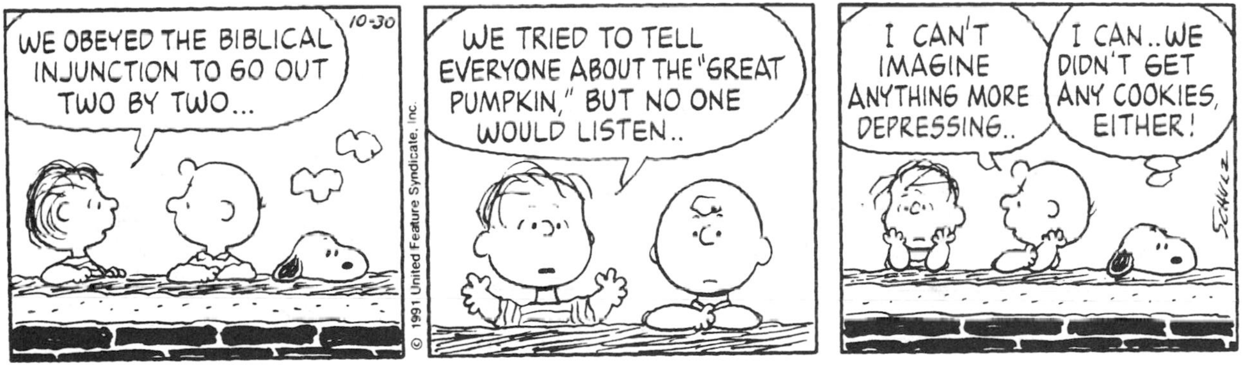
10-30
WE OBEYED THE BIBLICAL INJUNCTION TO GO OUT TWO BY TWO...
© 1991 United Feature Syndicate, Inc.
WE TRIED TO TELL EVERYONE ABOUT THE "GREAT PUMPKIN," BUT NO ONE WOULD LISTEN..
I CAN'T IMAGINE ANYTHING MORE DEPRESSING..
I CAN..WE DIDN'T GET ANY COOKIES, EITHER!
SCHULZ

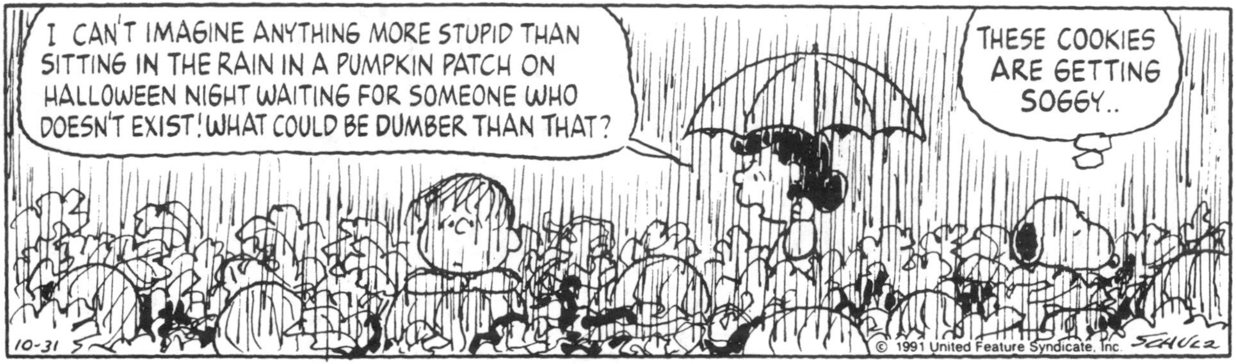
I CAN'T IMAGINE ANYTHING MORE STUPID THAN SITTING IN THE RAIN IN A PUMPKIN PATCH ON HALLOWEEN NIGHT WAITING FOR SOMEONE WHO DOESN'T EXIST! WHAT COULD BE DUMBER THAN THAT?
THESE COOKIES ARE GETTING SOGGY..
10-31
© 1991 United Feature Syndicate, Inc.
SCHULZ

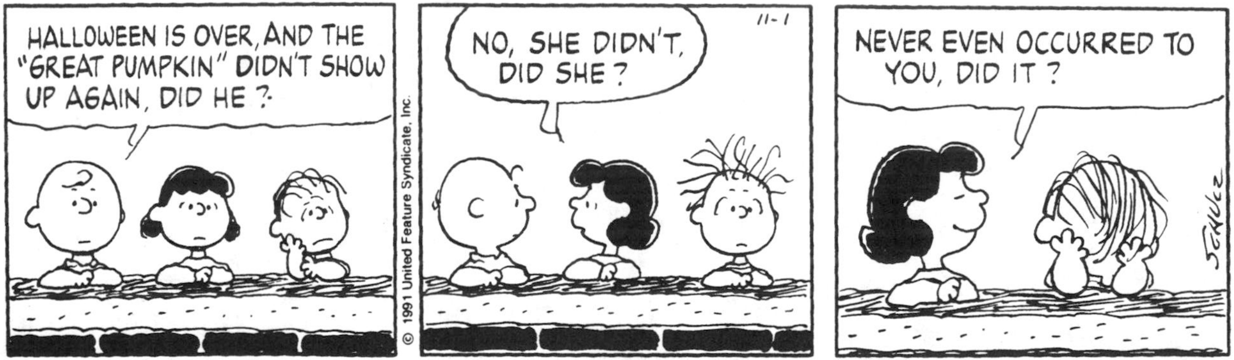
HALLOWEEN IS OVER, AND THE "GREAT PUMPKIN" DIDN'T SHOW UP AGAIN, DID HE?
© 1991 United Feature Syndicate, Inc.
11-1
NO, SHE DIDN'T, DID SHE?
NEVER EVEN OCCURRED TO YOU, DID IT?
SCHULZ

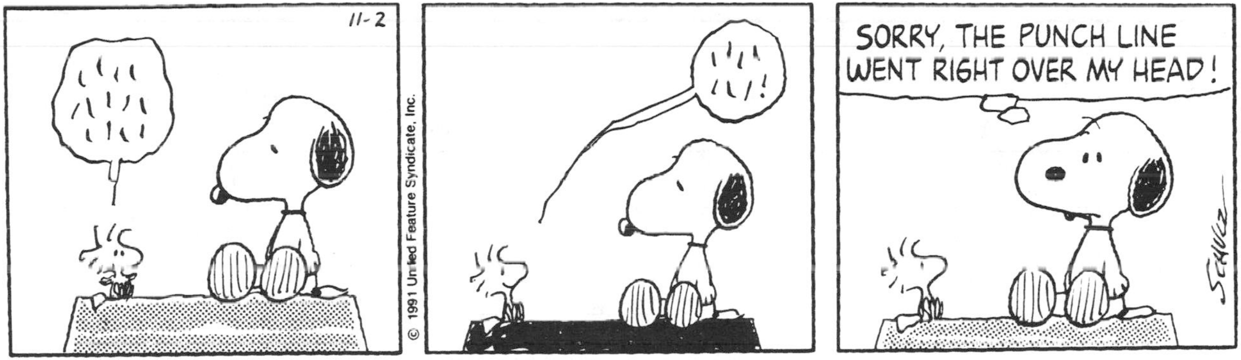
11-2
© 1991 United Feature Syndicate, Inc.
SORRY, THE PUNCH LINE WENT RIGHT OVER MY HEAD!
SCHULZ

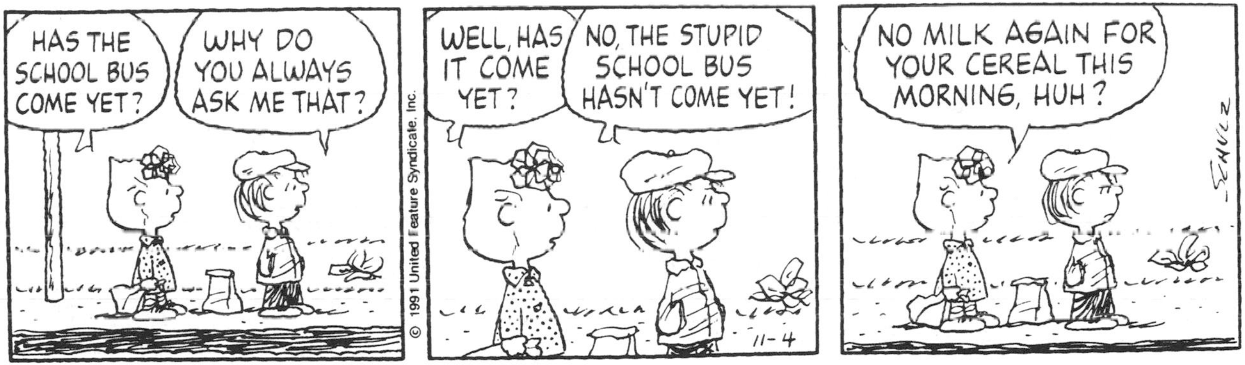
HAS THE SCHOOL BUS COME YET?
WHY DO YOU ALWAYS ASK ME THAT?
© 1991 United Feature Syndicate, Inc.
WELL, HAS IT COME YET?
NO, THE STUPID SCHOOL BUS HASN'T COME YET!
11-4
NO MILK AGAIN FOR YOUR CEREAL THIS MORNING, HUH?
SCHULZ

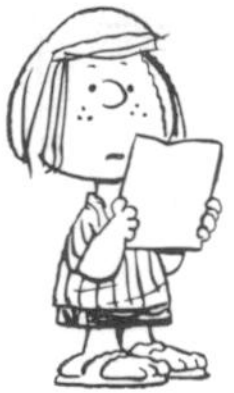

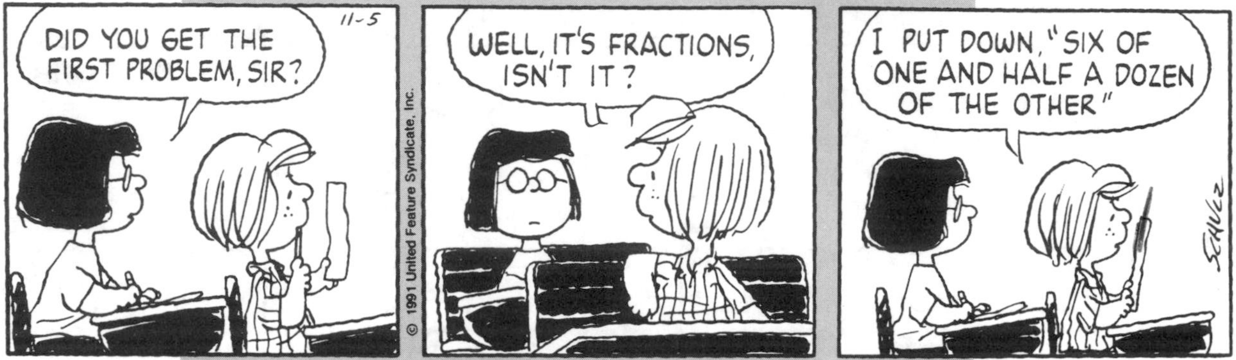
11-5
DID YOU GET THE FIRST PROBLEM, SIR?
© 1991 United Feature Syndicate, Inc.
WELL, IT'S FRACTIONS, ISN'T IT?
I PUT DOWN, "SIX OF ONE AND HALF A DOZEN OF THE OTHER"

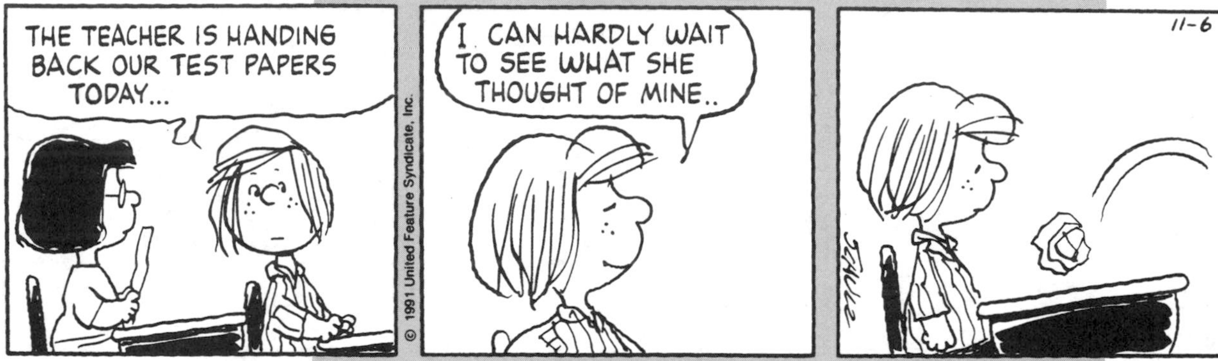
THE TEACHER IS HANDING BACK OUR TEST PAPERS TODAY...
© 1991 United Feature Syndicate, Inc.
I CAN HARDLY WAIT TO SEE WHAT SHE THOUGHT OF MINE..
11-6

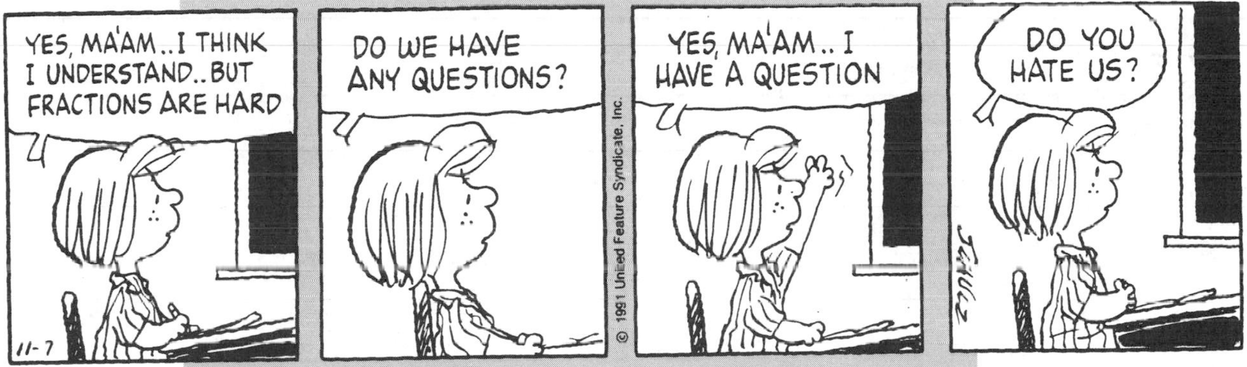
YES, MA'AM..I THINK I UNDERSTAND..BUT FRACTIONS ARE HARD
11-7
DO WE HAVE ANY QUESTIONS?
© 1991 United Feature Syndicate, Inc.
YES, MA'AM.. I HAVE A QUESTION
DO YOU HATE US?
SCHULZ

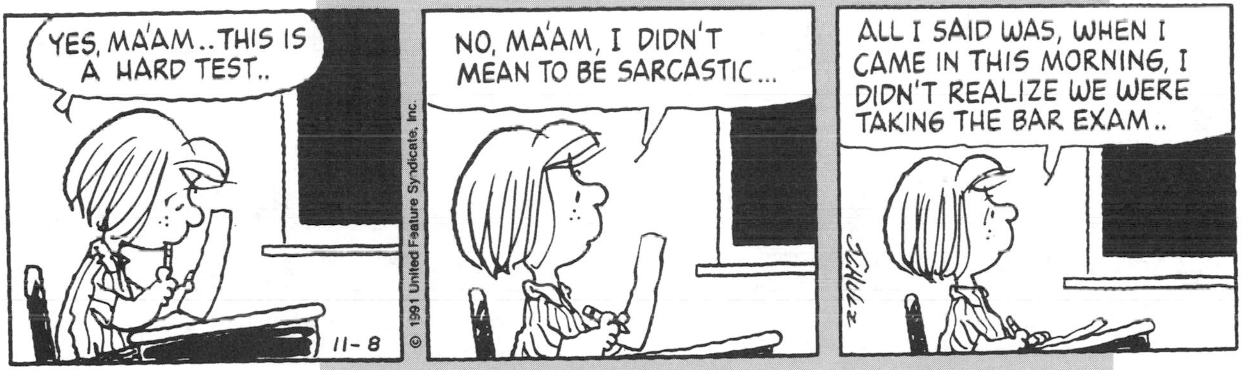
YES, MA'AM..THIS IS A HARD TEST..
11-8
© 1991 United Feature Syndicate, Inc.
NO, MA'AM, I DIDN'T MEAN TO BE SARCASTIC...
ALL I SAID WAS, WHEN I CAME IN THIS MORNING, I DIDN'T REALIZE WE WERE TAKING THE BAR EXAM..
SCHULZ

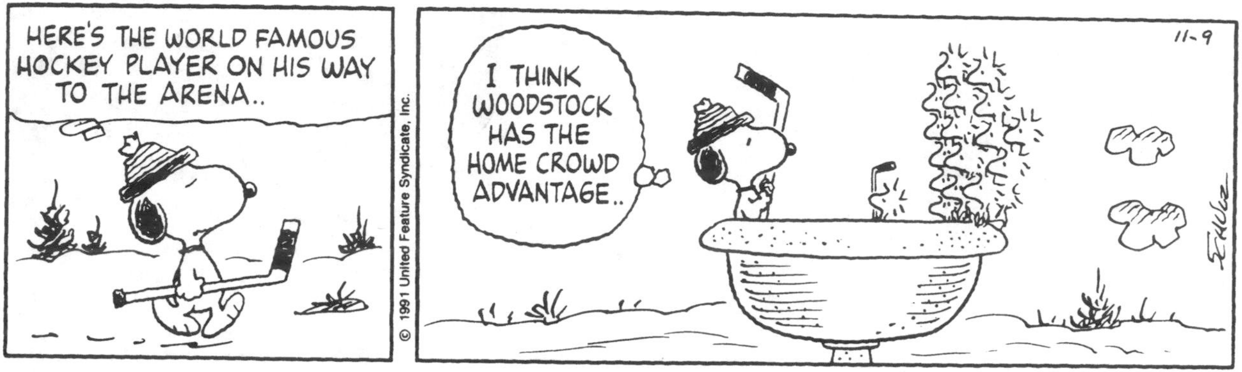
HERE'S THE WORLD FAMOUS HOCKEY PLAYER ON HIS WAY TO THE ARENA..
© 1991 United Feature Syndicate, Inc.
11-9
I THINK WOODSTOCK HAS THE HOME CROWD ADVANTAGE..
SCHULZ

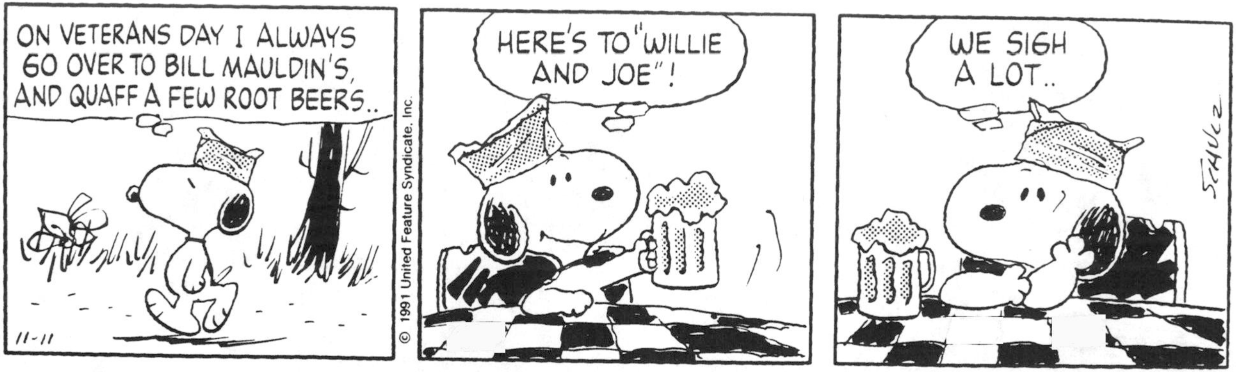
ON VETERANS DAY I ALWAYS GO OVER TO BILL MAULDIN'S, AND QUAFF A FEW ROOT BEERS..
11-11
© 1991 United Feature Syndicate, Inc.
HERE'S TO "WILLIE AND JOE"!
WE SIGH A LOT..
SCHULZ

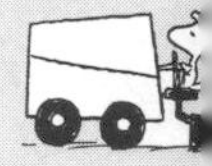

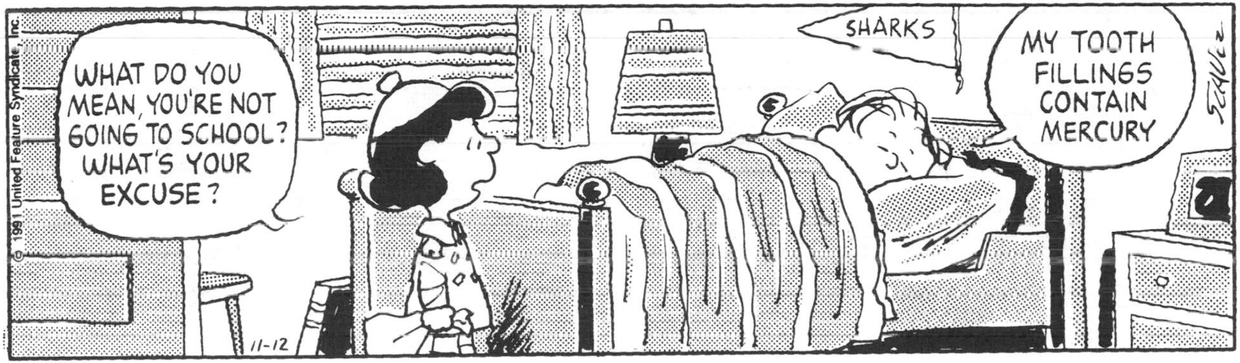
© 1991 United Feature Syndicate, Inc.
WHAT DO YOU MEAN, YOU'RE NOT GOING TO SCHOOL? WHAT'S YOUR EXCUSE?
SHARKS
MY TOOTH FILLINGS CONTAIN MERCURY
SCHULZ
11-12

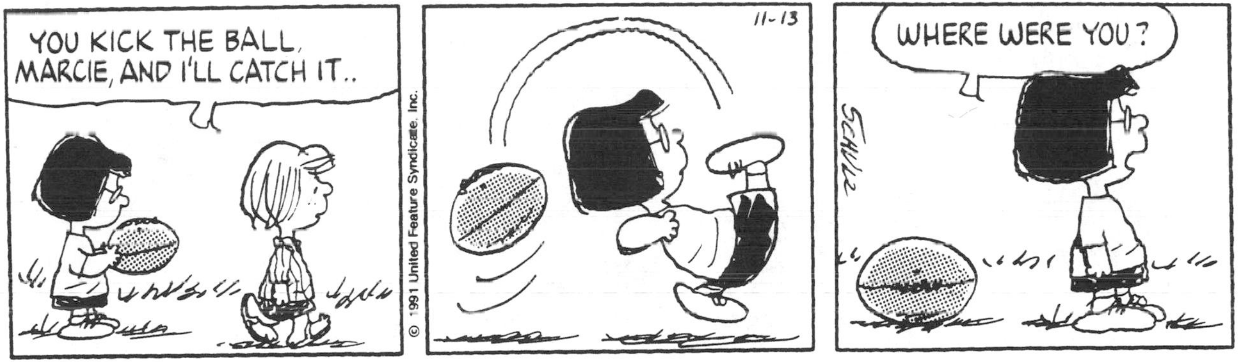
YOU KICK THE BALL, MARCIE, AND I'LL CATCH IT..
© 1991 United Feature Syndicate, Inc.
11-13
SCHULZ
WHERE WERE YOU?

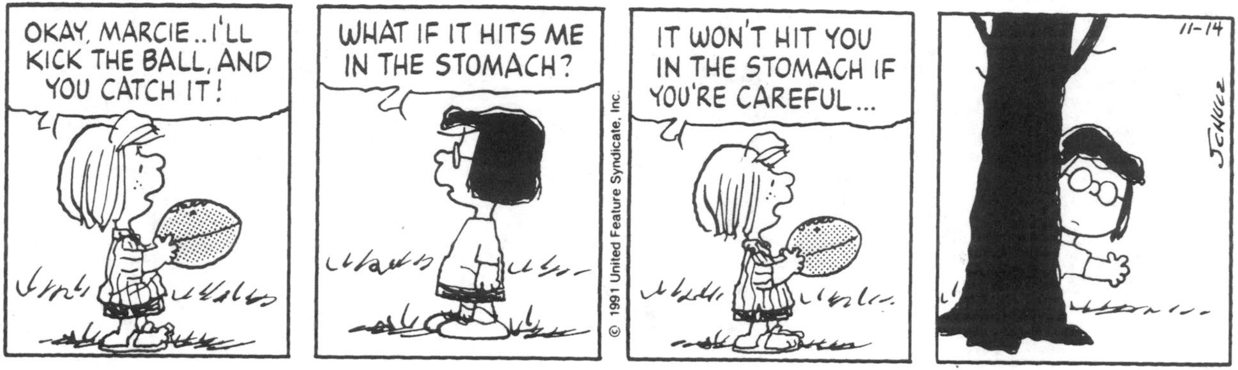
OKAY, MARCIE.. I'LL KICK THE BALL, AND YOU CATCH IT!
WHAT IF IT HITS ME IN THE STOMACH?
IT WON'T HIT YOU IN THE STOMACH IF YOU'RE CAREFUL...
11-14
SCHULZ

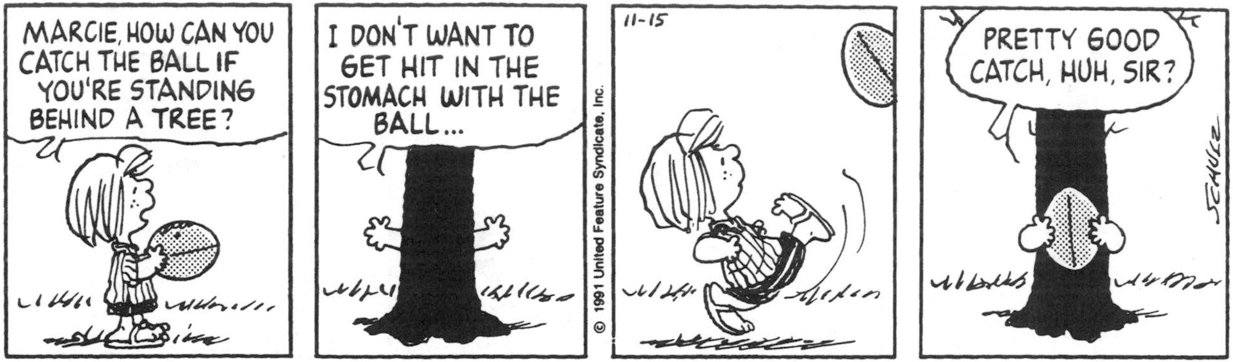
MARCIE, HOW CAN YOU CATCH THE BALL IF YOU'RE STANDING BEHIND A TREE?
I DON'T WANT TO GET HIT IN THE STOMACH WITH THE BALL...
11-15
PRETTY GOOD CATCH, HUH, SIR?
SCHULZ

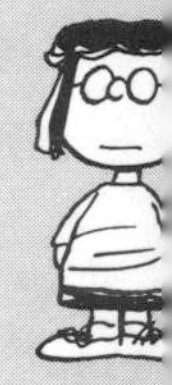

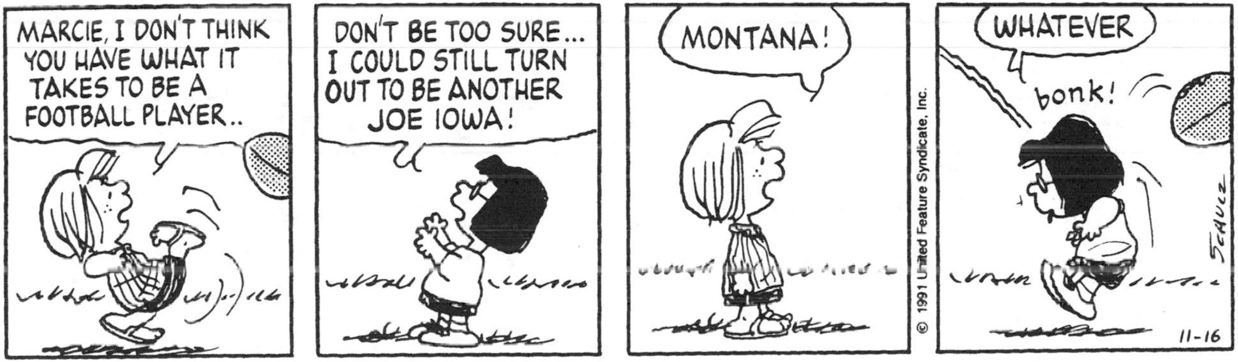
MARCIE, I DON'T THINK YOU HAVE WHAT IT TAKES TO BE A FOOTBALL PLAYER..
DON'T BE TOO SURE... I COULD STILL TURN OUT TO BE ANOTHER JOE IOWA!
MONTANA!
WHATEVER
bonk!
© 1991 United Feature Syndicate, Inc.
SCHULZ
11-16

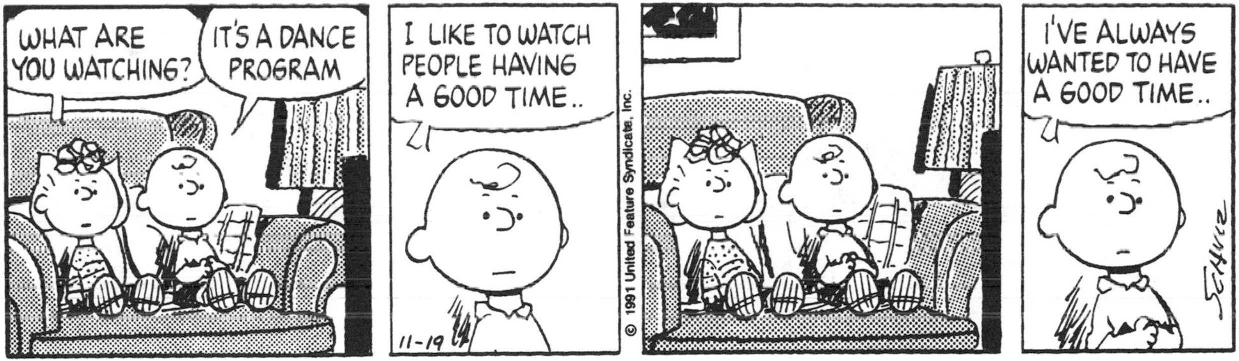
WHAT ARE YOU WATCHING?
IT'S A DANCE PROGRAM
I LIKE TO WATCH PEOPLE HAVING A GOOD TIME..
11-19
© 1991 United Feature Syndicate, Inc.
I'VE ALWAYS WANTED TO HAVE A GOOD TIME..
SCHULZ

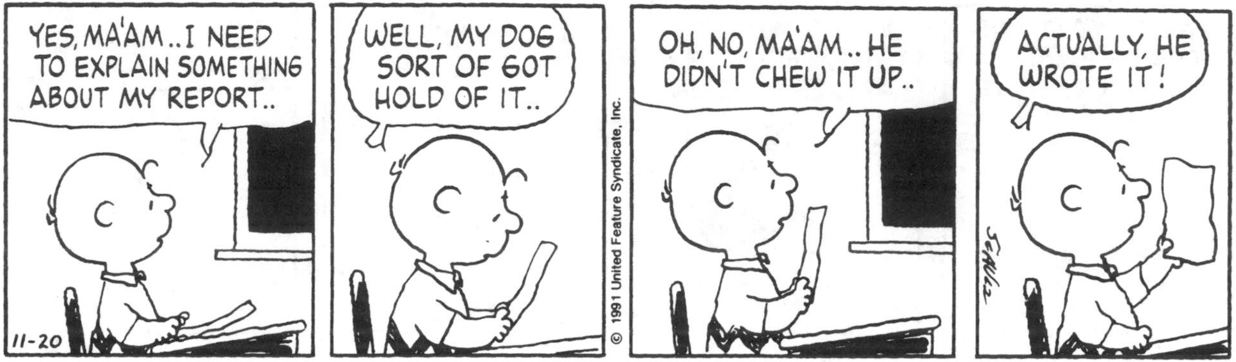
YES, MA'AM.. I NEED TO EXPLAIN SOMETHING ABOUT MY REPORT..
11-20
WELL, MY DOG SORT OF GOT HOLD OF IT..
© 1991 United Feature Syndicate, Inc.
OH, NO, MA'AM.. HE DIDN'T CHEW IT UP..
ACTUALLY, HE WROTE IT!
SCHULZ

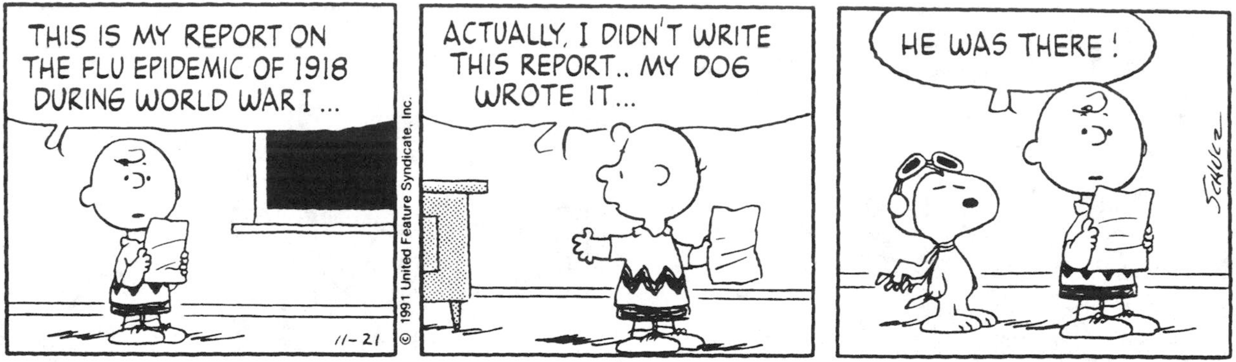
THIS IS MY REPORT ON THE FLU EPIDEMIC OF 1918 DURING WORLD WAR I ...
11-21
© 1991 United Feature Syndicate, Inc.
ACTUALLY, I DIDN'T WRITE THIS REPORT.. MY DOG WROTE IT...
HE WAS THERE!
SCHULZ

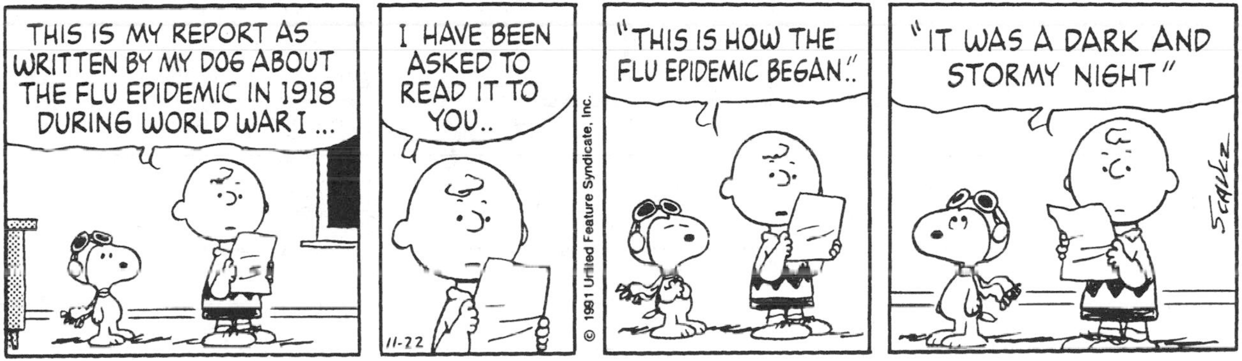
THIS IS MY REPORT AS WRITTEN BY MY DOG ABOUT THE FLU EPIDEMIC IN 1918 DURING WORLD WAR I ...
I HAVE BEEN ASKED TO READ IT TO YOU..
11-22
© 1991 United Feature Syndicate, Inc.
"THIS IS HOW THE FLU EPIDEMIC BEGAN."
"IT WAS A DARK AND STORMY NIGHT"
SCHULZ

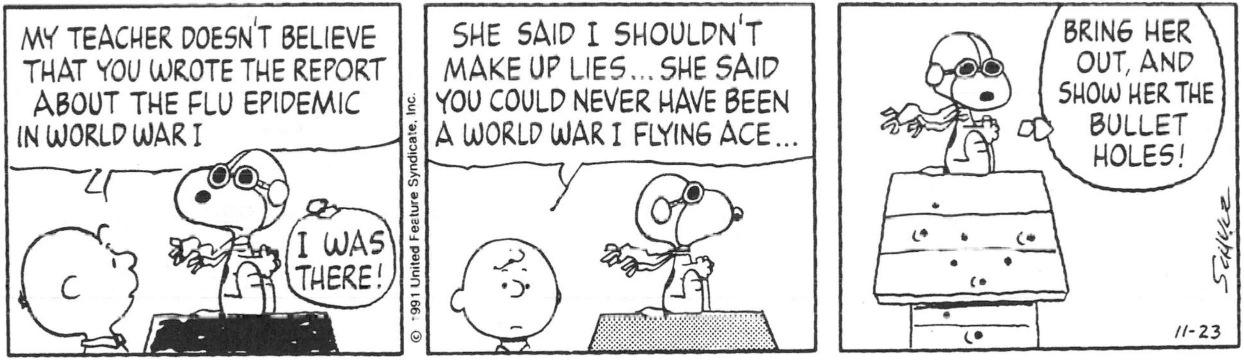
MY TEACHER DOESN'T BELIEVE THAT YOU WROTE THE REPORT ABOUT THE FLU EPIDEMIC IN WORLD WAR I
I WAS THERE!
© 1991 United Feature Syndicate, Inc.
SHE SAID I SHOULDN'T MAKE UP LIES... SHE SAID YOU COULD NEVER HAVE BEEN A WORLD WAR I FLYING ACE...
BRING HER OUT, AND SHOW HER THE BULLET HOLES!
SCHULZ
11-23

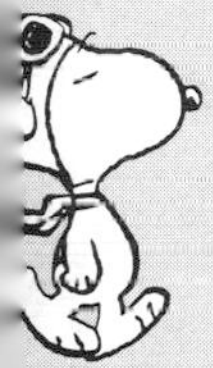

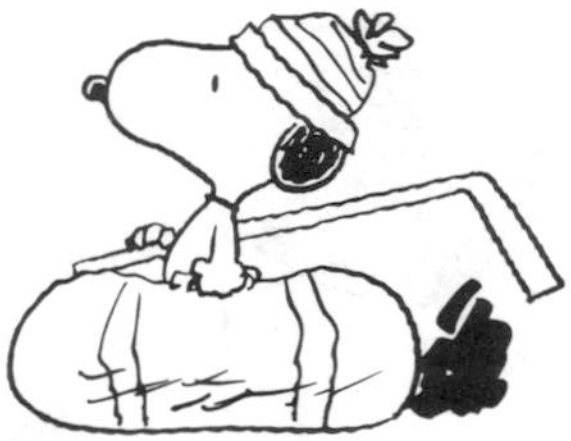

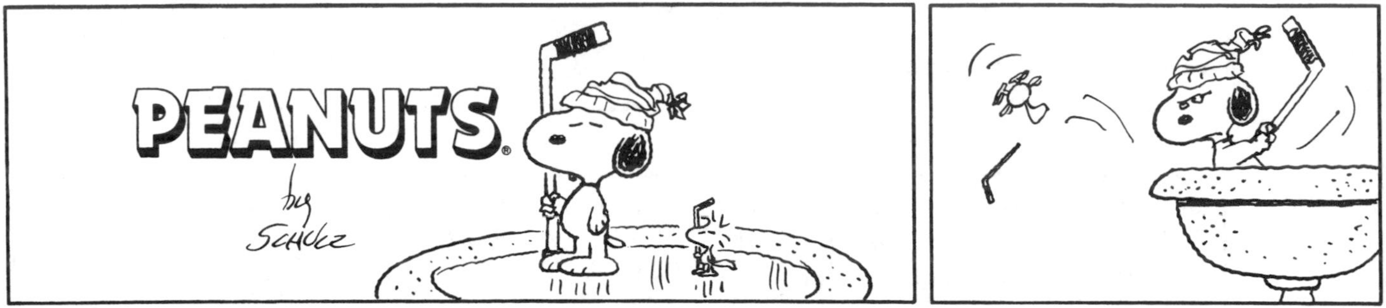
PEANUTS®
by SCHULZ

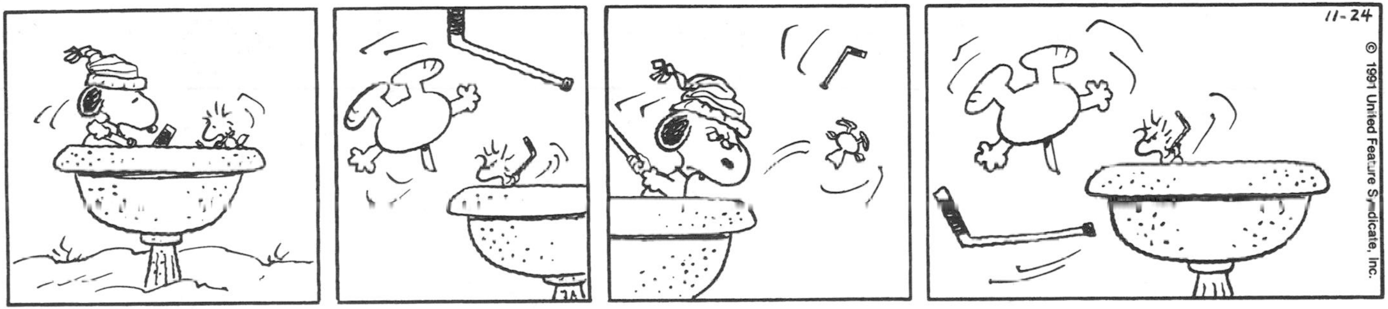
11-24
© 1991 United Feature Syndicate, Inc.

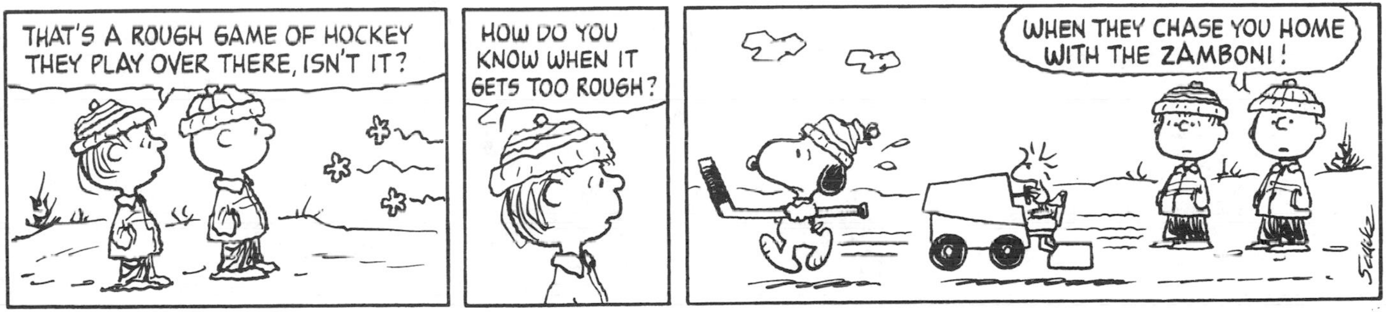
THAT'S A ROUGH GAME OF HOCKEY THEY PLAY OVER THERE, ISN'T IT?
HOW DO YOU KNOW WHEN IT GETS TOO ROUGH?
WHEN THEY CHASE YOU HOME WITH THE ZAMBONI!
SCHULZ

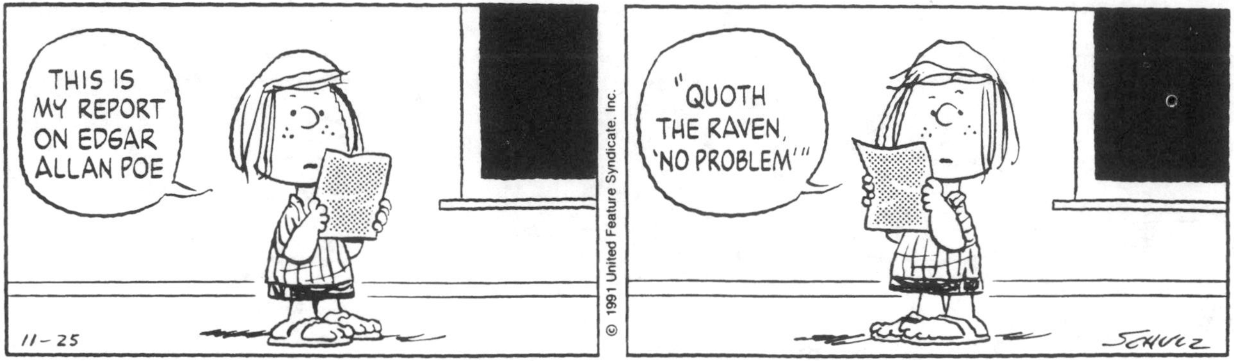

THIS IS MY REPORT ON EDGAR ALLAN POE
"QUOTH THE RAVEN, 'NO PROBLEM'"
11-25
© 1991 United Feature Syndicate, Inc.
SCHULZ

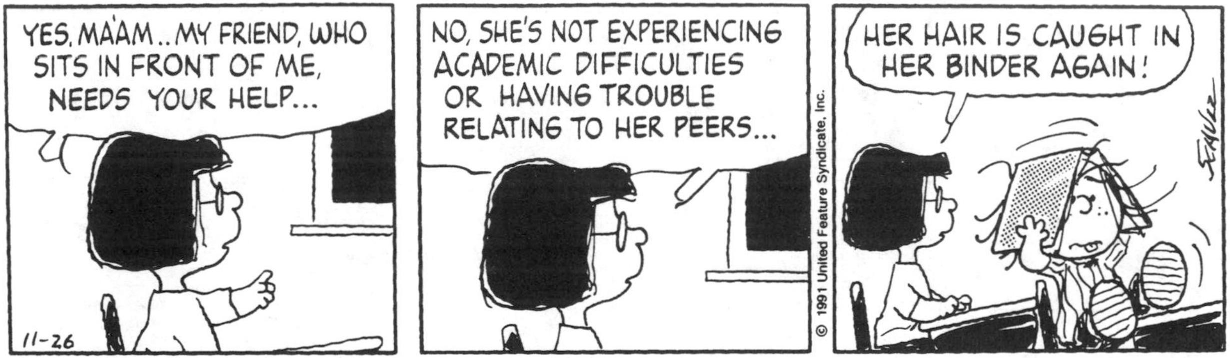

YES, MA'AM.. MY FRIEND, WHO SITS IN FRONT OF ME, NEEDS YOUR HELP...
NO, SHE'S NOT EXPERIENCING ACADEMIC DIFFICULTIES OR HAVING TROUBLE RELATING TO HER PEERS...
HER HAIR IS CAUGHT IN HER BINDER AGAIN!
11-26
© 1991 United Feature Syndicate, Inc.
SCHULZ

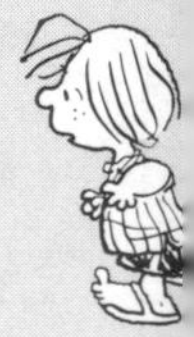

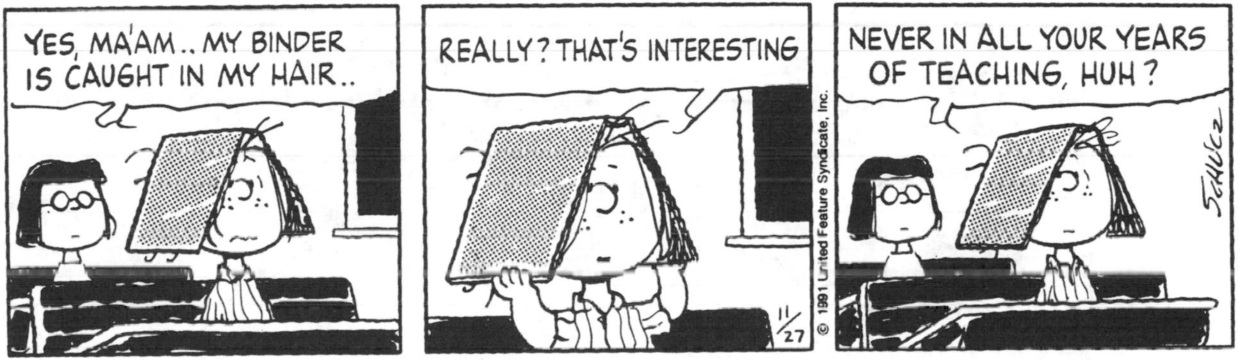
YES, MA'AM.. MY BINDER IS CAUGHT IN MY HAIR..
REALLY? THAT'S INTERESTING
11/27
© 1991 United Feature Syndicate, Inc.
NEVER IN ALL YOUR YEARS OF TEACHING, HUH?
SCHULZ

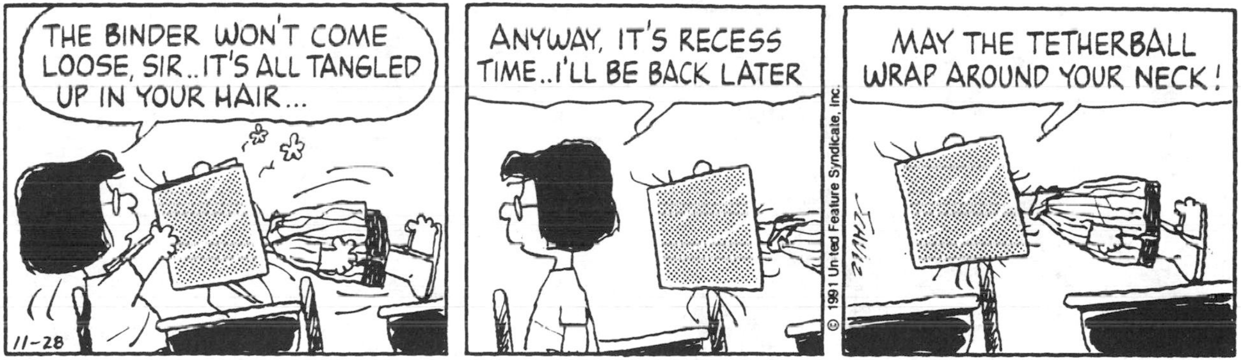
THE BINDER WON'T COME LOOSE, SIR.. IT'S ALL TANGLED UP IN YOUR HAIR...
11-28
ANYWAY, IT'S RECESS TIME.. I'LL BE BACK LATER
© 1991 United Feature Syndicate, Inc.
MAY THE TETHERBALL WRAP AROUND YOUR NECK!
SCHULZ

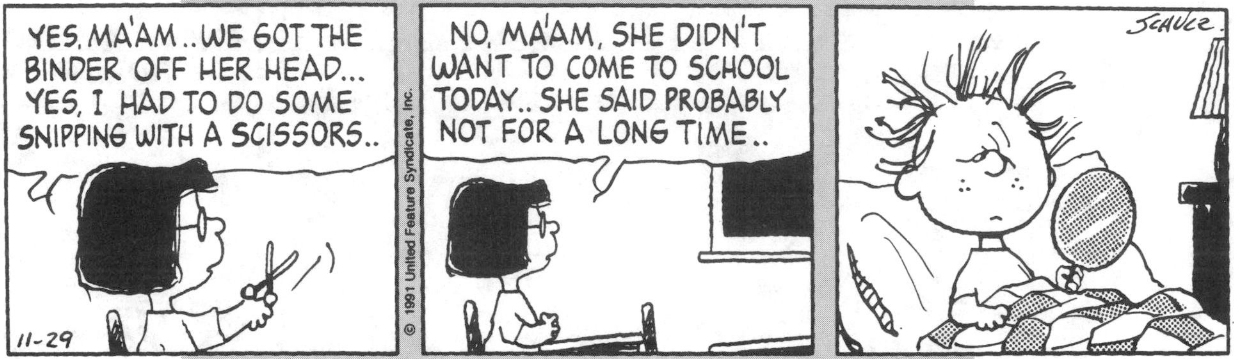
YES, MA'AM.. WE GOT THE BINDER OFF HER HEAD... YES, I HAD TO DO SOME SNIPPING WITH A SCISSORS..
11-29
© 1991 United Feature Syndicate, Inc.
NO, MA'AM, SHE DIDN'T WANT TO COME TO SCHOOL TODAY.. SHE SAID PROBABLY NOT FOR A LONG TIME..
SCHULZ

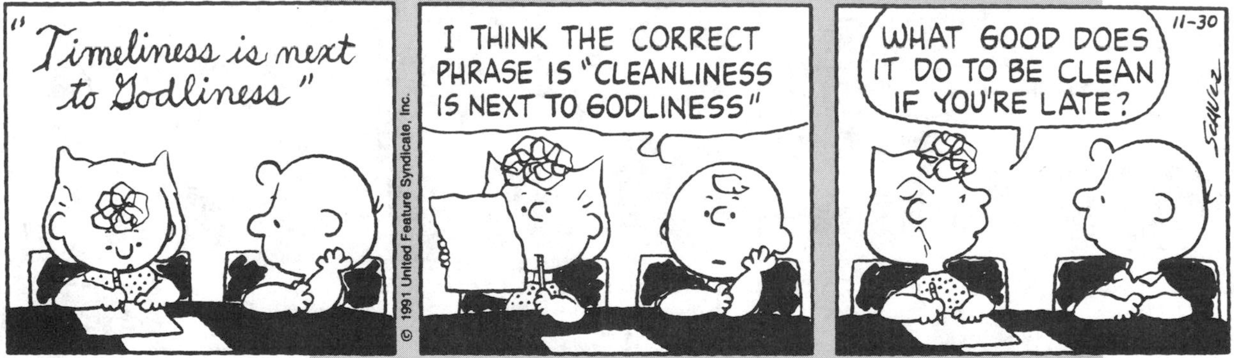
"Timeliness is next to Godliness"
© 1991 United Feature Syndicate, Inc.
I THINK THE CORRECT PHRASE IS "CLEANLINESS IS NEXT TO GODLINESS"
WHAT GOOD DOES IT DO TO BE CLEAN IF YOU'RE LATE?
11-30
SCHULZ

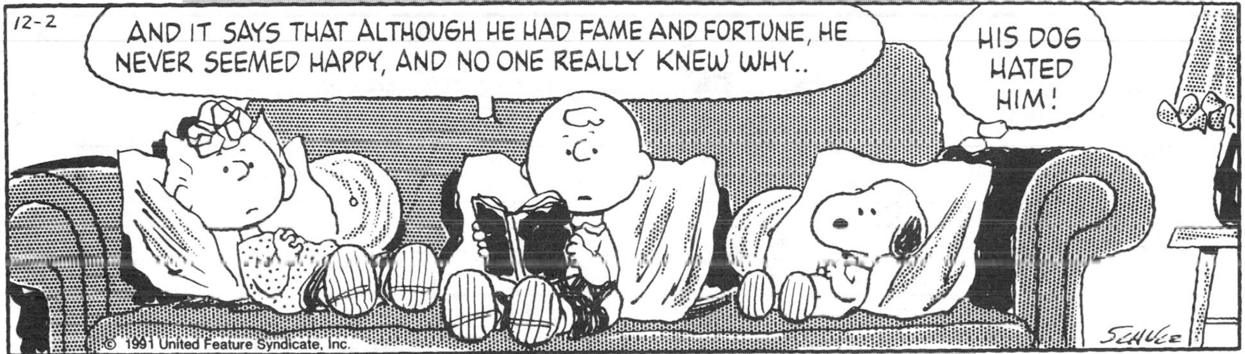
12-2
AND IT SAYS THAT ALTHOUGH HE HAD FAME AND FORTUNE, HE NEVER SEEMED HAPPY, AND NO ONE REALLY KNEW WHY..
HIS DOG HATED HIM!
© 1991 United Feature Syndicate, Inc.

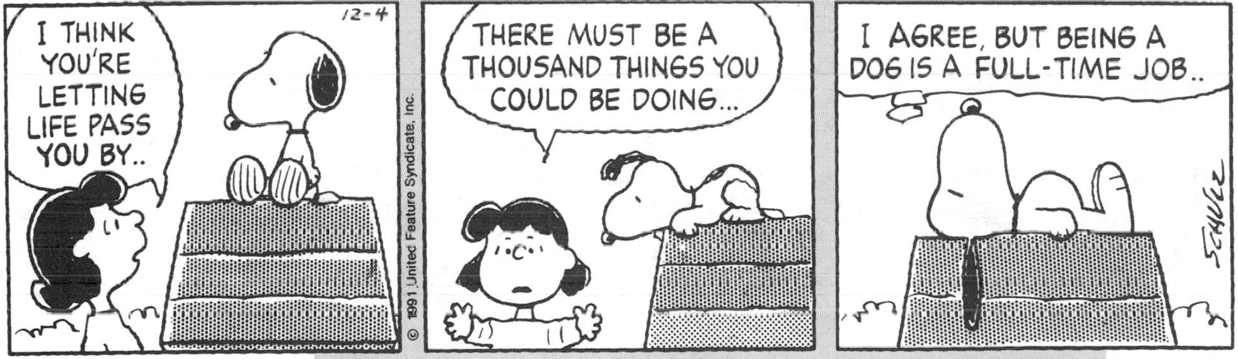
12-4
I THINK YOU'RE LETTING LIFE PASS YOU BY..
© 1991 United Feature Syndicate, Inc.
THERE MUST BE A THOUSAND THINGS YOU COULD BE DOING...
I AGREE, BUT BEING A DOG IS A FULL-TIME JOB..

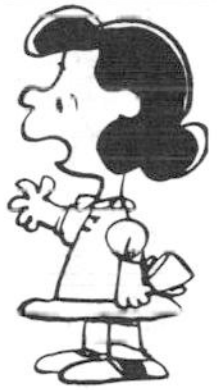

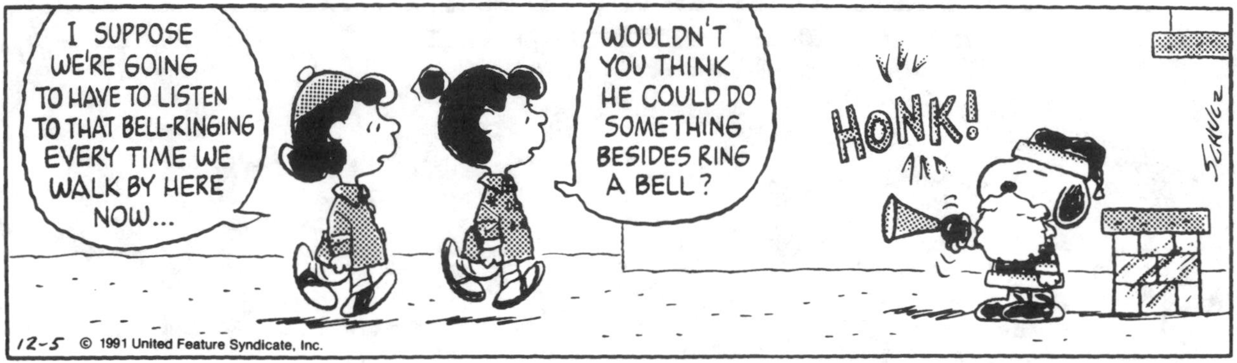
I SUPPOSE WE'RE GOING TO HAVE TO LISTEN TO THAT BELL-RINGING EVERY TIME WE WALK BY HERE NOW...
WOULDN'T YOU THINK HE COULD DO SOMETHING BESIDES RING A BELL?
HONK!
12-5 © 1991 United Feature Syndicate, Inc.

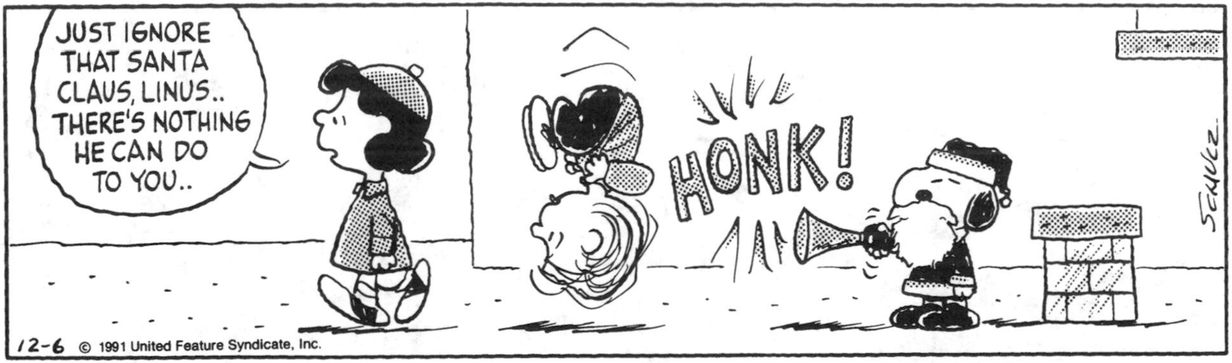
JUST IGNORE THAT SANTA CLAUS, LINUS.. THERE'S NOTHING HE CAN DO TO YOU..
HONK!
12-6 © 1991 United Feature Syndicate, Inc.

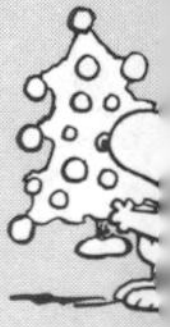

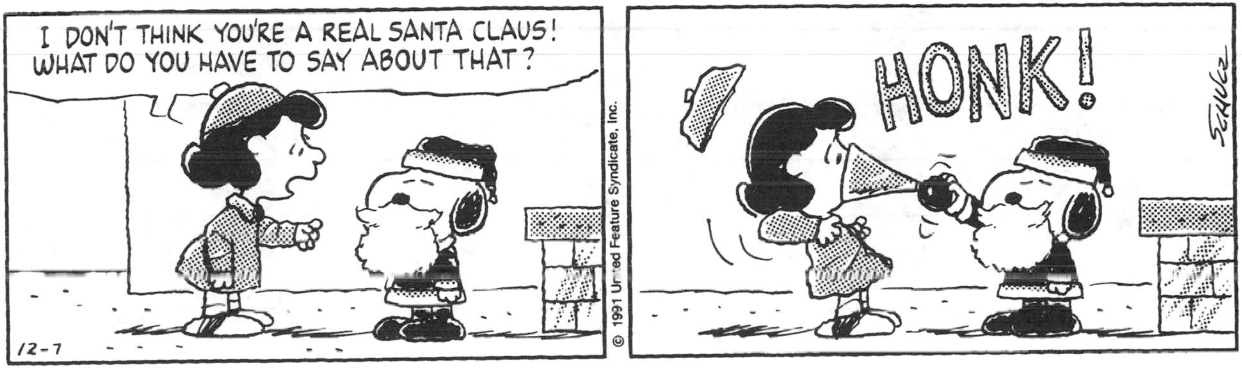
I DON'T THINK YOU'RE A REAL SANTA CLAUS! WHAT DO YOU HAVE TO SAY ABOUT THAT?
12-7
© 1991 United Feature Syndicate, Inc.
HONK!
SCHULZ

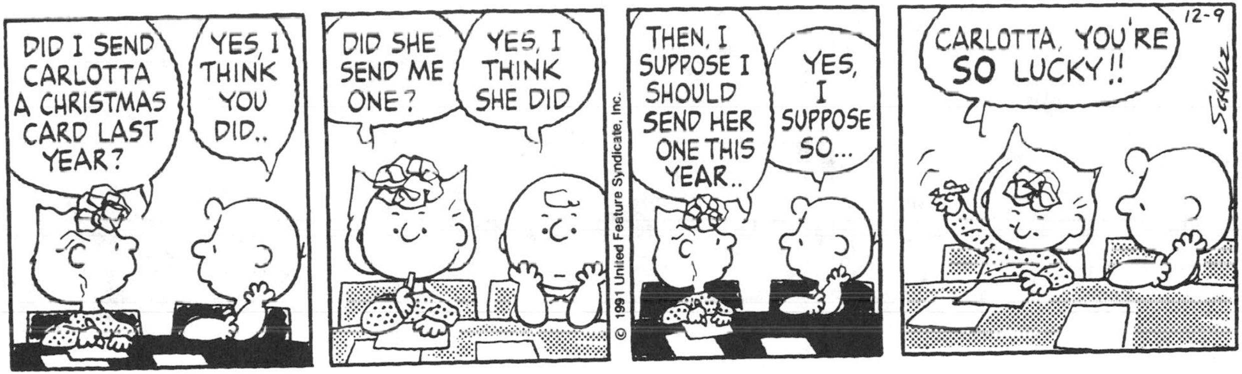
DID I SEND CARLOTTA A CHRISTMAS CARD LAST YEAR?
YES, I THINK YOU DID..
DID SHE SEND ME ONE?
YES, I THINK SHE DID
© 1991 United Feature Syndicate, Inc.
THEN, I SUPPOSE I SHOULD SEND HER ONE THIS YEAR..
YES, I SUPPOSE SO...
12-9
CARLOTTA, YOU'RE SO LUCKY!!
SCHULZ

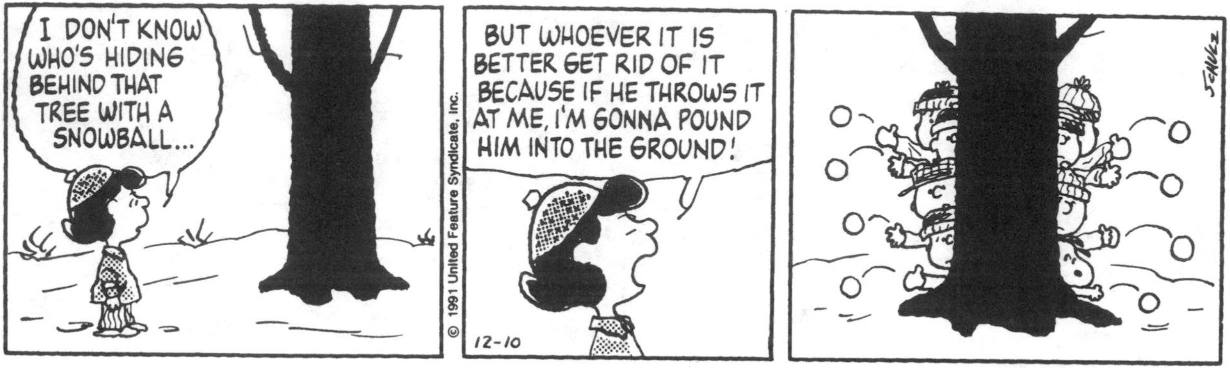
I DON'T KNOW WHO'S HIDING BEHIND THAT TREE WITH A SNOWBALL...
BUT WHOEVER IT IS BETTER GET RID OF IT BECAUSE IF HE THROWS IT AT ME, I'M GONNA POUND HIM INTO THE GROUND!
12-10
SCHULZ

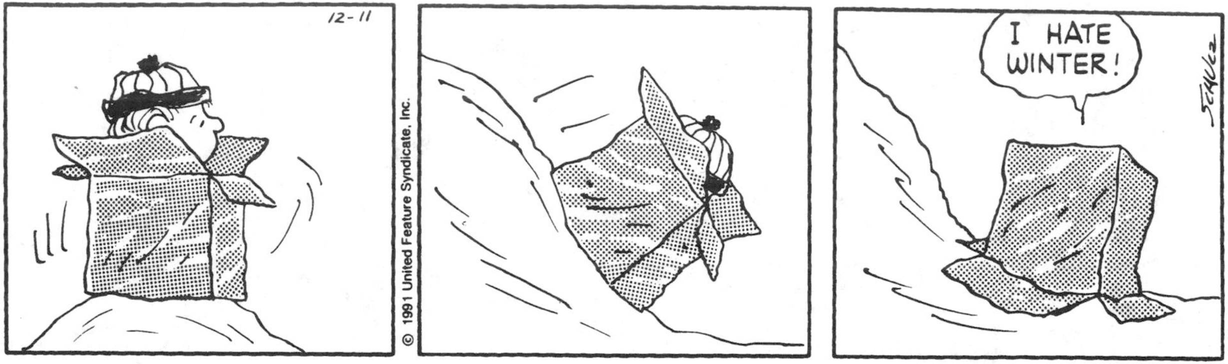
12-11
I HATE WINTER!
SCHULZ

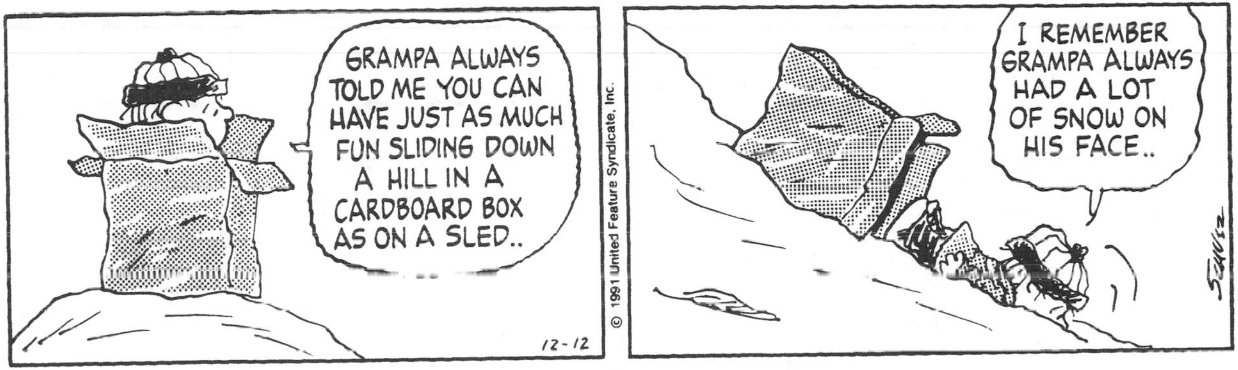
GRAMPA ALWAYS TOLD ME YOU CAN HAVE JUST AS MUCH FUN SLIDING DOWN A HILL IN A CARDBOARD BOX AS ON A SLED..
12-12
© 1991 United Feature Syndicate, Inc.
I REMEMBER GRAMPA ALWAYS HAD A LOT OF SNOW ON HIS FACE..
SCHULZ

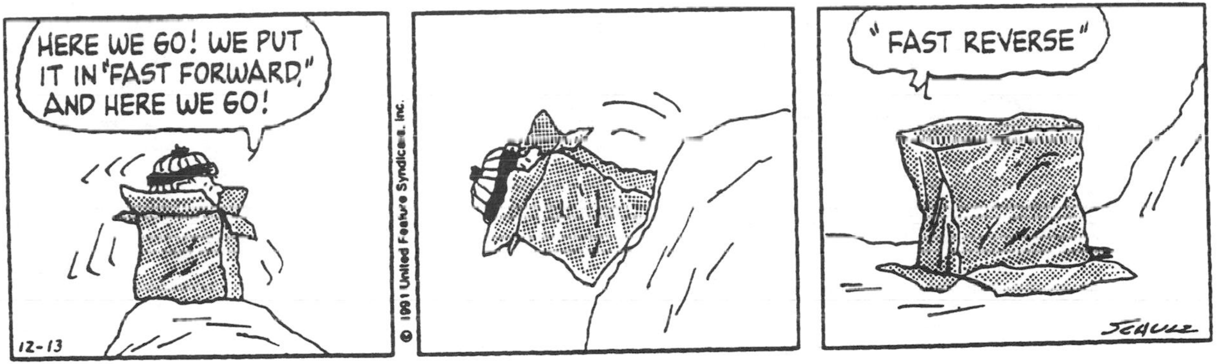
HERE WE GO! WE PUT IT IN "FAST FORWARD," AND HERE WE GO!
12-13
© 1991 United Feature Syndicate, Inc.
"FAST REVERSE"
SCHULZ

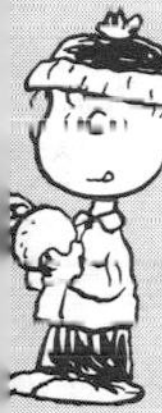

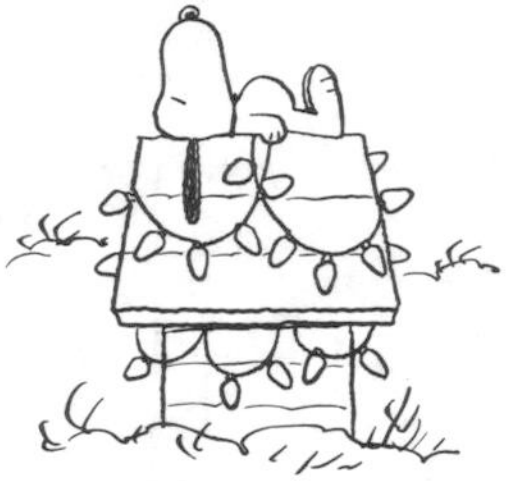

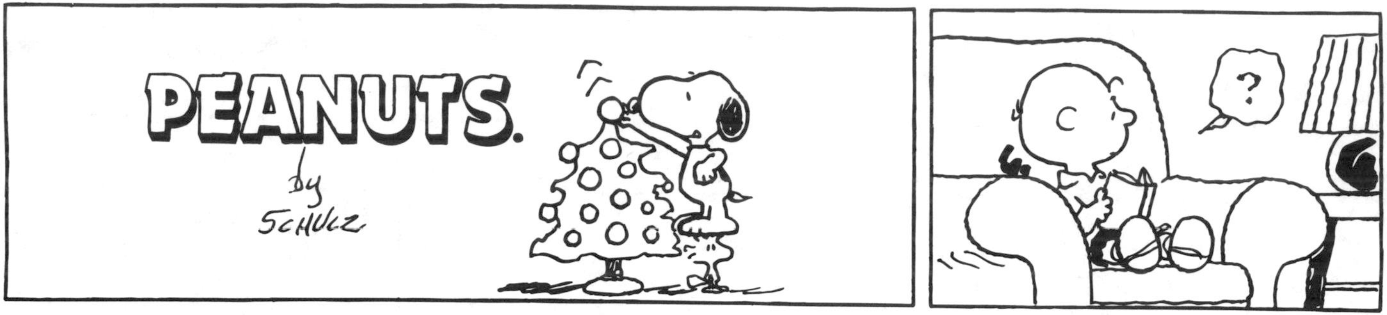
PEANUTS.
by SCHULZ
?

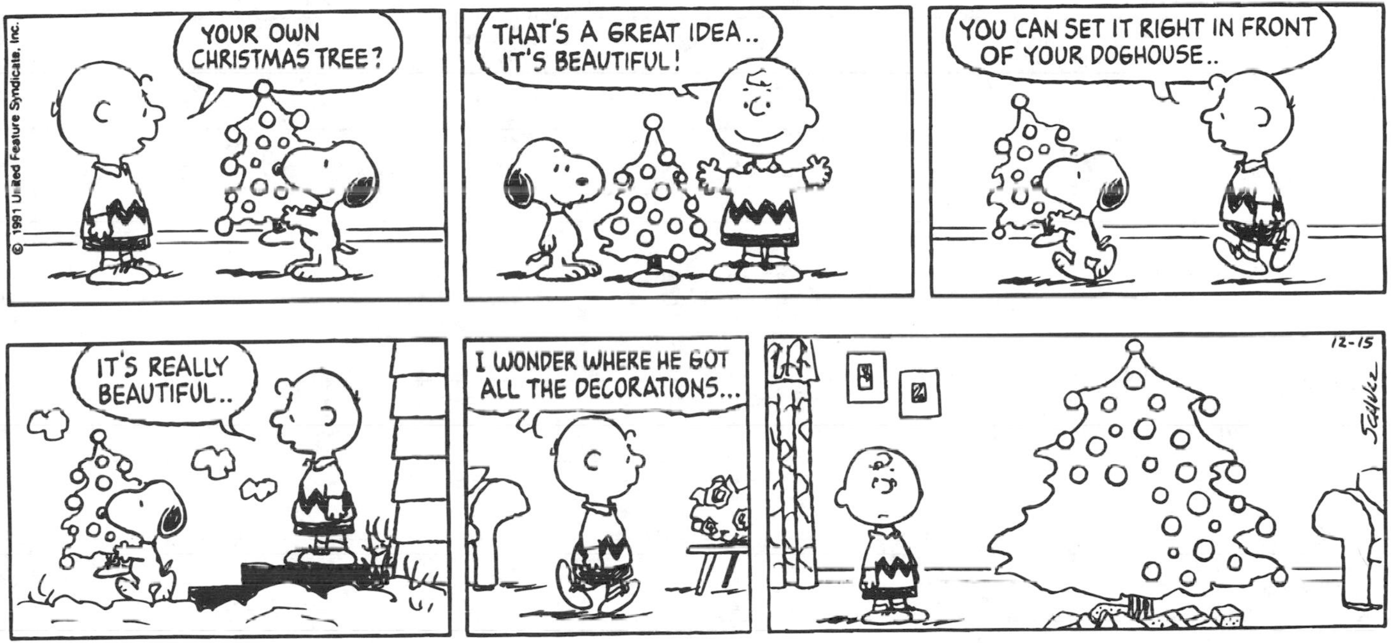
© 1991 United Feature Syndicate, Inc.
YOUR OWN CHRISTMAS TREE?
THAT'S A GREAT IDEA.. IT'S BEAUTIFUL!
YOU CAN SET IT RIGHT IN FRONT OF YOUR DOGHOUSE..
IT'S REALLY BEAUTIFUL..
I WONDER WHERE HE GOT ALL THE DECORATIONS...
12-15
SCHULZ

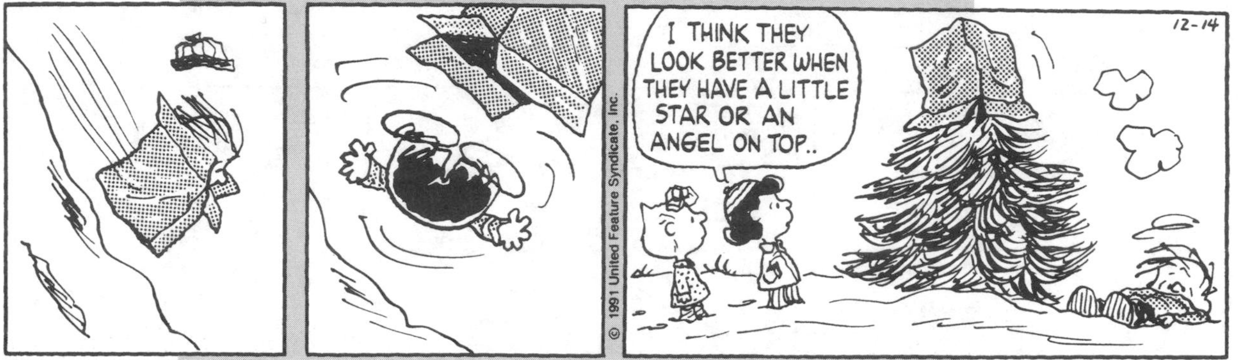
© 1991 United Feature Syndicate, Inc.
I THINK THEY LOOK BETTER WHEN THEY HAVE A LITTLE STAR OR AN ANGEL ON TOP..
12-14

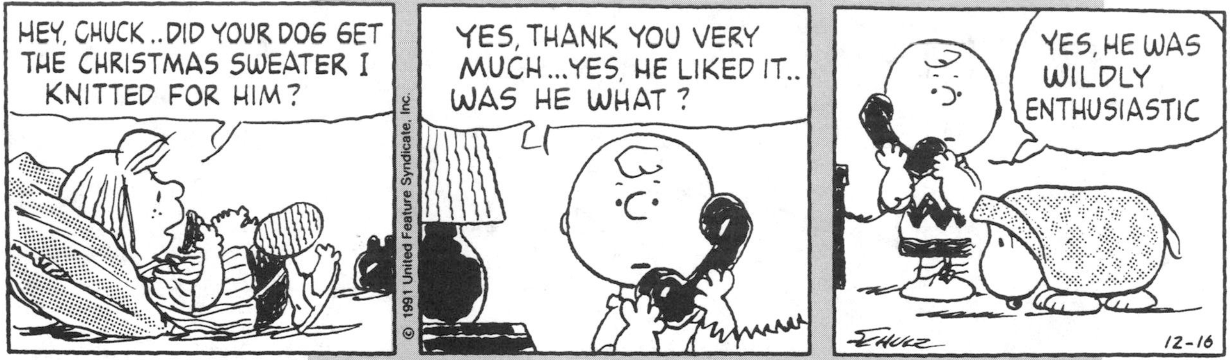
HEY, CHUCK..DID YOUR DOG GET THE CHRISTMAS SWEATER I KNITTED FOR HIM?
© 1991 United Feature Syndicate, Inc.
YES, THANK YOU VERY MUCH...YES, HE LIKED IT.. WAS HE WHAT?
YES, HE WAS WILDLY ENTHUSIASTIC
SCHULZ
12-16

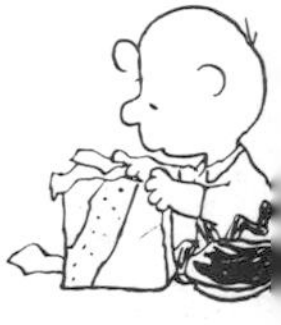

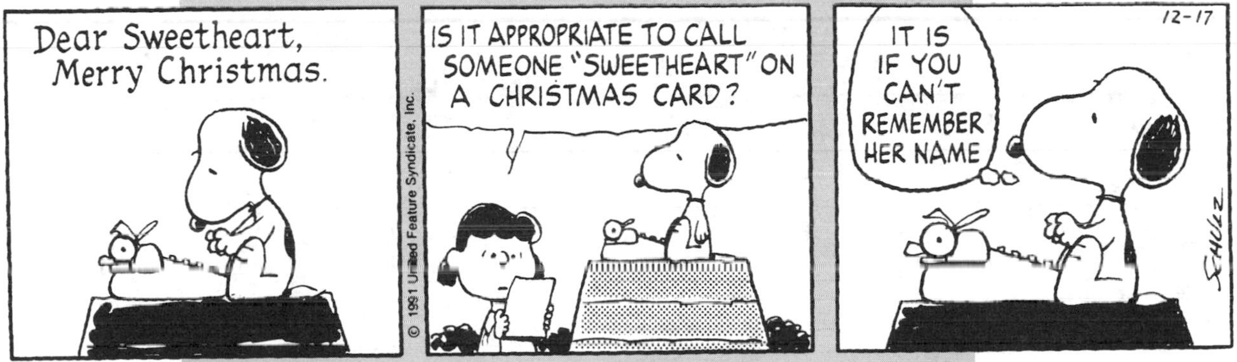
Dear Sweetheart,
Merry Christmas.
© 1991 United Feature Syndicate, Inc.
IS IT APPROPRIATE TO CALL SOMEONE "SWEETHEART" ON A CHRISTMAS CARD?
12-17
IT IS IF YOU CAN'T REMEMBER HER NAME
SCHULZ

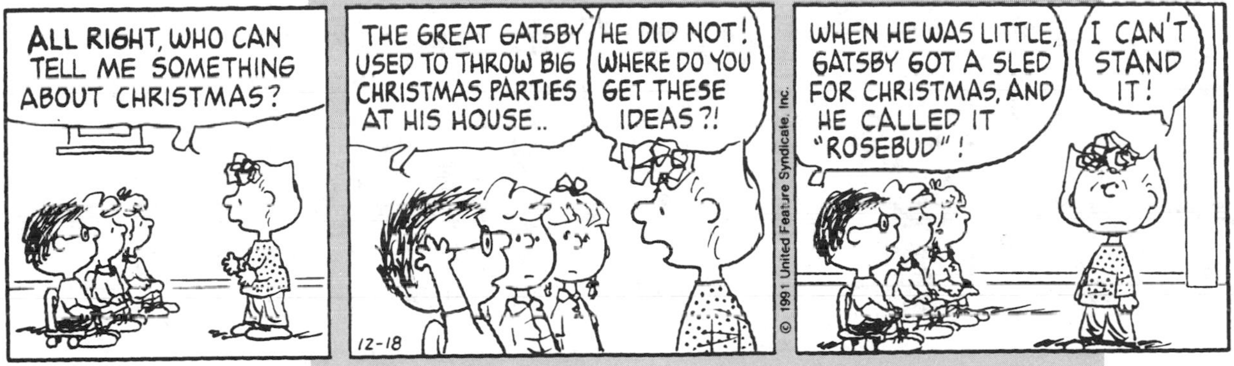
ALL RIGHT, WHO CAN TELL ME SOMETHING ABOUT CHRISTMAS?
THE GREAT GATSBY USED TO THROW BIG CHRISTMAS PARTIES AT HIS HOUSE..
HE DID NOT! WHERE DO YOU GET THESE IDEAS?!
12-18
© 1991 United Feature Syndicate, Inc.
WHEN HE WAS LITTLE, GATSBY GOT A SLED FOR CHRISTMAS, AND HE CALLED IT "ROSEBUD"!
I CAN'T STAND IT!

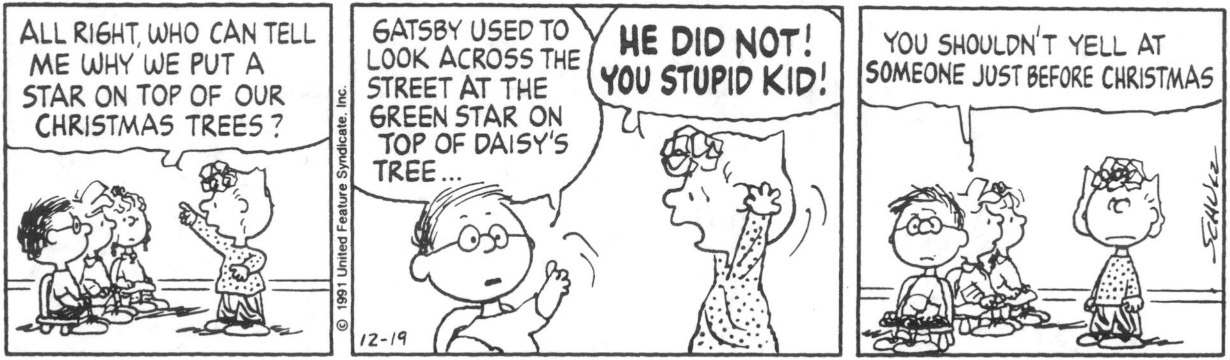
ALL RIGHT, WHO CAN TELL ME WHY WE PUT A STAR ON TOP OF OUR CHRISTMAS TREES ?
© 1991 United Feature Syndicate, Inc.
GATSBY USED TO LOOK ACROSS THE STREET AT THE GREEN STAR ON TOP OF DAISY'S TREE...
HE DID NOT! YOU STUPID KID!
12-19
YOU SHOULDN'T YELL AT SOMEONE JUST BEFORE CHRISTMAS
SCHULZ

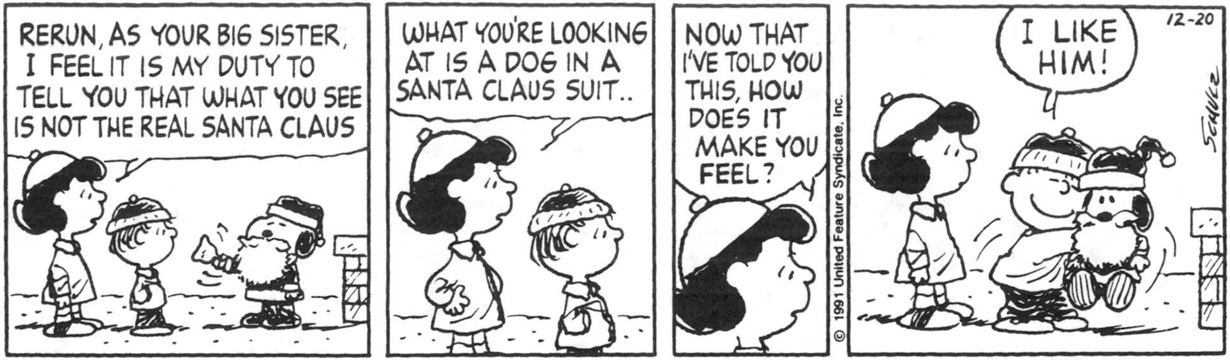
RERUN, AS YOUR BIG SISTER, I FEEL IT IS MY DUTY TO TELL YOU THAT WHAT YOU SEE IS NOT THE REAL SANTA CLAUS
WHAT YOU'RE LOOKING AT IS A DOG IN A SANTA CLAUS SUIT..
NOW THAT I'VE TOLD YOU THIS, HOW DOES IT MAKE YOU FEEL?
© 1991 United Feature Syndicate, Inc.
12-20
I LIKE HIM!
SCHULZ

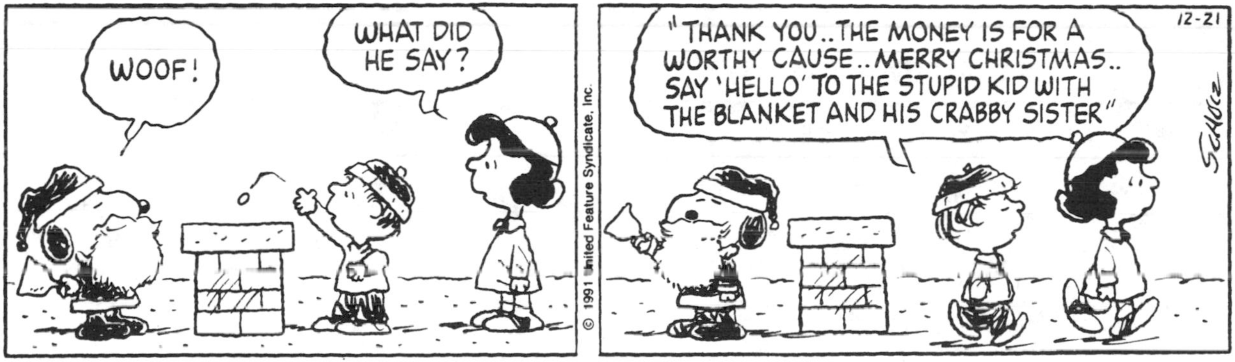
WOOF!
WHAT DID HE SAY?
© 1991 United Feature Syndicate, Inc.
12-21
"THANK YOU..THE MONEY IS FOR A WORTHY CAUSE..MERRY CHRISTMAS.. SAY 'HELLO' TO THE STUPID KID WITH THE BLANKET AND HIS CRABBY SISTER"
SCHULZ

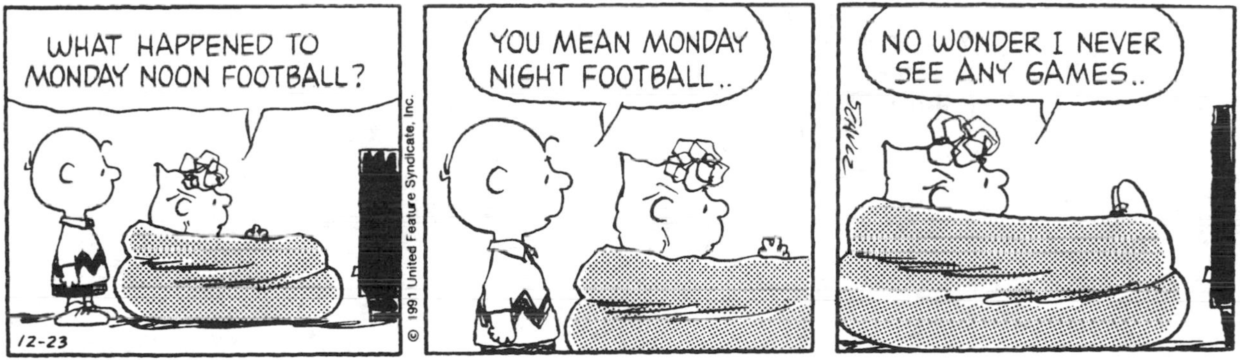
WHAT HAPPENED TO MONDAY NOON FOOTBALL?
12-23
© 1991 United Feature Syndicate, Inc.
YOU MEAN MONDAY NIGHT FOOTBALL..
NO WONDER I NEVER SEE ANY GAMES..
SCHULZ

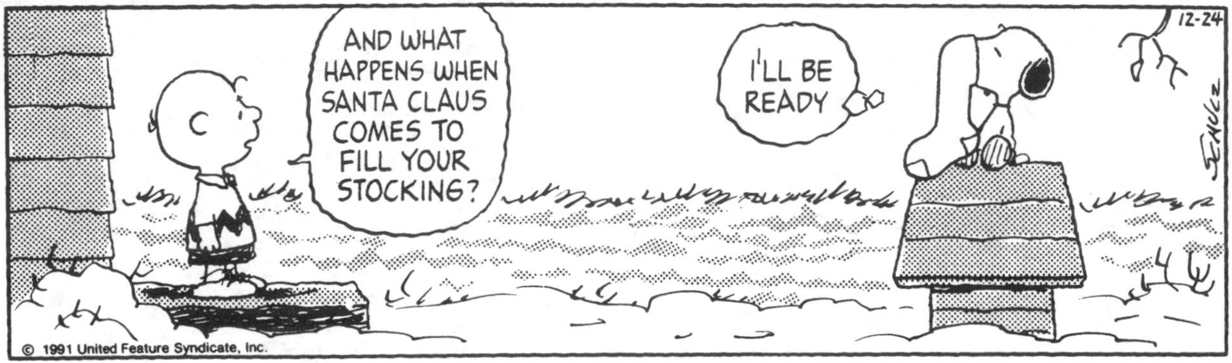
12-24
AND WHAT HAPPENS WHEN SANTA CLAUS COMES TO FILL YOUR STOCKING?
I'LL BE READY
© 1991 United Feature Syndicate, Inc.

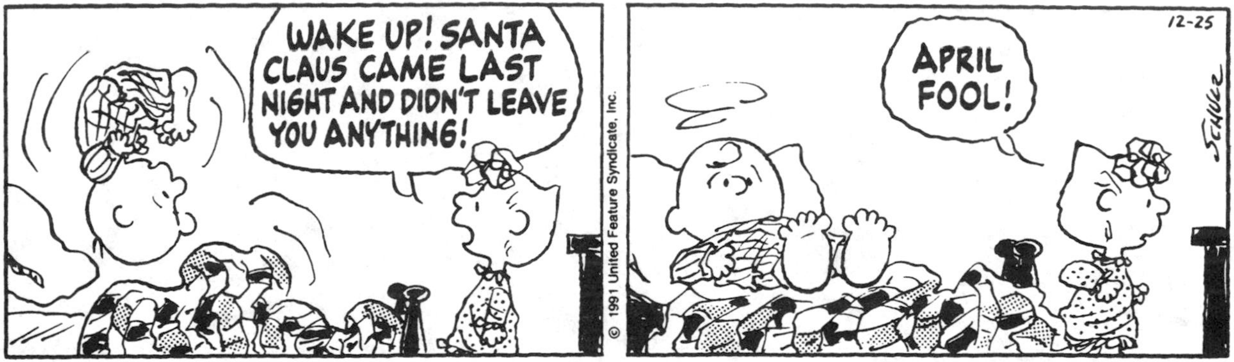
WAKE UP! SANTA CLAUS CAME LAST NIGHT AND DIDN'T LEAVE YOU ANYTHING!
© 1991 United Feature Syndicate, Inc.
12-25
APRIL FOOL!

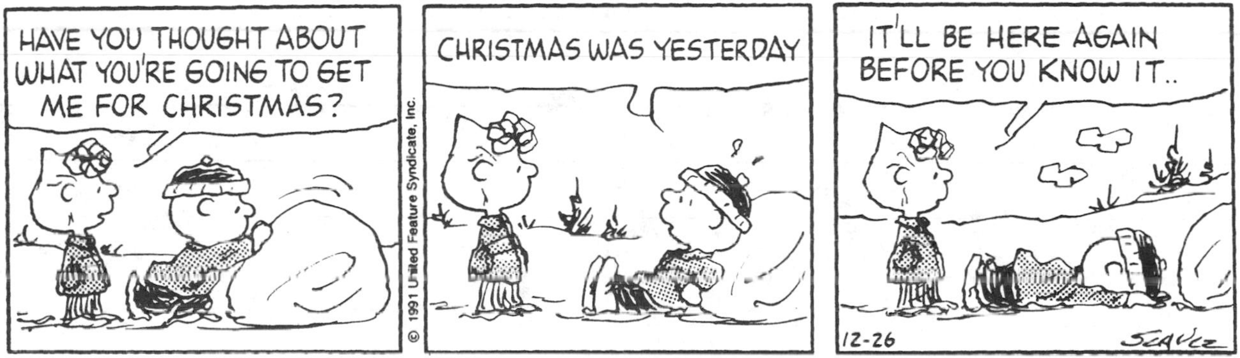
HAVE YOU THOUGHT ABOUT WHAT YOU'RE GOING TO GET ME FOR CHRISTMAS?
CHRISTMAS WAS YESTERDAY
IT'LL BE HERE AGAIN BEFORE YOU KNOW IT..
© 1991 United Feature Syndicate, Inc.
12-26

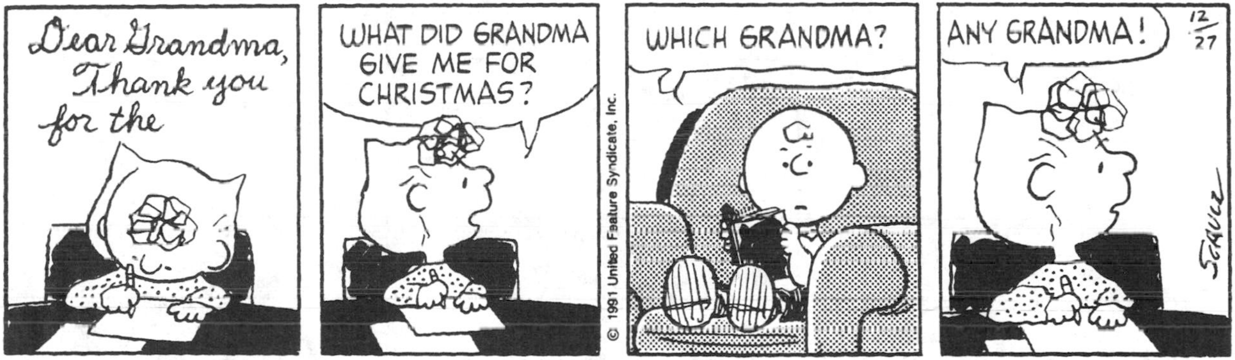
Dear Grandma,
Thank you for the
WHAT DID GRANDMA GIVE ME FOR CHRISTMAS?
WHICH GRANDMA?
ANY GRANDMA!
12/27
© 1991 United Feature Syndicate, Inc.

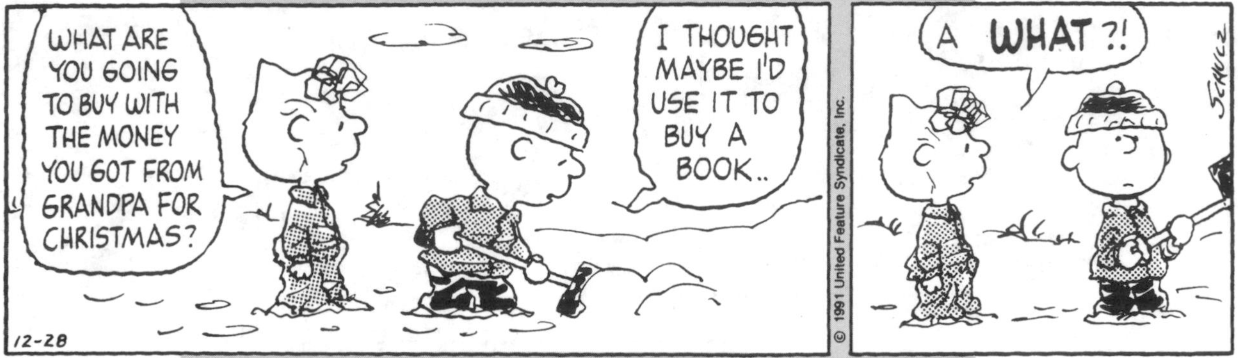
WHAT ARE YOU GOING TO BUY WITH THE MONEY YOU GOT FROM GRANDPA FOR CHRISTMAS?
I THOUGHT MAYBE I'D USE IT TO BUY A BOOK..
A WHAT?!
© 1991 United Feature Syndicate, Inc.
SCHULZ
12-28

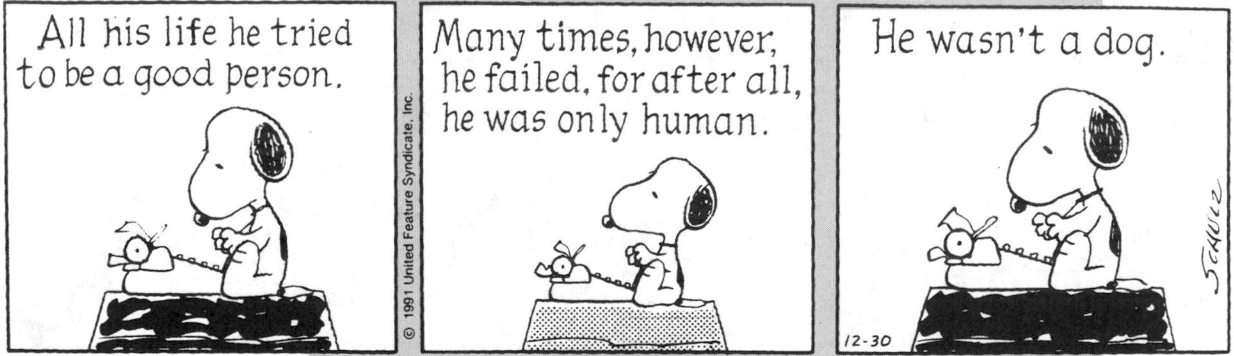
All his life he tried to be a good person.
© 1991 United Feature Syndicate, Inc.
Many times, however, he failed, for after all, he was only human.
He wasn't a dog.
SCHULZ
12-30

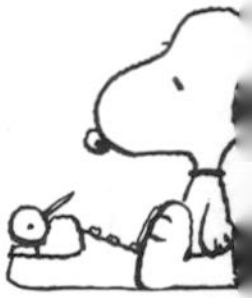